# *Breaking the Fine Rain of Death*

# *Breaking the Fine Rain of Death*

## African American Health Issues and a Womanist Ethic of Care

Emilie M. Townes

CONTINUUM • NEW YORK

2001

The Continuum Publishing Company
370 Lexington Avenue, New York, NY 10017



Printed in the United States of America

---

**Library of Congress Cataloging-in-Publication Data**

Townes, Emilie Maureen, 1955–
Breaking the fine rain of death : African American health care and a womanist ethic of care / Emilie M. Townes.
p. cm.
Includes bibliographical references and index.
**ISBN 0-8264-1121-5 (hc) ISBN 0-8264-1368-4 (pbk)**
1. Afro-Americans – Health and hygiene – Moral and ethical aspects – United States. 2. Afro-Americans – Medical care – Moral and ethical aspects – United States. 3. Afro-Americans – Health and hygiene – United States – Cross-cultural studies. 4. Afro-Americans – Medical care – United States – Cross-cultural studies. 5. Health services accessibility – United States – Cross-cultural studies. I. Title.
RA448.5.N4T68 1998
362.1′089′96073–dc21 98–8470

*for the aunts*

Agnes Moore
Helen McLean

I give you my eyes at this hour of hunger
breaking African children into a fine rain of death.

SONIA SANCHEZ, "On the Occasion of
*Essence's* Twenty-Fifth Anniversary"

# Contents

## *Introduction and Acknowledgments*

# To Heal the Wounded Spirit

There has been a great deal of recent literature from a feminist perspective on the nature of an ethic of care and on the concept of caring. Such writers as Nel Noddings (*Caring: A Feminine Approach to Ethics and Moral Education,* 1984), the authors in Mary Jeanne Larrabee's edited volume (*An Ethic of Care: Feminist and Interdisciplinary Perspectives,* 1993), and Nancy N. Rue (*The Value of Compassion,* 1991) offer compelling insights into the nature of care and caring as seeking compassion and justice. These writings emerge out of the debate between Lawrence Kohlberg and Carol Gilligan and, as such, tend more toward drawing distinctions between gender-based understandings of moral reasoning and examining their impact on developing an ethic of care.

This book explores a different tract. The attempt to understand gender-based distinctions, while helpful, is much too narrow a focus for analyzing the dynamics of care and developing an interstructured moral theory of care to address an increasingly complex and distressed social order. In this book, I turn to the broader social constructs of health and health care from which to develop an ethic of care. With recent public debates on the nature of national health care in the United States and with the explosion of the fitness industry that shows few signs of slowing, it is imperative that we explore the issues that feed the public debate about our national health. It is my contention that an ethic of care must emerge out of this conundrum of competing moralities.

These complexities in addressing issues of health care undergird my contention that an ethic of care must address these issues in a rigorous manner that employs a praxeological (reflection-and-action) methodology. It is only through employing such a methodology that the possibilities for a relevant ethic of care can emerge. I propose a womanist methodology in which race, gender, and class are necessary theoretical tools to carry out developing an ethic of care that takes into consideration gender, but as a part of a more rigorous theo-ethical analysis that seeks a realism about the social order that then moves to a consideration of the steps needed for transformation.

Therefore, this praxeological framework will employ an interdisciplinary methodology. The disciplines of social ethics, biblical hermeneutics, philosophical ethics, social history, public health, and sociology help tease through the thorny problems of addressing health care at the turn of this century in an attempt to shape a womanist ethic of care. I will use the African American community as a "test case" for exploring these issues that frame my attempt to do a womanist theo-ethical analysis that provides a more extensive ethic of care. My goal is to paint a more accurate and encompassing picture of African American life in order to set the backdrop for an ethic of care that truly addresses the labyrinthine relationships that comprise any social group. My analysis is, by necessity, both descriptive and prescriptive.

I attempt to integrate two things. First, I take up the debate on health and health care. Although medical ethicists have entered this fray, social ethicists have been less willing to do so. I think the concerns of social ethics — structures, institutions, processes, systems, and the ways in which individuals and groups both respond and shape them — provide a helpful lens to consider the nature of health and health care. Second, I attempt an ethic of care that emerges not only out of this consideration of health and health care but also out of the biblical theme of communal lament. I am struck, as I continue to explore the book of Joel, how genuine lament (both individual and corporate) precedes healing. I attempt to explore lament in an integrated way with health and health care to shape a womanist ethic of care that moves beyond concerns centered solely on identity politics that are exclusively gendered, economic, or racial. Rather, I focus on caring and hope.

I want to explore models of healing that are sensitive to social location and cultural context. My hope is that I will lay a foundation that, though grounded in the lives of Black folk, has universal dimensions. My concern is both academic and practical. I hope to enrich scholarly debate and insights through an interdisciplinary analysis that is more than a hodgepodge of ideas and insights and that points the way to a rigorous methodology. As a womanist methodology, it must first be practical and relevant to the needs and cares of the Black Church and the African American community. It then expands its horizon to inform academic discourse and other communities beyond the worlds of Black folks. This means that part of the methodology of this book is the rejection of a closed, fixed system of ideas about health and health care.

The medical model that defines health as the absence of disease or illness is not my focus. That model is based on curative medicine that aims to diagnose illness and restore health. Health is not simply the absence of disease — it comprises a wide range of activities that foster healing and wholeness. My focus is on the personal and public dimensions of health. In this view, health is a cultural production in that health and illness alike are social constructs and dependent on social networks, biology, and environment. As it is embedded in our social realities, health also includes the integration of the spiritual (how we relate to God), the mental (who we are as thinking and feeling people), and the physical (who we are biologically) aspects of our lives.

A subtext that runs throughout the book is a concern for the ways in which we, in the United States, are quickly moving toward an overly individualistic medical model that obscures, if not denies, the communal aspects of our health. This individualistic impulse often drives a wedge between the person and the community he or she resides in. This has enormous ramifications for the kind of health-care systems we create or do not create. We do not survive or live in an equitable health-care system. Those who can afford excellent care are able to receive it. Those who cannot, do not — as a rule.

Part 1, "Context and Pretext," is an exploration of the basic elements necessary to develop a womanist ethic of care. In chapter 1, I begin with a sermon fragment based in the book of Joel, a book that is an example of a communal lament. This type of lament — because it has a clear form and is expressed corporately — can help shape our vision of ourselves as we become more attuned to the world around us. By extension, it has a deep moral character that helps the discipline of social ethics do its work. A communal lament happens in community, and this corporate experience of calling for healing makes pain bearable and manageable in the community. It is only then that we can begin to heal.

It is from this exploration of salvation and healing that I move, in chapter 2, to an overview of the health-care system in the United States. We live in a troubling health-care delivery system. More than two million people lose their health coverage each month, although many will get their coverage back within a few weeks or months. There are 37 million U.S. citizens who have no health care at all. Of this number, 9.5 million are children. Eighty-five percent of the uninsured belong to families that include an employed adult. Obtaining group insurance is difficult for part-time workers or the self-employed. Some people are in jobs they dare not leave because of their health benefits, and many people on welfare remain so because they can receive health benefits that they could not obtain if they were employed in minimum-wage jobs. With the advent of managed care, health delivery systems have moved away from the fee-for-service plans that many of us grew up with to the prospective-payment plans of health maintenance organizations. It is imperative that we understand that we are health consumers, and we must become aware of, at the very least, the basic structure of health-care delivery in the United States and the ways in which we can enter into the emerging world of health-care delivery (or lack thereof) as informed advocates for our health and the health of others.

Chapter 3 delves more specifically into the worlds of Black folks and the impact of the health-care delivery system of the United States on their lives. This chapter is historical and analytical as I argue for understanding health as a cultural production. As such, I begin with slave culture and explore some of the biological realities of slaves and the racial stereotypes and assumptions that medical personnel operated with concerning the Black body. This racialist ideology continues into the twentieth century, as the rise of public health had a profound effect on the health of Americans. It also had a strong effect on Black health care in the United States, although it was not as far-reaching as in the general population. Black medical professionals founded medical schools and hospitals to treat the illnesses that visited African American life. The chapter ends by addressing the various stereotypes and realities of health in the contemporary lives of African Americans.

In part 2, "Exploring Health and Health Care in Black America," three specific areas of African American life are explored. The first, in chapter 4, is the tragedy of the Tuskegee Syphilis Study. This study was conducted by the U.S. Public Health Service and involved four hundred southern Black men for forty years — 1932 to 1972. These men were not told that they had syphilis, and they were not treated so that researchers could discover the "natural history" of the disease. The end of the study was death, when the men were autopsied to see what havoc the disease had wrought on their internal organs. In much of the literature regarding Black health, the Tuskegee Study is often referred to as a key reason that there is much distrust and suspicion among African Americans when they face the medical establishment. A consideration of this study crystallizes the structural issues involved in health care. Issues of class, race, and complicity are the marrow of this chapter.

Where chapter 4 concentrates on men, chapter 5 concentrates on women. Taking a historical perspective, this chapter explores the ways in which sexist ideologies were reified in medical opinion, practice, and prescription. On the contemporary scene, rather than explore the traditional women's health issues that concentrate on reproductive health, I want to explore what I believe to be a more powerful set of issues regarding women's health and health care in the United states. These issues are those surrounding clinical trials and the dreadful lack of access and participation of women in these trials. From these issues, the chapter moves into the world of Black women to explore the ways in which they are accounted for (or not) in health-care delivery in the United States.

The final chapter in part 2 looks at the impact of HIV/AIDS in the African American community — it is a story of men and women. The 1992 report from the President's Commission on AIDS alarmed many. The statistic that 47 percent of the people in the United States with AIDS came from groups making up only 21 percent of the total population caught many off guard. African Americans were 12 percent of the U.S. population, but nearly 30 percent of those with AIDS were Black. Hispanics/Latinos comprised 9 percent of the population and 17 percent of the AIDS cases. The 1997 midyear numbers continued to rise with Blacks and Hispanics/Latinos accounting for more than 60 percent of the reported AIDS cases.

Beginning with a discussion of the Black body as icon, chapter 6 explores issues of sexuality and drug abuse in relation to HIV/AIDS in African American life. I then move to explore the ways in which HIV/AIDS has global dimensions, the ways in which the lack of HIV/AIDS research for women may be sowing the seeds of Black genocide, and the role of the Black Church in meeting the growing devastation wrought by AIDS in African American communities.

Part 3, "Communal Repentance," turns to develop an ethic of care that responds to the various theo-ethical issues raised in parts 1 and 2. By naming some issues of health and health care in the African American community, I suggest that we begin the process of awareness and repentance. It is only out of this repentance that the lament is genuine, and then can begin the process of healing based on caring and hope.

Chapter 7 begins the concrete development of an ethic of care that utilizes the PEN-3 model developed by Collins Airhihenbuwa of the Pennsylvania State University Department of Health Education. This conceptual model is used in the planning and development of culturally appropriate health education/promotion programs. This model provides a helpful framework for a theo-ethical theory and exploration that seek to maintain the womanist concern for an interstructured analysis based on race, gender, and class considerations. I then integrate the PEN-3 model with the assets-based model of Jon Kretzmann and John McKnight to explore the ways in which culturally sensitive and responsive, community-based strategies can help various African American communities address issues of health and health care. The chapter includes examples of community-based and religious-based models of care already operative in the African American community.

The final chapter begins with a sermon fragment based on Hebrews 10. The structure of this chapter varies from the others in that I intersperse sermon fragments throughout the chapter in an interplay between more academic and linear discourse and discourse that is more lyrical and metaphorical. In large measure, this strategy helps me develop an ethic of care that is directed to body and soul. It must be realistic regarding the realities of social conditions and the impact that they have on Black health, but it must also seek transformatory themes and practices that encourage a form of caring that heals the corporate body and soul. These themes involve eschatology, salvation, despair, and hope.

•

There are many who contributed to this project. I owe great thanks to the faculty, trustees, and administration of Saint Paul School of Theology for granting me sabbatical time to work on major portions of this book. My colleagues Tex Sample, Harold Washington, and Kris Kvam either read or listened to me think through various portions of the manuscript and offered helpful and insightful feedback. My student assistants, Annalise Fonza and Mark Pridmore, spent many hours tracking down references and transcribing notes with great care and detail. The students and my team-teaching partner, Derrel Watkins, in the fall 1997 Koinonia class listened with patience as I lectured from portions of the manuscript to get their feedback and suggestions. Their comments have shaped this final product more than most of them can imagine.

In my wider circle of colleagues, I owe a debt of thanks to the women and men who participate in the American Academy of Religion's Womanist Approaches to Religion and Society Group. Also, the program committee of the Society of Christian Ethics allowed me to read through sections of the manuscript for their critique and evaluation. The staff and fellows of the Association of Religion and the Intellectual Life's Research Colloquium have been valuable associates in this manuscript. For the past three years John Downey, Carol Ochs, and James Breeden have heard this manuscript unfold and been both supportive and probing in their feedback. I have had the invaluable opportunity to lecture on the material in this book in many venues. Through keynote speeches, church workshops, and public lectures on university and seminary campuses, I have had a wider pool of response that have helped strengthen my work.

As always, my family and friends have held me to the task — even when they were not aware of doing so. My mother, sister, aunts, and uncles are just plain good folk, and I am blessed to be a part of such a human family as I have. Among my many friendships that are precious and rich I want to thank Katie Cannon, Delores Williams, Patricia Hunter, Karen Baker Fletcher, Frances Wood, and Leslie Williams. Each, in her own way, reminds me that writing is a craft, and analysis and critique are essential.

As always, I also thank the Spirit. It was through the teachings and examples I saw growing up in Durham and Southern Pines, North Carolina, that I began to understand how the Spirit works beyond human folly and design. I cannot blame any inconsistency or faltering critique on the Spirit — they are my own. But I do know that the Spirit has everything to do with those places in this text where readers sense that they are meeting themselves and their communities. It is through the Spirit that we can heal our wounded spirits — body and soul.

*Part 1*

# CONTEXT AND PRETEXT

## *Chapter 1*

# The Formfulness of Communal Lament

*Joel 1–2*

what is it about the day of the Lord
  that captures our imagination
  that challenges our souls
  that calls us up
    into a hope
    a wish
    a challenge
    a ministry
what is it about the day of the Creator
  that prompts us to take cover
  to deny we hear a voice
    calling
    insisting
    that we move beyond our todays
      into better, richer, fuller
        more faithful tomorrows
what is it about the day of God
  that we begin to see who we are
  how we are
  what we are
  and realize
    that our worship is full, but incomplete
    our mission is strong, but lacks power
    our caring is deep, but needs more compassion
that great day of Joel's people
  in which sons and daughters prophesy
  in which the old dream dreams
  and the young see visions
in which the spirit is poured out
  so that all this can happen
that great day only comes *after* the locusts
  *after* the trumpet of lament has blown in Zion

it comes *after* the day of darkness and gloom
*after* the fire has devoured in front and the flame burns behind
*after* the war horses and rumbling chariots
*after* the invading army that makes the people's faces grow pale
that scales the wall
that keeps its own course, not swerving
not jostling
that climbs through the windows of the houses like a thief
*after* the earthquakes and the thunder and the sun and moon are darkened
and the stars withdraw their shining
the great day comes after the people of the land
have been reduced to trembling
and the great and powerful army comes
like none before it and none after it
and it devours everything
they are relentless
they are devastating
they are relentless
they are devastating

these people do not start out happy
they are in full lament
they are being more than whiny, cranky Israelites
they are in trouble
no, Joel doesn't condemn Judah for its injustice
or its vile behavior
Joel doesn't mention Judah's departure from God's standards
like the other prophets
(someone once said, well he did only have 3 chapters, he didn't have time to "say more")
we know that all this is true
but Joel has lament on his mind
and he sees the problem differently
the problem is not what Judah has done or not done
he knows all that
the problem is the inhumanity and evil of others toward the people of Israel
Joel's is a plea to God to come to the aid of those who trust in God
no matter what the trials and tribulations they face
no matter what the adversity is — this time
a lament, for Joel, is about repentance

Joel tells the folk to *turn* to God
to turn to God for assistance in meeting these bugs
this drought
that army
those signs from heaven
turn to God
for this is the God of the covenant
this is the God who cares and controls the full sweep of time and space
this is the God who upholds justice
this is the God whose actions are designed to make God's own self be known to us
turn to God for salvation and hope
for if you are in big trouble, says Joel,
if you've got any faith at all
it is God you must turn to
it's only then that we can talk about sons and daughters prophesying
and dreams and visions and the spirit
this is the rending of the heart
this is the pouring out of the spirit in our lives
when we immerse ourselves
in turning again and again to God
when we open ourselves up to God's promise
what is important is the content of faith
for it is only after the people enter honest lament
through a faith that leads them to hope
that God's answer is: grace
it is only after the people enter into
genuine assembly
genuine weeping
genuine sorrow
that God answers with a divine yes
this is when the day of the Lord comes
this is when we can truly prophesy as a church
this is when we have dreams that move us beyond where we are and how we are
this is when we have a vision worth sharing as a church
this is when we can gather and celebrate ministry
that seeks to be faithful
and responds to God's call: return to me with all your heart
by saying I am willing to try to be a prophet, a dreamer, a visionary
Joel gives us moving, powerful language

we know this passage
we are captured by the power of

> Then afterward
> I will pour out my spirit on all flesh;
> your sons and your daughters shall prophesy,
> your old ones shall dream dreams,
> and your young ones shall see visions.
> Even on the male and female slaves,
> in those days, I will pour out my spirit.

but Joel does not give us this passage
without stipulations
it comes only after the people have been brought low by the injustices and evil of others
and they *choose* to turn to God with all their hearts
the call to give up our certainty
give up our comfort zone
give up our structures and plans
is before us
then we can claim the hope found in Joel's words
then we can meet the challenges of God's grace
for in the Hebrew Bible
laments mark the *beginning* of the healing process
and people need and want to be healed
if we learn anything from Joel
it is to know that the healing of brokenness and injustice
the healing of social sin and degradation
the healing of spiritual doubts and fears
begins with an unrestrained lament
one that starts from our toenails and is a shout by the time it gets to the ends of the strands of our hair
it's a lament of faith
to the God of faith
that we need help
that we can't do this ministry alone
we can't witness to the world in isolation
we can't fight off the hordes of wickedness and hatred with a big stick
we can't do this by ourselves anymore, God
we need some *divine* help

## History and Context

The book of Joel is an inspiring puzzle. Joel presents contradictory facts that look back toward preexilic prophecy and forward toward postexilic prophecy. It is not surprising that biblical scholars disagree about its approximate dating. Some date it as early as King Joash of Judah and the priest Jehoiada in the ninth century B.C.E. Others date it sometime in the years immediately preceding the fall of Jerusalem between 597 and 587 B.C.E. Still others believe that it dates to the time of the rebuilding of the temple between 515 and 500 B.C.E., which would make Joel a contemporary of Haggai and Zechariah. Other scholars believe that it dates to the end of the fifth century B.C.E. and as late as the third century B.C.E. The introduction to Joel in the Oxford Annotated Bible (NRSV) suggests that the majority of historical references, the omission of the Assyrians and Babylonians, and Joel's great use of earlier prophets make the period from 400 to 350 B.C.E. most likely.[1] This diversity of opinion makes the precise dating of Joel impossible.

Two things are certain: it is one of the shortest books of prophecy in the Hebrew Bible, and it is placed second in the Book of the Twelve Prophets. It begins with a call to fasting and lament in response to a devastating locust plague and drought. It ends with a judgment of the nations in the Valley of Jehoshaphat. Joel is a book of public prophecy, not private oracle.[2] The book arose from a time when worship and covenant between God and Israel were linked intimately in a robust and compelling manner.

*The Land Is Ruined*

Hear this, O elders,
  give ear, all inhabitants of the land!
Has such a thing happened in your days,
  or in the days of your ancestors?
Tell your children of it,
  and let your children tell their children,
  and their children another generation.

Such are the first three verses of the book of Joel. A brief but powerful story is about to unfold. It is a story that must be told to generations, for it is a story of crisis, repentance, assurance, and salvation. Judah experienced a crisis of monumental proportions — nothing like it had ever happened in the memory of the elders of the present generation or of their parents. The present generation was to repeat the story for the generation in their midst, who would pass it to the generations yet to come.

Telling the children has a long tradition in the Hebrew Bible.[3] One example is Psalm 78:2–8.[4] Here the people resolve to keep the process of telling alive by telling of the "glorious deeds of God" and the "wonders" of God so that the next generation will have a source of hope. What is more important, the story must be told to the children so that they, and the generations yet to come, will not forget the works of God. The hope of the psalmist is that the children will not be like their ancestors, "stubborn and rebellious," a generation "whose heart was not steadfast, whose spirit was not faithful to God." It was important to the ancient peoples of the Bible, as it is for us today, to tell their children about the things God had done in their individual and collective histories so that all generations may have steadfast hearts and faithful spirits. What Joel calls the people to do, so that the children may remember and pass it on to generations to come, is what gives lament its power, the call to fasting.

Claus Westermann maintains that no worship observance in ancient Israel is better known to us today than the rite of lament.[5] Further, Westermann notes that deliverance from Egypt is a fundamental element in the theology of the Hebrew Bible.[6] There is a formula for deliverance: distress, a cry of distress, a promise of deliverance, deliverance, and the praise of God. Therefore, lament is set within the context of an account of deliverance. This deliverance, for Westermann, is the basis of Israel's relationship with God and God's saving acts in the history of the people of Israel.[7]

Joel turns to the nature of crisis. There is a deadly plague of locusts:

> What the cutting locust left,
> the swarming locust has eaten.
> What the swarming locust left,
> the hopping locust has eaten,
> and what the hopping locust left,
> the destroying locust has eaten. (1:4)

Such a plague as this must be a sign that the Day of the Lord (Yhwh) is near. Plagues of locusts were familiar to the Israelites. However, nothing like the plague had ever happened before in Israel's collective memory. This is a plague that must be remembered, for all are called to realize its awful presage.

It is the cry of distress that is so powerful, this lament. As Joel presents a situation of crisis, of distress, the lament comes forth in potent language:

> Wake up, you drunkards, and weep;
> and wail, all you wine-drinkers,
> over the sweet wine,
> for it is cut off from your mouth.
> For a nation has invaded my land,
> powerful and innumerable;

its teeth are lions' teeth,
and it has the fangs of a lioness.
It has laid waste my vines,
and splintered my fig trees;
it has stripped off their bark and thrown it down;
their branches have turned white. (1:5–7)

These words are unequivocal in their anguish. They mark the outlines of the devastation and ruin that have befallen the nation. Westermann notes that only a rending of the heart such as this can lead to the events of deliverance.[8] Lament is an inevitable part of what happens between God and humanity.

Because we live in worlds of sin and destruction, we must come upon times of despair and crisis. Because we rely too much on human design and purpose, we will fall victim to the folly of our arrogance and conceit. Westermann notes the lament of the dead that looks backward and finds its voice in those who mourn the loss of someone.[9] However, it is the lament of affliction that looks forward that marks Joel's words:[10]

To you, O God, I cry.
For fire has devoured
the pastures of the wilderness,
and flames have burned
all the trees of the field.
Even the wild animals cry to you
because the watercourses are dried up,
and the fire has devoured
the pastures of the wilderness. (1:19–20)

Here, Joel calls out to God as he has already encouraged the people of Judah to reach out, cry out for life. The only other alternative is death and destruction.

The lament of affliction is directed toward God in the Hebrew Bible, for it is God who can change the suffering, the source(s) of the crisis. Joel's cry of lament recognizes the power and timelessness of God and the finite quality of human existence. Humanity is not idealized or spiritualized for Joel. His imagery is clear: concrete life is threatened and despairing. Joel draws humanity's limitations in clear, bold lines. There are no longer the grain or drink offerings in the temple; the fields and very ground mourn; the grain is destroyed; the wine has dried up; and the oil fails (1:9–10). Humanity's ability to stop the devastation sits mute as Joel calls the people to realize that human schemes cannot control the scope of this devastation. Rather, Judah must turn to God.

For the people of Judah, the call to lament was familiar. The limitations of humanity were well known, and the need to cry to God with all of one's heart was natural. Also natural was a God who was deeply concerned about the cries of distress.[11] There was (and is) no boundary that forbids lamentation. Joel uses this freedom to cry out and to urge the people of Judah to cry out, to fast:

> Put on sackcloth and lament, you priests;
> wail, you ministers of the altar.
> Come, pass the night in sackcloth,
> you ministers of my God!
> Grain offering and drink offering
> are withheld from the house of your God.
>
> Sanctify a fast,
> call a solemn assembly.
> Gather the elders
> and all the inhabitants of the land
> to the house of Yhwh your God,
> and cry out to God. (1:13–14)

## The Fire and the Flame

It is important to Joel that Judah awake to the reality of the crisis. Joel urges Judah to plead publicly for Yhwh's help — as an act of penitence and as a plea for assistance. As we move through Joel, we do not see the crisis as a punishment for disobedience, but it is a deeply distressing reality that Judah longs to correct (1:5–14). The only way to get there is to repent from sin. There is an urgent sense of repentance in Joel, and it must be more than a set of external rites, it must be a matter of the heart — for the God who judges sin is the God of compassion and mercy.

It is at this point that verse 15 rings out:

> Alas for the day!
> For the day of the Lord is near,
> and as destruction from the Almighty it comes.

The phrase "the Day of the Lord" is used five times in Joel[12] and only sixteen times in the entire Hebrew Bible. There are other occurrences of related terms, but not this exact phrasing. Hans Wolff suggests that no other witness from the Hebrew Bible gives this phrase as detailed and systematic a treatment as Joel.[13] The phrase cuts both ways — it could be an oracle of judgment against Israel and Judah or against foreign nations.[14] In its broadest sense, it describes the moment when God acts in judgment or salvation. It is God's day because God is the supreme actor, and the object of God's action is either Israel, Judah, or other nations. For Joel there are two alternatives—the salvation of Israel or its destruction. Both are possibilities: 1:4–2:17 is a prophecy of judgment, and 2:18–3:21 shifts to a prophecy of salvation.

In the Hebrew Bible, the Day of the Lord is God's holy war against evil, God's judgment of sin. In Joel, it threatens Israel's ongoing existence as a covenant people, but it is a day whose consequences *may* be averted through repentance.[15] The "Day of the Lord" is a biblical phrase used by prophets to describe the immediate future or the ultimate eschatological consummation.[16]

Most of the Day-of-the-Lord passages refer to judgments of God, but some, such as Zechariah 14:1–21, speak of God's blessing. There are times when it appears as a past day, such as in Zechariah 1:7, Malachi 2:23, and Ezekiel 13:5. In Amos 5:18, 20, it is a coming day. As in Obadiah 14 and Isaiah 13:6, 9, the phrase points to a time when nations will be punished. In Joel 1:15 and 2:1, 11, there are times when the phrase indicates the punishment of Israel. Joel 1:16–20 emphasizes this dimension of punishment:

> Is not the food cut off
>   before our eyes,
> joy and gladness
>   from the house of our God?
>
> The seed shrivels under the clods,
>   the storehouses are desolate;
> the granaries are ruined
>   because the grain has failed.
> How the animals groan!
>   The herds of cattle wander about
> because there is no pasture for them;
>   even the flocks of sheep are dazed.
>
> To you, O God, I cry.
> For fire has devoured
>   the pastures of the wilderness,
> and flames have burned
>   all the trees of the field.
> Even the wild animals cry to you
>   because the watercourses are dried up,
> and fire has devoured
>   the pastures of the wilderness.

Joel recognizes a crisis in the land — the locusts and drought are signs that the Day of the Lord is near. There is cultic lamentation of the economic crisis in 1:16–20. Although locust plagues were common and dreaded, Joel sees this plague as a unique new act of God. Within the Hebrew Bible, locust plagues often have the role of divine visitations as a retaliation for a breach of the covenant.[17] In this plague Joel points to the economic devastation and sees it as the first signs of Israel's eschatological day of judgment. For Joel, Judah stands on the rimbones of disaster and must choose to turn back to God.

Joel's lamentation induces an eschatological alarm found in 2:1–11. Again Joel tells the people:

> Blow the trumpet in Zion;
> sound the alarm on my holy mountain!
> Let all the inhabitants of the land tremble,
> for the day of the Lord is coming, it is near —
> a day of darkness and gloom,
> a day of clouds and thick darkness!
> Like blackness spread upon the mountains
> a great and powerful army comes;
> their like has never been from of old,
> nor will it be again after them
> in ages to come. (2:1–2)

As Joel makes good use of the ideas and vocabulary associated with the Day-of-the-Lord sayings, he is mining the rich memories of the power and destruction of God's wrath that the image evokes. The call to blow the trumpet is in the same form found in Hosea 5:8, in which the warning of the unnamed enemy goes forth. As in Jeremiah 3:5–6, this enemy draws near.

The wall towers of an ancient city were staffed by guards who were to remain vigilant and sound the alarm should an enemy launch an attack. In this passage, God acts as the guard on the tower and through Joel as prophet sounds the alarm so that Judah can take precautions.[18] However, it is not a military defense that Judah must mount. Rather, it is one in which the priests must lead the people to the temple to repent.

In the verses that follow, the scope of the impending calamity unfolds:

> Fire devours in front of them,
> and behind them a flame burns.
> Before them the land is like the garden of Eden,
> but after them a desolate wilderness,
> and nothing escapes them.

They have the appearance of horses,
  and like war-horses they charge.
As with the rumbling of chariots,
  they leap on the tops of the mountains,
like the crackling of a flame of fire
  devouring the stubble,
like a powerful army
  drawn up for battle.

Before them peoples are in anguish,
  all faces grow pale.
Like warriors they charge,
  like soldiers they scale the wall.
Each keeps to its own course,
  they do not swerve from their paths.
They do not jostle one another,
  each keeps to its own track;
they burst through the weapons
  and are not halted.
They leap upon the city,
  they run upon the walls;
they climb up into the houses,
  they enter through the windows like a thief. (2:3–10)

Joel leaves unspoken that God would punish the people for their sins. Indeed, a puzzle within Joel is Joel's silence about the nature of the national sins that prompted the locust plague that is the forerunner of God's awful day. Joel does not report any covenant violations.

Again the memories of the Day of the Lord evoked by Isaiah 13:6, 9 and Zephaniah 1:15 are woven into Joel's warning. This time he reminds the people of its perfect destructive power:

The earth quakes before them,
  the heavens tremble.
The sun and the moon are darkened,
  and the stars withdraw their shining.
Yhwh utters God's voice
  at the head of God's army;
how vast is God's host!
  Numberless are those who obey God's command.
Truly the day of the Lord is great;
  terrible indeed — who can endure it? (2:10–11)

Wolff notes that this arresting description of the coming Day of the Lord concludes with a startling question: "Who can endure it?"[19] Here Joel makes the transition from rhetoric to imminent threat. However, as Joel holds out the awe-fullness of God's wrath and judgment, he turns immediately to possibilities found in repentance:

> Yet even now, says Yhwh,
>   return to me with all your heart,
> with fasting, with weeping, and with mourning;
>   rend your hearts and not your clothing.
> Return to Yhwh, your God,
>   for God is gracious and merciful,
> slow to anger, and abounding in steadfast love,
>   and relents from punishing.
> Who knows whether God will not turn and relent,
>   and leave a blessing behind,
> a grain offering and a drink offering
>   for Yhwh, your God? (2:12–14)

Key for Joel is that repentance be a matter of the heart and not a set of empty, external rites done in perfunctory weariness. Prayer and fasting must now be done with the heart and not as a matter of rote. The people are called to remember that the God who judges sin is also the God of compassion and mercy. The God of Israel remains sovereign even as the people begin genuine lament and repentance. Repentance no more controls God than the magic incantations of pagan priests.[20] Joel is clear that neither rites nor sincere contrition automatically guarantees the result.

God initiates and invites the nation to repentance. As the urgency of repentance unfolds in verse 13, a familiar and quite old story is also unfolding. The time for decision has come. The people can choose to repent and move closer to the possibility of salvation, or they can continue the activities that brought first the locust plague and then the violent and arresting imagery of the relentless, wrathful army of God.

Joel tells Judah to blow the trumpet and begin a genuine lament that involves the whole community, not just those of privilege or the dispossessed:

> Blow the trumpet in Zion;
>   sanctify a fast;
> call a solemn assembly;
>   gather the people.
> Sanctify the congregation;
>   assemble the aged;

gather the children,
   even infants at the breast.
Let the bridegroom leave his room,
   and the bride her canopy.

Between the vestibule and the altar
   let the priests, the ministers of Yhwh, weep.
Let them say, "Spare your people, O Yhwh,
   and do not make your heritage a mockery,
   a byword among the nations.
Why should it be said among the peoples,
   'Where is their God?'" (2:15–17)

Again, it is the community that must gather. As the community laments, so must it gather as a solemn assembly and be sanctified as a congregation. The call to repentance, to lament, takes on a new quality. Joel, the prophet who was well acquainted with the temple, wants *all* the people to seek a rending of the heart that will lead them into true faithfulness before God.

As with other laments, an oracle of salvation answers the prayer of the people:

Then God became jealous for the land,
   and had pity on the people.
In response to the people God said:
I am sending you
   grain, wine, and oil,
   and you will be satisfied;
and I will no more make you
   a mockery among the nations.

I will remove the northern army far from you,
   and drive it into a parched and desolate land,
its front into the eastern sea,
   and its rear into the western sea;
its stench and foul smell will rise up.
   Surely God has done great things!

Do not fear, O soil;
   be glad and rejoice,
   for God has done great things!
Do not fear, you animals of the field,
   for the pastures of the wilderness are green;
the tree bears its fruit,
   the fig tree and vine give their full yield.

O children of Zion, be glad
  and rejoice in Yhwh your God;
for God has given the early rain for your vindication,
  Yhwh has poured down for you abundant rain,
  the early and the later rain, as before.
The threshing floors shall be full of grain,
  the vats shall overflow with wine and oil.

I will repay you for the years
  that the swarming locust has eaten,
the hopper, the destroyer, and the cutter,
  my great army, which I sent against you.

You shall eat in plenty and be satisfied,
  and praise the name of Yhwh your God,
  who has dealt wondrously with you.
And my people shall never again be put to shame.
You shall know that I am in the midst of Israel,
  and that I, Yhwh, am your God and there is no other.
And my people shall never again
  be put to shame. (2:18–27)

As the people lament and repent with their hearts, God chooses salvation for all. The present crisis ends. The plague withdraws; the land becomes fertile again; and the covenant is restored. The future is one of blessings for Judah and judgment for Judah's enemies.

The final Day-of-the-Lord saying in chapters 1 and 2 begins with the reminder that God's spirit is poured out on *all* flesh:

Then afterward
  I will pour out my spirit on all flesh;
your sons and your daughters shall prophesy,
  your old men shall dream dreams,
  and your young men shall see visions.
Even on the male and female slaves,
  in those days, I will pour out my spirit.

I will show portents in the heavens and on the earth, blood and fire and columns of smoke. The sun shall be turned to darkness, and the moon to blood, before the great and terrible day of God comes. Then everyone who calls on the name of God shall be saved; for in Mount Zion and in Jerusalem there shall be those who escape, as Yhwh has said, and among the survivors shall be those whom God calls. (2:28–32)

Here the strong eschatological themes in Joel come to the fore again. The compelling words of Ezekiel 39:29 ("And I will never again hide my face from them, when I pour out my spirit upon the house of Israel") find voice again in Joel. The people whom God has called to life are to be a nation of prophets.

Joel announces a radical transformation of the social order, if not social revolution. In traditional Jewish society, the free, older male was at the top of the social structure.[21] Most of Israel's prophets belonged to this group. Now the distinctions between the sons and daughters, old and young, slave (male and female) and free are swept aside. All people will become prophets, visionaries, and seers. The new people of God no longer recognize privileged individuals. All will live their lives into the future in an intimate relationship with God.

As verse 32 ends chapter 2, Joel refers to the announcement of salvation in verse 27: "And my people shall never again be put to shame." The divine promise will become a final fortress of refuge, for "everyone who calls on the name of Yhwh" shall be saved.[22]

## The Formfulness of Communal Lament

Joel gives us a communal lament of affliction that, with full hearts and genuine worship, evokes an oracle of salvation from God. Such public lament was frequent and familiar — consider the number of individual and communal laments found in the book of Psalms.[23] In the Hebrew Bible, the communal lament is used by and/or on behalf of a community to express complaint, sorrow, and grief over impending doom that could be physical or cultural. It could also be used for a tragedy or a series of calamities that had already happened. Yet the appeal is always to God for deliverance.[24]

By putting their suffering into the form of lament, the people of Judah had to first acknowledge the crisis in their midst. This fuels much of Joel's great pains to draw out the marks of suffering: the grain and cereal offering that is cut off, the devastation of the fields, the very ground in mourning, the wine that has dried up, and the oil that has failed. The crops have failed and fruit trees have dried up. Then Joel ends "surely, joy withers away among the people" (1:12).

By putting words to their suffering, the community could move to a pain or pains that could be named and then addressed. Lament is, in a word, formful.[25] When done as communal lament, it helps the community to see the crisis as bearable and manageable — in the community. Joel, as the one calling the people to lament, remains in the community to help it deal with the experience of crisis and devastation.

Walter Brueggemann notes that laments are genuine pastoral activities.[26] In an essay in which Brueggemann reflects on our contemporary moves away from genuine lament, he suggests that this loss of lament is also a loss of genuine covenant interaction with God.[27] The result is that the petitioner either becomes voiceless or has a voice permitted to speak only praise. When lament is absent, covenant is created only as celebration of joy and well-being. Without lament, covenant is a practice of denial and pretense that sanctions social control.[28]

As Joel shows so well, the power of lament, particularly communal lament, is that the community must recognize its condition and act in faith-filled ways. It is this biblical vision from Joel that fuels much of the present book as I focus on the tragic consequences of an inadequate health-care system that we all endure and its particular impact on the lives of African Americans and the mission and ministry of the church in light of this. Let me be clear to the reader: Black folk may be the focus, but these are issues that affect us all. That is why I believe that *communal* lament can help us best get at these complex issues. For lament enables us and even requires of us to acknowledge and to experience the fullness of our suffering.

As noted earlier, the formfulness of communal lament has a deep moral character that helps the discipline of social ethics do its work in our contemporary contexts. As Joel moves into our present, I believe that we are drawn to explore anew what communal lament can mean for us. Communal lament, as a corporate experience of calling for healing, makes suffering bearable and manageable *in* the community. When we grieve, when we lament, we acknowledge and live the experience rather than try to hold it away from us out of some misguided notion of being objective or strong. We hurt; something is fractured, if not broken. A foul spirit lives in us and among us. We are living in structures of evil and wickedness that make us ill. We must name them as such and seek to repent — not out of form but from the heart. It is only then that we can begin to heal.

Communal lament helps us move to responsible faith — one of praise and thanksgiving and also grief and mourning. We can, as communities of faith, question the nature of radical evil in systems of health and health care that deny the humanity of many. Communal lament in our contemporary world helps us ask questions of justice as we remain in the stream of our religious traditions. For when Israel used lament as rite and worship on a regular basis, it kept the question of justice visible and legitimate.[29]

As Joel reveals, God asks us to return to God with all our hearts. In what we do, be it fasting, weeping, or mourning, we are to rend our hearts, not our clothing. This call to return to God is alive for us today. We are living in whirlpools of catastrophes concerning health and health care in the United States. Only a heart-filled return to God can help us seek ways to work for excellent health and health care for all the members of our society. So I begin with a lament that I hope will become communal.

Communal lament, as I attempt in this book, names problems, seeks justice, and hopes for God's deliverance — so that we may not see that terrible Day of the Lord made real in our lives. Although I cannot declare God's deliverance, the first two tasks are very much within the scope of this book. I believe that Joel's call for repentance and lament to escape the Day of the Lord is apt for us today. It is more than apt: it is necessary because we are in a situation of crisis, and more and more of us are moving into despair.

## Chapter 2

# Fragmented Efforts

## *Health Care in the United States*

As compelling as the words of Joel are, social ethics draws on scripture as only one of its groundings to do its work. As a discipline, social ethics looks at social structures, processes, and communities — especially those that are large and complex. It also looks at socially shared patterns of moral judgments and behavior. A social ethicist asks the question of how we all belong together under God and what our responsibilities are for one another because of this soul-deep relationship with the divine. Some of the questions that arise for the social ethicist again and again are Why? How? What are we to do? How are we to respond? What have we created? What are we called to create? What leads to freedom? Are we on the path to salvation?

Social ethics pays close attention to social contexts and how they shape and direct our sense of a moral self and moral action — our moralities. Social ethicists know that the social context influences the perspectives and incentives of the individuals acting within it. They explore issues of individual and collective moral responsibility and what is right action. So they look at what policies and practices institutions should follow and not only at how individuals should behave within the framework of existing policies and practices.

This chapter explores some of the contextual dimensions of health and health care in the United States. I begin with an overview of our current health-care delivery system. I then turn to the health insurance industry and move into overviews of Medicare and Medicaid. I conclude with a consideration of health maintenance organizations (HMOs) and managed-care programs and a brief discussion of national health-care plans. The words of Joel continue to guide this chapter — Joel's words of a communal lament that say there *is* hope for this world. We all deserve affordable and excellent health care.

### The Context of the Fragmentation

In July 1969 President Richard Nixon voiced the lament that the U.S. health-care delivery system was in crisis. With media such as *Time, Fortune, Business*

*Week*, CBS, and NBC picking up the call, the public heard that our health-care system was "chaotic," "archaic," and "unmanageable."[1] In an essay the following year, Barbara and John Ehrenreich identified five problem areas of medicine that exacerbated the situation: "finding a place where the appropriate care is offered at a reasonable price," "finding one's way amidst the many available types of medical care," "figuring out what they are doing to you," "getting a hearing if things don't go right," and "overcoming the built-in racism and male chauvinism of doctors and hospitals."[2] It is both striking and disheartening that these issues first raised in 1970 remain germane for a contemporary examination of the health-care delivery system in one of only two industrialized nations (South Africa is the other) that do not guarantee health-care access for all their citizens. And it is ironic that the United States has one of the highest physician-to-patient ratios in the world.[3]

In 1940, people in the United States spent $4 billion on health care. By 1989, that figure had risen to almost $670 billion. In 1996, it was a staggering $1 trillion. Health care is 12 percent of the gross national product (GNP).[4] In 1994, some analysts projected that the figure will rise to $1.5 trillion or 15 percent of the GNP by the year 2000. However, it is now clear that we may not have to wait until 2000 to see this figure made a reality.[5] This makes health care the third largest industry in the United States. Each year, the percentage of health-care costs in the GNP increases by nearly 20 percent. The federal and state governments also spend more and more monies for health care — growing from about 10 percent of the budget in 1965 to 30 percent in 1985.[6]

## Appropriate Care/Affordable Price

All of us in the United States face a many-tiered labyrinth when we search for appropriate and affordable health care. Factors of income and class, accessibility, ability to pay, and time management often conspire in ways that make achieving health care a part of the dailiness of life difficult.

Regardless of racial-ethnic identity or geographic location, working-class and poor folks face an almost insurmountable challenge in finding appropriate, affordable care.[7] The urban and rural poor suffer from a dearth of health services in their respective communities.

A problem that affects both poor and middle-class people is finding a way to pay for the care they need. In the federal 1997 budget, $4.434 billion were appropriated for low-income discretionary health programs. This staggering figure becomes sobering when we realize that this is actually 4 percent lower than the 1995 prerecession level as adjusted for inflation.[8] Some of the figures within this massive appropriation are troubling.[9] The $802 million appropriated for the Consolidated Health Centers is the same as 1995 when adjusted for inflation. These centers provide health care to more than 8 million people, including 3.5 million children. The Maternal and Child Health Block Grant that supports health care for low-income mothers and children received $681 million — a 6 percent reduction from 1995 when adjusted for inflation. The Indian Health Services Program received $1.806 billion — virtually the same funding as the 1995 inflation-adjusted level.

Finding the time to access the care that is available can be an enormous challenge. Those in nonsalaried positions can face the prospect of losing a full work day for a routine doctor's appointment in either a clinic or a private setting.

The numbers of charitable facilities that provide free health care continue to decline, and we are faced with the reality that health care is a commodity that we purchase as consumers from providers that were, until recently, unregulated and charged steadily increasing prices. Our health-care system is a private system, unlike much of our educational system.

## (Un)Insurance

From 1980 to 1989, the number of uninsured U.S. citizens increased by nearly 7 million. In 1993, 39 million people in the United States did not have medical insurance. In 1996, that number had risen to 42 million. At least 2 million of the uninsured are considered "uninsurable" because of pre-existing conditions. At least 18 percent of the children in the United States have no medical insurance.[10] When the American College of Physicians (ACP) released the 1996 figures, it attributed the increase to the continued decline in employer-provided coverage and to Medicaid funding cuts.[11] The ACP noted that the problem was not confined to the poor but extended to households with annual incomes of more than $33 thousand, which is more than twice the poverty level for a family of four. These households made up 14 million of those without insurance.

The ACP deemed the declining coverage a "moral and economic issue" and urged Bill Clinton and Robert Dole to address this in the platforms being shaped by their respective parties for the upcoming presidential election in the fall of 1996. The ACP also called for a public debate to explore alternatives to our current employer-based health insurance system. The group saw this as pressing given that the percentage of workers receiving health insurance as a fringe benefit declined from 66 percent in 1983 to 62 percent in 1996. This translates to 12.5 million people (almost 9 percent of the nonelderly population) who lost employer-sponsored coverage between 1988 and 1993.[12]

According to U.S. Census Bureau figures released in 1990, workers in agriculture, household employment, construction, forestry, and fishing had uninsurance rates higher than 30 percent.[13] Workers employed in entertainment, retail trade, repair, and personal services had uninsurance rates between 20 and 30 percent. Sobering among all these numbers is the fact that only 7 percent of the uninsured were unemployed adults.

The uninsured are a panorama of U.S. society.[14] In 1990, 33 percent were Hispanics/Latinos; 20 percent were African Americans; 10.7 percent were White (not Hispanic). For Hispanics/Latinos, 46 percent of Mexicanos, 39 percent of Central and South Americans, 35 percent of Chicanos, 27 percent of Mexican Americans, 21 percent of Cubans, and 16 percent of Puerto Ricans were uninsured. Within these statistics for Hispanics/Latinos was the startling figure that 21 percent of those whose family incomes were above $50 thousand were uninsured, and 39 percent of those with family incomes below $25 thousand were uninsured. Those Hispanics/Latinos 65 years or older were at a much greater risk of being uninsured (5 percent compared to 0.9 percent) than any other racial-ethnic group of seniors. Only 45 percent of all Hispanics/Latinos had private insurance compared to 77 percent of Whites.[15]

The figures for African Americans in 1990 are also disturbing.[16] Considering gender, 24 percent of men and 18 percent of women were uninsured. In terms of income, 16 percent of those with family incomes above $50 thousand annually and 24 percent of those below $25 thousand annually were uninsured. Fifteen percent of Black children and 30 percent of young adults between the ages of 18 and 39 were uninsured. Only 46 percent of African Americans had private insurance, compared to 77 percent of Whites.

In terms of income, 5.3 million of the uninsured had family incomes above $50 thousand, and an additional 7.2 million had family incomes between $25 thousand and $50 thousand annually. The uninsured of 1990 included 18,600 lawyers, 29,000 physicians, 52,500 clergy, 58,000 college professors, 90,000 engineers, and 270,000 teachers. Among occupational groups, only judges and legislators had universal coverage.

The ironic twist here is we have these alarming figures for the uninsured when, as a nation, we are constantly increasing our use of health services even as those services continue to rise in cost. Many of us pay for our health care directly out-of-pocket. However, it is more common for us to pay for services through third-party payers (insurance companies).[17] In the United States, employers pay for most private insurance coverage (two-thirds of U.S. workers are covered through employee plans).[18] Traditionally, insurance companies reimburse doctors, hospitals, and/or patients after the care has been given and a bill submitted to the company. This is known as fee-for-service.

Most policies cover only part of the bill, and most have deductibles, which means that patients must pay a set amount before the insurance coverage covers part or all of the rest of the expense. This arrangement is known as cost-sharing. Unfortunately, one effect of cost-sharing is that the poor often have less access to needed health care because of the out-of-pocket expenses that cost-sharing demands from the patient. It is also possible that treatment for mental health or dental care may not be covered. This set of circumstances becomes even more pressing when youth, income, and access are combined.

Parents with moderate incomes are finding it almost impossible to get affordable health insurance policies for their children.[19] As the number of employers offering health coverage to families declines, the insurance industry has not filled the gap with affordable health coverage plans. From 1987 to 1995, there was an 8 percent drop (67 to 59) in the coverage for children in employer-based insurance plans. Between 1995 and 1996, nearly 23 million children under the age of eighteen (33 percent) were without health insurance for at least one month. Most of these children were from working families with incomes of $15 thousand or more. Almost half of these children were uninsured for twelve months or longer, and fewer than 7 percent were uninsured less than three months. Wendy Lazarus, the director of the Children's Partnership, a Santa Monica, California, advocacy group notes: "Parents are willing and eager to invest their money on their kids, but what we are seeing is there are very few companies marketing child-only plans. You have to be very persistent to find them."[20]

Often policies are as high as $100 per month per child. This is a stiff figure for families who are juggling a host of demands on a limited budget and constricted income. The price and availability of children's insurance vary by state and community with no set standard. For instance, in southern California, the children's health insurance market is large and competitive. There, it may be the case that parents find it more affordable to purchase plans for their children outside of their employers' plans. In Missouri, parents can purchase individual adult policies for their children, but there is no market designed specifically for children.

A young, White, Kansas couple with an income of about $1 thousand per month discovered that Blue Cross and Blue Shield could insure their four-year-old daughter for a $50 premium. This was within their budget, but they found that they could not get similar coverage for their nine-month-old son. Kansas Blue Cross and Blue Shield stopped accepting children under the age of one in 1996 because of the costs associated with birth problems, immunizations, and frequent office visits. Blue Cross and Blue Shield spokeswoman Janet Cooper stated that "if we included it [coverage for the previously named services] from birth, the rates would have just been unaffordable for the vast majority."[21] At least one health-care-policy analyst, Deborah Chollet of the Alpha Center (a nonprofit health policy think tank based in Washington, D.C.), believes that it is unlikely that private insurers will ever meet the demand for insurance for children.

There are private and government initiatives, however, that are trying to fill the need for affordable children's health insurance. Most states have made Medicaid available to more children in low-income families, but there are still many more children who remain without insurance. Missouri and Kansas are among twenty-three states with "caring programs" sponsored by local Blue Cross and Blue Shield companies that offer insurance to low-income children. For example, in Kansas City, Missouri, the Missouri Valley Caring Program for children combines public donations and doctors who volunteer to provide free outpatient care to 1,004 children. The midyear 1997 waiting list for this program was 216 children.[22] In the Daytona Beach, Florida, area, the Health Kids program begun in 1992 now covers 37,000 children in sixteen counties. The families enrolled in this program are typically "two married adults, one or both working, . . . high school graduates or have some college."[23] The executive director of this program suggests that there are many families nationwide who fit this profile.

But to return to the young, White, Kansas couple for a moment. They were reluctant to seek help from Medicaid, but eventually had no other option. They planned to use this coverage only in the case of a medical emergency for their nine-month-old son. The mother's words are quite telling about the ways in which poverty has been moralized with a stigma: "I feel guilty doing this and some people may look down on me, but it's for the health and safety of my child."

Our current health-care insurance options did not emerge until the early 1950s. This is when private commercial insurers who covered lower-risk individuals became the norm.[24] By the end of the 1980s, commercial insurers handled 40 percent of the market. These companies, such as Prudential, Aetna, Metropolitan Life, and Cigna, were profit-oriented businesses. (This distinction is important given the dominance of Blue Cross and Blue Shield until this time. Until 1994, Blue Cross was a nonprofit association of eighty insurance companies. Blues now have the freedom to convert to for-profit companies. Some have done so, and others are considering doing so.)[25] The commercial insurers are concerned because as the cost of medical care rises and as people access that care in greater numbers, the insurers' profit margins are falling. This has prompted insurers to explore alternatives to the traditional, retrospective, fee-for-service method of payment and move into prospective methods of payment for health care.

Some theorized that a more competitive arena between insurance providers and health-care providers would lower medical costs to the consumer. The reality is that many insurance companies and health-care provider networks do not accept or make it difficult for those with expensive medical problems to join those health-care plans.[26] What is happening is that the older form of setting insurance rates and coverage, community rating, is being replaced by experience rating. With community rating, the health-care costs of entire communities were averaged so that those with more expensive medical problems were included with those with minor to no medical problems. The community shared the cost of health care so that all could be covered. Experience rating means that insurance premiums and accessibility to insurance depend on the projected level of an individual's health-care needs.

## Medicare and Medicaid

The Federal Health Care Financing Administration (HCFA) administers the Medicare and Medicaid programs that help pay the medical bills for more than 72 million beneficiaries. Of those, 6 million were dually entitled (covered by both Medicare and Medicaid). The majority of beneficiaries in these plans are in fee-for-service programs; however, an increasing number of beneficiaries are in managed-care programs. In 1967, national health costs were $51 billion (6.3 percent of the GNP). By 1995, the HCFA expenditures were $248.9 billion (16.4 percent of the federal budget). Paralleling this massive shift, the expenditure per-person increased from $247 in 1967 to $3,510 in 1994.

Medicare was created by the 1965 Federal Social Security Act to provide hospital and medical insurance for those over sixty-five, those with permanent kidney failure, and those with certain disabilities. This program covers 37 million people. Medicaid was also created in 1965 to provide assistance for needy and low-income people. This population includes children, the aged, those who are blind and/or disabled, and those eligible to receive federally assisted income maintenance payments. The federal government and state governments work together in this program with each state having its own eligibility criteria and administering the program. This program covers more than 36 million people — making it the largest program providing medical and health-related services to the poor in the United States. To qualify in some states, a person must be *poorer* than the federal poverty standard and meet other state-specific standards such as being a single parent.

The range of services covered by these plans is an important part of understanding how Medicare and Medicaid function in our society.[27] The number of inpatient hospital facilities decreased from 6,707 in 1975 to 6,376 in 1996. With this came a decrease of 45 percent for inpatient hospital beds per 1,000 enrolled (51.5 to 28.4). The number of psychiatric hospitals grew to almost 400 by 1976 and remained at that number until 1983 with the start of the prospective-payment system. Since then, the number of psychiatric hospitals has grown to 682. Skilled nursing facilities had a rapid increase during the 1960s, then decreased in the first half of the 1970s. By 1996, there were 13,444 facilities (a 6.4 percent increase since the beginning of 1995). The number of home-health agencies peaked in December 1970 and then remained stable until the passage of the Omnibus Budget Reconciliation Act of 1980, which permitted the certification of proprietary agencies in states not having licensure laws. Between 1995 and 1996, there was a 7.2 percent growth of such agencies (7,827 to 8,437). This from a previous high of almost 6,000 agencies in 1986.

## *Medicare*

This is the largest health insurance program in the United States. It covers roughly 37 million Americans who are sixty-five or older and the disabled. There are two parts to Medicare: Part A is Hospital Insurance, and Part B is Medical Insurance. Part A provides coverage for inpatient hospital services, dialysis, skilled nursing facilities, home-health services, and hospice care. It is anticipated that unless the federal government takes action, there will be a budget shortfall of $90 to $120 billion over the next seven years. Medicare Part B helps pay for physician costs, outpatient hospital services, medical equipment and supplies, and other health services and supplies. To use Part A, one must have certain financial difficulties, but Part B has no such stipulations. To enroll in Part B, those who qualify must simply complete an application form at their local Social Security Administration office.

Those enrolled in Medicare increased from 19.5 million in 1967 to 38.1 million in 1996 — a 95 percent increase. Medicare State Buy-In Programs, in which states enroll people in Medicare Part A and Part B, have grown from about 2.9 million recipients in 1975 to over 4.8 million in 1995 — a 66 percent increase. Enrollees with end-stage renal disease increased from over 66,700 in 1980 to nearly 257,000 in 1995 — a 285 percent increase. The total number of Medicare certified beds in short-stay hospitals peaked at just over 1 million in 1984–85 and then dropped to the current level of 926,000.[28]

Medicare skilled-nursing benefit payments increased from $7.1 billion in 1994 to $9.1 billion in 1995 — a 28.2 percent increase. Medicare home-health-agency benefit payments grew from $12 billion in 1994 to $15.1 billion in 1995 — a 25.8 percent increase. Hospice expenditures grew from $1.4 billion in 1994 to $1.9 billion in 1995.

These massive outlays of money are ripe for fraud and mismanagement. Unfortunately, both have found a home in this system. The HCFA is well aware of the billions of dollars lost to Medicare fraud. In its July 31, 1996, World Wide Web bulletin, "Medicare Fraud and Abuse" (see www.hcfa.gov/medicare/mbfraud.htm), the HCFA notes that a cooperative effort among beneficiaries, Medicare contractors, providers, and state and federal agencies is needed to curb abuse. As of 1995, Texas, New York, Florida, California, and Illinois were home to 40 percent of all Medicare and Medicaid beneficiaries. These states have been the focus of the federal government's efforts to curb fraud through Operation Restore Trust (ORT). ORT targets home-health agencies, nursing homes, durable medical equipment suppliers, and hospice centers because these industries receive about 40 percent of all Medicare and Medicaid dollars each year, and they have been identified as problem industries in terms of fraud.

The guidelines from the HCFA bulletin are clear about the ways in which beneficiaries can identify possible fraud. In a section entitled "Most Common Medicare Rip-offs," the HCFA suggests that beneficiaries be suspicious if any of the following happen:

- Services are not rendered or equipment is not received
- You are offered free testing or screening in exchange for your Medicare card number
- Your provider performs services that exceed what is needed
- Your provider offers or accepts referral fees from another provider in exchange for the referral
- Your provider has misrepresented the services billed to Medicare
- You are charged for filling out claim forms
- A doctor or durable medical equipment supplier claims that you will not have to pay the 20 percent coinsurance or deductible that Medicare generally requires if you use his or her services. These charges can only be waived in special cases of financial hardship

If a beneficiary suspects fraud or has any questions about the bill, he or she is urged to call the Medicare carrier or intermediary who sent the Explanation of Benefits notice.

In the next section, "Tips to Prevent Fraud," the HCFA urges beneficiaries to review payment notices from Medicare for errors and report all suspected instances of fraud and abuse. The payment notice shows what Medicare was billed for, what Medicare paid, and what the beneficiary owes. The bulletin ends with a list of tips to prevent fraud:

- Don't ever give out your Medicare Health Insurance Claim Number (on your Medicare card) except to your doctor or other Medicare provider.
- Don't allow anyone, except appropriate medical professionals, to review your medical records or recommend services.

- Don't contact your physician to request a service that you do not need.
- Do be careful in accepting Medicare services that are represented as being free.
- Do be cautious when you are offered free testing or screening in exchange for your Medicare card number.
- Do be cautious of any provider who maintains they have been endorsed by the Federal government or by Medicare.
- Do avoid a provider of health-care items or services who tells you that the item or service is not usually covered, but they know how to bill Medicare to get it paid.

As the HCFA seeks to educate beneficiaries about fraud, the disturbing facts and figures concerning fraud continue to come to public attention. One example of the scope of this kind of fraud is that of a Florida businessman who defrauded Medicare and private insurance companies of more than $51 million by selling adult diapers to nursing homes as "female urinary collection devices" through his nursing-home supply business.[29] His sentence was without parole, and the district court judge ordered him to pay $4.1 million of restitution. This was in addition to the $2.5 million already paid and the $32 million the government had seized from bank accounts. Between January 1993 and May 1994 alone, this businessman defrauded the system of more than $4.1 million in the state of Kansas. His biggest fraud took place in Florida.

The home-health-care industry, which serves 7 million people, is another area that suffers from fraud. In August 1997, federal authorities issued a 102-count indictment against twelve people associated with Mederi (an agency in Dade County, Florida) for defrauding Medicare of $15 million worth of fictitious patient visits.[30] Federal audits in 1997 found that 40 percent of home-health visits paid for by Medicare in California, Illinois, New York, and Texas did not qualify for reimbursement. Further, 25 percent of home-health-care agencies that are certified to bill Medicare have defrauded or exploited the program. In 1996, Medicare spent $17 billion in home-health care.

## *Medicaid*

The number of recipients of Medicaid — a program designed to provide medical and health-related services to the poorest among us — increased from about 10 million in 1967 to 37.5 million in 1996 — a 275 percent increase. Dependent children rose from 9.8 million in 1985 to 18.2 million in 1996 — an 86 percent increase. In terms of our total population (not including military personnel), those on Medicaid were 13.8 percent of the population in 1996. This is a 35 percent increase from 1990 when they were 10.2 percent of the population.

Medicaid follows national guidelines provided by the federal government, and each state then establishes its own eligibility standards; determines the type, amount, duration, and scope of services; sets the rate of payment for services; and administers its own program. This means that Medicaid varies from state to state as well as within each state over time.

When Medicaid was created in 1965 it carried the promise that it would help end a dual-class medical-health delivery system. Inadequate funding, low physician payment rates, and increasing costs of long-term care have thwarted the realization of its promise. This is particularly true for poor mothers and their children. For instance, a 1986 California study found that pregnant women in twelve California counties could not find a single obstetrician willing to accept the California Medicaid program (Medi-Cal) pay of $518 for prenatal care, delivery, and postpartum care.[31]

As is the case with Medicare, the HCFA must deal with fraud. The HCFA World Wide Web page that deals with Medicaid fraud, "Medicaid Bureau Fraud and Abuse Information,"[32] notes that "fraud and abuse in the Medicaid program is costing tax payers billions of dollars each year." The Medicaid program's price tag has risen from $3.9 billion in 1968 to more than $130 billion in 1993. Although the HCFA is clear that this rising cost is due to a variety of factors, it has decided to focus "on the tremendous amount of money lost to fraud and abuse."

Using a partnership (of beneficiaries, Medicaid providers, contractors, and state and federal agencies) similar to the one it uses to combat Medicare fraud, the HCFA notes "states are primarily responsible for policing fraud in the Medicaid program," so the role of HCFA is to provide increased technical assistance and guidance.

This HCFA bulletin, like the Medicare bulletin, gives a detailed description of common methods used to defraud the system. They are:

- Billing for phantom patient visits
- Billing for goods and/or services not provided, or old items as new
- Billing for more hours than are in a day
- Billing for medically unnecessary testing
- Paying kickbacks in exchange for referrals
- Charging personal expenses to Medicaid
- Inflating the bills for services and/or goods provided

- Concealing ownership of related companies
- Falsifying credentials and double billing

It also gives a list of ways to prevent fraud:

- Review your Medicaid bill to make sure that they actually rendered services and/or items being billed to you. (Verify that the date of service is correct.)
- Do not give your Medicaid claim number to anyone except your doctor or another Medicaid provider.
- Do not contact your doctor/physician to request a service that you do not need.
- Do not share your Medicaid records or recommended services with anyone besides appropriate medical professionals.
- Be suspicious when you are offered free testing or screening in exchange for your Medicaid card number.
- Be careful in accepting Medicaid services represented as free of charge.
- Avoid providers claiming to know how to have Medicaid pay for health care services or items not usually covered.

The recent plan to balance the federal budget by 2001 included the Medicaid Reform Plan. Although details are sketchy at the time of this writing, there are some major directions that have been set. First are the cuts. The plan is designed to cut $22 billion from Medicaid by 2001. This is in addition to dramatic Medicaid reductions (nearly $80 billion) projected in 1995. These reduced spending projections are due to changes in "medical inflation and programmatic changes initiated by states, including requiring enrollment in managed care, reductions in provider reimbursements, services and certain population groups."[33] Roughly two-thirds of the cuts are from the Department of Human Services, which provides funds for hospitals serving a disproportionate share of low-income and Medicaid beneficiaries. Judy Waxman and Joan Alker suggest that this reduction may not be harmful to beneficiaries if "funds remaining in this program are properly targeted to essential community providers who really serve low-income and Medicaid beneficiaries."[34] The remaining one-third of cuts comes from a per-capita cap on all Medicaid spending.

Second is flexibility. The Medicaid Reform Plan includes a repeal of the Boren Amendment, which requires that certain standards be set for hospital and nursing home reimbursements; the plan allows states (without waiver requirements) to require that beneficiaries enroll in managed-care plans; and it allows states (without waiver requirements) to enroll beneficiaries in home- and community-based programs. It also includes a proposal giving states the option to let disabled SSI beneficiaries who earn more than a certain amount to buy into Medicaid.

Third is reinvestment. The plan adds $13 billion in new Medicaid expenditures. This allows states to extend continuous Medicaid coverage for a year at a time to children. It also will use Medicaid dollars to fix some coverage problems created by the previous welfare reform bill instituted during the Bush presidency.

The final piece is the Children's Care Initiative, which is designed to extend coverage to about 5 million of the estimated 10 million children who lack health insurance. This program is estimated to cost $10 billion. There are some advocates, such as Waxman and Alker, who are concerned that the cuts to Medicaid will be used to pay for this initiative. In response, the federal government acknowledges that some of the funding is coming from the existing Medicaid program. However, it also states that these cuts in Medicaid are offset, in part, by some proposals in the children's initiative that are called "Medicaid reinvestment."[35]

The Children's Care Initiative has a five-pronged strategy. First is the workers-between-jobs initiative. This helps pay health insurance premiums for those temporarily unemployed and their families. This includes annual grants to states to pay for COBRA (Consolidated Budget Reconciliation Act) costs or other private plans for up to six months. There is a full subsidy to families who are 100 percent under the poverty level with subsidies continuing on a sliding scale up to persons who are 240 percent above the poverty level. The government estimates coverage of 3.3 million people, including 700,000 children, in 1998 at a cost of $9.8 billion over the five-year budget cycle.

Second is state partnership grants. This is a very small program to states to cover children whose parents' incomes are too high for Medicaid but who can't afford private coverage. The federal government estimates that this will cover 1 million children at a cost of $750 million over the five-year budget cycle.

Third is a plan to help adolescents in low-income families. Under the current plan, low-income children between thirteen and eighteen are phased into Medicaid. The federal government estimates that 1 million uninsured will gain coverage under this plan. There is no additional cost associated with this plan because it is not a new initiative.

Fourth is Medicaid twelve-month continuous eligibility. This would allow children who sign up for Medicaid to remain on the program a full year, regardless of changes in their families' incomes. Although it is not clear at the time of this writing, this feature is likely to become a state option and not a requirement. The federal government estimates that more than 1 million children will be continuously covered at a cost of $3.7 billion over the five-year budget cycle.

The final prong is Medicaid outreach. This is aimed at enrolling 3 million poor children who are eligible for, but not receiving, Medicaid. No money was authorized to accompany this initiative, and there are few details available about how it will be implemented. The federal government estimates that this will provide coverage for an additional 1.6 million children.

## The Maze of Types of Care

As we face the complex questions of affordability and accessibility, we must also sort through the tangled threads of the type of care we can receive. Health care is tangibly different from other commodities. We often cannot predict when we need it; it may be delayed, but it is rarely optional; far too often we, as consumers, receive limited information about the nature and options we have for our care; and there is scant knowledge of the ultimate price of the care we do and will receive.[36]

Two major age groups have the most illnesses and are in greatest need of health care — people between twenty and thirty and those over sixty-five. In the twenty to thirty age group, acute conditions such as colds, influenza, and a variety of injuries predominate. With those over sixty-five, chronic illnesses that present the greatest cost to society predominate. Nearly 86 percent of those over sixty-five have one or more chronic illnesses.[37] As we continue to live longer, the prevalence of chronic disease increases as well. The three most frequent illnesses are arthritis, hypertension, and heart disease.

The poor live shorter, unhealthier, and more disabled lives. The realities of mental illness, poor educational systems, crime, inadequate housing, environmental racism, limited income, and drug use create a deadly conundrum. People who earn less than $9,000 a year have the highest death rates and are more likely to have hypertension, arthritis, upper respiratory illnesses, speech difficulties, and eye disease.[38]

Given the ways in which we are (un)healthy, options for our care are vital. As noted previously, the U.S. health-care delivery system is moving away from fee-for-service plans to prospective-payment plans. Perhaps the best known of the prospective-payment plans is the health maintenance organization (HMO). More than 36 million people in the United States belong to one of the HMO plans. Generally, those enrolled in an HMO pay a monthly, quarterly, or annual prepayment (capitation) fee that covers all health-care services for that period of enrollment. There may be an additional fee from $5 to $10 for each office visit, and prescriptions may cost $3 to $10.

Some HMOs allow the patient to select a doctor from the list of physicians on staff or may assign a doctor at the time of enrollment. HMO doctors receive an annual salary for each patient they see annually. This amount is the same no matter how often the patient sees the doctor. The major feature of an HMO is that it offers the most cost- or labor-effective treatments. This is largely because the doctor or hospital no longer receives a fee for each service (office/clinic visit, procedure, hospitalization).

The preferred provider organization (PPO) is like the HMO in that it works on the prospective-payment model. Hospitals and doctors in a PPO provide their services to companies' employees at a reduced, prearranged rate. Patients select their doctors from a list of those who participate in the PPO. Both the HMO and PPO limit the number of new hospitalizations and cut down on the number of days patients spend in hospitals.

As the medical care system moves increasingly away from fee-for-service care, understanding the structure of managed care becomes more and more vital. With managed care, insurance companies have a major voice in determining the services delivered by doctors and hospitals. Managed-care companies will only pay for medical procedures and hospitalizations that they have preapproved. This means that doctors and other health-care professionals may spend a sizable amount of energy and time negotiating with managed-care companies.[39] Insurance or managed-care companies decide if services are unnecessary or inappropriate and can and do refuse to pay for these services.

Four measuring systems and organizations are used to determine the efficacy of care and service. Diagnosis Related Groups (DRGs) are a classification system adopted by the federal government to determine reimbursement for Medicare patients. State and federal payments to hospitals are based on set fees related to the patient's diagnosis. An important feature of this system is that the hospital knows how much it will receive based on the particular DRG it is rated as. The hospital makes money if the actual cost of treatment is less than the predetermined amount; it loses money if the treatment costs more than the DRG allowance.

The Resource-Based Relative Value Scale (RBRVS) is designed to help third-party payers (e.g., insurance companies) determine how much to reimburse doctors. Health-care services and providers are rated for length of procedure, the expense of overhead, the cost of running a doctor's office, and the cost of the doctor's training. Professional Standards Review Organizations (PSROs) were created by the federal government to review the quality of health care paid for with federal funds. These are also set up on a local basis by medical associations for monitoring the practice standards of physicians. Finally, Peer Review Organizations (PROs) have replaced PSROs as the federal system that reviews the hospital costs to Medicare.

There was, however, an important transition that occurred before the present managed-care system emerged, and that transition needs to be addressed. John Lantos, a University of Chicago physician who worked on the failed attempt by the Clinton administration to reform health care, notes the move doctors made from multispeciality group practices to speciality group practices.[40] For Lantos, this means that doctors failed to respond to contemporary political, moral, and economic challenges, and instead

> identified with a particular speciality, and imagined a profession that was infinitively divisible. They thought a lot about what was good for pediatricians, surgeons, or gastroenterologist, what was good for academic medical centers or rural family practices, but not about what they all had in common. . . . Proposals for reform come from subspecialty groups, and usually reflect rather transparent attempts to benefit those subspecialities. Though unsuccessful in its attempt at health-care reform, the Clinton administration did learn that it could effortlessly play off primary-care doctors against specialists, salaried doctors against those who still worked in fee-for-service arrangements, doctors who care for the young against doctors who care for the old.[41]

With all the changes in philosophy, delivery, and actual care that the prospective-payment model engenders, many doctors have turned to physician-practice management for relief. This industry promises the doctor a lucrative salary and deals with HMOs and other administrative hassles to free the doctor to concentrate on patient care. Advocates say that physician-practice management puts the doctor back in charge of medicine while critics suggest that this is simply trading one corporate overseer for another.[42]

Part of the reason for the rise in physician-practice management is the decline in physician income caused by HMOs. With the focus on keeping patients well, all goes well unless too many patients get sick. In the worst-case scenario, doctors can be (and are) pressured to restrict treatment or risk losing income. HMOs also require doctors to document the need for expensive drugs and treatment — an administrative nightmare for some physicians. With most doctors still working in one- or two-person practices, they have little bargaining power with an HMO.[43] When doctors use a practice-management company, the company uses the numbers of physicians it manages to negotiate higher fees from HMOs; relieve doctors of billing, payroll, and scheduling; and supply them with medical technologies that can improve and track patient health.[44]

As these new options for health-care delivery join the traditional model, we are faced with the need to be even wiser consumers about our health care. Health care has moved firmly into the camp of big business and profit margins.

Another development is an increase in the number of medical students who are specializing in primary-care medicine — pediatrics, internal medicine, or family practice. Because of the structure of managed care, primary physicians are the "gatekeepers" to specialized referrals. In 1996, more than half of the physicians graduating from U.S. medical schools who participated in the National Residency Matching Program specialized in primary care.[45] Medical school personnel believe that the number of students who choose primary-care specialities will continue to rise, but that this will not leave a dearth of specialists.

## Figuring Out What They Are Doing to You

Our health care sits in the midst of a field of ironies. Between 1970 and 1982, the number of health-care providers increased by 57 percent while the number of health-care administrators increased by 171 percent.[46] We make heroic and extremely expensive efforts to save low-birth-weight premature babies while childhood immunization rates have a lower priority. Four out of ten children between the ages of one and four are not immunized against mumps, polio, rubella, or measles. The rate of nonimmunization is even higher among children in racial-ethnic groups.[47] Depression is one of the underrecognized and undertreated serious, long-term medical conditions.

The percentage of the national health-care budget for prevention is only 0.3 — three-tenths of 1 percent. U.S. medical professionals from across the range of expertise suggest that major improvements to our life expectancy are mostly due to preventive efforts in our lives — such as improved diet and housing conditions.[48] By at least one estimate, up to 70 percent of all illness — especially diabetes, high blood pressure, heart disease, and cancer — may be related to our self-destructive lifestyles.[49] We are a nation of overeaters, with high-fat and high-salt diets, who lack exercise. Among the youngest of us, prenatal care and vaccination are crucial to enhancing life expectancy and decreasing infant mortality. For the oldest of us, improved life expectancy means caring for chronic illnesses, but our current health-care system still falters when it comes to providing for nursing homes and other extended-care facilities.

As health care moves increasingly toward prospective payment, it is crucial that we understand what is being prescribed as care and as healthy for our bodies. It is imperative that we understand the nature of our illnesses and the options of treatment available, and that we become advocates for our own care and that of others. As health care has become a big business, our lives have become far too much like commodities.

We are quickly moving away from the era when our concerns may have been unnecessary procedures and unnecessary and inappropriately long hospitalizations to one in which we have to fight for procedures and advocate for longer hospital stays. The demands of profitability have changed the shape of health care in this nation. We are, as Jane Bryant Quinn suggests, in a new world of medical rationing.[50] She notes that as patients, their relatives, their friends, and community advocates place pressure on legislators, almost every state in this country has passed at least one law reversing new cuts in treatment. Managed-care companies argue that the government should not be involved in the insurer-patient relationship, and HMOs take the position that legislatures should not micromanage medical care. Both concerns are valid, but added to this mix are patients who often feel as if they are up against a monopoly where they have few options.

According to the National Conference of State Legislatures, common consumer questions that states have dealt with include: Which doctor should you call? When are emergencies paid for? Whom can you trust? Will you be offered a last chance at life? Will your health plan stabilize your newborn? Can you stay in the hospital after a mastectomy?[51] These kinds of basic questions contain some interesting twists and turns.

A 1993 Gallup Poll revealed that most women consider gynecologists to be their primary doctors. Under managed care, gynecologists are considered specialists and a woman must be referred to one by a primary-care physician in the managed-care plan. Twenty states now have laws that allow women in managed-care plans to see gynecologists and obstetricians without first getting another doctor's permission.

HMOs do not cover unauthorized treatment in nonmember hospitals as a rule. They will pay if there is an emergency, but they may decide, upon reviewing the claim, that there was no emergency. Seventeen states have passed laws that the require HMOs to pay for emergency treatment at nonmember hospitals if it seems reasonable that the patient considered the condition an emergency.

Some managed-care plans require that doctors not tell patients about alternative treatments or about whether the doctor has a financial incentive not to treat. Such doctors are also told not to discuss competing plans. Twenty states have made these kind of gag rules illegal and bar managed-care plans from retaliating against doctors who do discuss alternatives.

The question of being offered a last chance at life is one of the most complex health-care issues. For instance, only a few states require managed-care plans to allow bone marrow transplants for women with advanced breast cancer. Many plans pay voluntarily, but there is no consistency in the industry regarding this and other expensive medical procedures that may help to prolong life.

The recent uproar concerning length of hospital stays after childbirth has helped pass a federal law that is to go into effect in 1998 that makes insurers pay for a stay of up to forty-eight hours for normal births and ninety-six hours for Cesareans. Currently, twenty-nine states require health insurance payments for longer maternity stays.

An equally irate uproar ensued concerning hospitalization after a mastectomy. Some HMOs do not let patients stay overnight after the surgery. As of this writing, fifteen states have introduced bills requiring HMOs to allow inpatient stays for mastectomy patients.

We absolutely must learn to ask questions about our health care. Medical technology is complex and mystifying, but it is not completely unfathomable. When the Ehrenreichs wrote their essay in 1970, they were concerned about overbilling, more affordable treatment, and expensive and unnecessary procedures. In the late 1990s, we now are faced with the other side of the coin.

## Patient Advocacy If Things Go Awry

"Patients' rights" is a relatively new term. It covers aspects of the patient-physician and patient-provider relationship. It includes the right to responsible medical care, confidentiality of personal information and conversations, the right to be informed about treatments and their likely consequences, the right to either accept or reject treatment once informed, and access to private records kept by a physician, hospital, or other organization.[52] It does not necessarily include full disclosure of the patient's prognosis, however.

Until the 1960s, patients had little choice in their course of treatment. But the rise of claims for medical malpractice, the consumer-rights movement's demands that manufacturers provide more product information, and the growth of alternative medicine and therapies have contributed to the movement away from the more paternalistic attitude that dominated the patient-physician and patient-provider relationship.

Patient-directed care, a new concept, is a further development in this trend. The focus here is primarily on the patient's or consumer's satisfaction, in contrast to the traditional model that focused on the condition — not the patient with the condition.[53]

These newer forms of advocacy are important in helping us vigorously address the changes that managed care has wrought within the health-care delivery system in this country. Unlike the Ehrenreich's world of the 1970s, we now have opportunities to challenge breakdowns or incompetencies in our care. But it is not an easy task even today. Those among us who have greater financial resources have a greater ability to seek redress if something goes wrong.

## Overcoming Systemic Paternalism and Racism

Most of us desire good health for ourselves and for others. As more information becomes available through various print media and the Internet, we are able to sort through issues of proper diet, to better understand the role of nutritional supplements such as vitamins, and to learn more about medical conditions such as hypertension, menopause, various cancers, and depression. As we begin to make greater use of these resources, we become better able to assert our rights as patients for competent and excellent health care.

Like the rest of our society, the U.S. medical system suffers from interstructured paternalism and racism. One of the foundational aspects of this problem is the way the majority of doctors receive their training and the lack of rigorous and ethically responsible clinical trials that include racial-ethnic men and women and White women. I will discuss this in greater detail in chapter 5.

Another key aspect is the recent development that hospitals are limiting the number of physicians they train. Many hospitals are making this move because of rising medical costs. In addition, health-care analysts have argued since the early 1980s that the United States produces more doctors than it needs.[54] However, others are warning that making such cuts threatens providing medical care for racial-ethnic communities that are already suffering from a lack of doctors and medical services because they never received the benefit of the increased numbers of physicians being trained in the first place.

Nationally, there are approximately 222 physicians for every 100,000 people. Yet in some urban areas, the ratio is as low as 50 physicians per 100,000. This prompted Floyd Malveaux, the vice president of Howard University Medical School in Washington, D.C., to note that the combination of widespread limits on the number of new doctors being trained and rollbacks in affirmative action policies for African American medical school students could increase the disparities already present between White and Black health care.[55] This is because Black doctors are more likely than other doctors to treat Black patients, and most Black doctors practice in areas where the percentage of African American residents is high.[56] Also, Black doctors are more likely to care for patients covered by Medicaid, and Hispanic/Latino doctors are more likely than other doctors to care for uninsured patients.

The National Medical Association (NMA — representing more than twenty thousand racial-ethnic physicians), the American Medical Association (AMA), and other medical organizations have submitted recommendations to federal officials to fund medical training in underserved areas and to increase the number of racial-ethnic medical students. In addition, this coalition of health-care providers also seeks to expand and create programs that recruit medical school graduates to work in underserved areas.[57]

Hopefully, such initiatives will help solve the dilemmas of providing adequate health care to all segments of U.S. society. However, at the heart of all of this is the need to value human beings. There is something horribly wrong when recent studies reveal that seriously ill Blacks receive less and inferior care than Whites for the "the same medical conditions under the same circumstances in virtually every type of hospital in the United States."[58]

## Fragmented Results

Given the vexing nature of health care in the United States, it is not surprising that the issue of a national health-care plan continues to surface as an option. The debate is heated and unfortunately has descended into bombastic rhetoric on all sides. Regardless of the level of the debate, some points need to give us pause as we consider the nature and scope of this lament over our nation's health. It is a sobering reality that countries such as Canada, Great Britain, France, and Germany — countries with national-health plans — do not experience the rising percentage of medical costs in their GNP as we do in the United States.

Much of our current debate would suggest that the idea of a national health-care plan is new or a "liberal" notion. However, President Harry S. Truman proposed a national health insurance plan, which was defeated by the American Medical Association, the rapid growth of Blue Cross and Blue Shield, and the inclusion of health insurance as a fringe benefit for many workers.[59] In the face of a recession, President Richard M. Nixon presented a national insurance plan, but his proposal was defeated with the creation of COBRA, which assures that those who have lost their jobs can continue to pay for their health plans for an additional eighteen months.

Most countries with national health care do not pass on the major costs of medical care to patients and have lower medical costs than the U.S. overall. What has evolved in the United States is a system based on profit priorities rather than need *and* it is the most costly medical care in the world. This cost is not solely technology and expertise, it is also administration. Managing the paperwork mountain required by insurers, Medicare, and Medicaid is daunting.

Countries with national health plans use a form of prospective payment called global budgeting. Global budgeting creates an annual upper limit on how much the local, regional, and national government can spend on health care. The point of global budgeting is to prioritize health-care needs.[60] In Great Britain, the government owns most of the hospitals and pays the doctors' salaries. Other doctors' services are contracted for by the government, which then reimburses them a fixed amount for each patient they see in their practice annually. Doctors receive additional income from administering vaccinations and preventive exams. Patients choose their doctor, and some allowances are made for those who desire private hospital beds or private care for certain operations. All patients must register with a general practitioner who decides if the patient needs to see a specialist. This system costs only a fraction of what we pay in the United States.

Germany has 1,100 sickness funds, which are private, nonprofit insurance providers affiliated with doctors' associations. These funds provide coverage for all low-income workers and their dependents and for all employers who, by law, must join them. Insurance costs are equally divided between workers and employers with the unemployed and retirees covered in a separate arrangement. Sickness funds use global budgeting where the worker and employer premiums cannot rise faster than the income of the workers. Income figures provide the basis for how sickness fund managers set the annual payment rates for providers.

Neither of these global budgeting plans for national insurance is without drawbacks. However, one important element of both of these is that they are based on health-care *need.* The system begins with the assumption that caring for the person, and by extension the community, should be the basis for how to think about and shape health-care delivery. Unlike the situation in the United States, the need to make a profit as a business is secondary to the plan for health.

There is a growing movement of doctors in the United States who are responding to the stresses and demands placed on them by health-care insurers to unite and implement doctor-owned and operated health-care plans. These organizations, physician directed networks (PDNs), are owned, operated, and controlled by doctors.[61] Doctors who are involved in these networks argue that the pressures related to cost, access, and availability in managed-care health plans interfered with the doctor-patient relationship.

The goal of PDNs is to have doctors decide proper patient treatment. Some PDNs are structured so that subscribers can only go to member doctors. If a patient decides to go outside of the system, it becomes an out-of-pocket expense for her or him. Other PDNs are structured more like preferred provider organizations (PPOs), in which if the patient decides to go outside the network, he or she is at least partially reimbursed.

As with all health plans, there are important questions that need to be asked: How are the doctors compensated? What are the review policies? Can the insured go outside the system? If they can, what is the reimbursement rate? What hospitals are involved? What is the overall philosophy of health and health care of the provider?

As we raise these and other questions in order to better understand our options for health care as well as to advocate for health care that considers people's lives and spirits, we approach the full lament that Joel speaks of. We are naming the illnesses, the evils, the realities, and the need to seek salvation from the parts of our health-care delivery system that are inhumane and fueled by a crass drive for greater profitability that disregards the preciousness of life.

## *Chapter 3*

# Shutting Down America When Collard Greens Started Tasting Like Water

## *Black Health and Health Care in the United States*

Our fragmented efforts thus far are pieces to a much larger puzzle that African Americans bring to the health-care debate. We live in a less-than-adequate health-care delivery system in the United States. Forty-two million Americans did not have *any* health insurance for at least one month in 1996. For many included in this figure the average was three months. Less wealth and jobs with fewer or no benefits contributed to the fact that African Americans were a disproportionate number in this group.

These figures are framed within a set of theoretical assumptions about the nature of health and disease that I will explore as groundings for this chapter. Collins Airhihenbuwa points to a deadly tendency in Western medicine to overemphasize health promotion and disease prevention in such a manner that there is little or no meaningful participation of peoples and their cultures in "positive behavioral transformation."[1] He points to practices of health promotion and disease prevention that are driven by a Westernized model that has a heavy emphasis on medicine and individual psychology. Airhihenbuwa notes that such an orientation is continually challenged within public health circles because of its cultural inappropriateness.

Airhihenbuwa emphasizes that health is a cultural production. Therefore, it is imperative that we hold history, politics, education, class, gender, race — all that makes up culture(s) — within the frame of our lament. Because cultures are forms of social interaction accepted by discrete communities within time and place, they evoke worldviews and historical experiences that mark our humanity and inhumanity. Far from being static, cultures are dynamic.

Black cultures in the West are the expressions of African American and Afro-Caribbean syncretism in diaspora. They are based on experience rather than nature and/or biology and are transmitted through language, symbols, and instruction. A key challenge for African Americans is the commodification of this culture — expensive designer clothes based on hip-hop fashion that become a status symbol and are then sold back into the community at exorbitant prices (a process that can involve the loss of life); music that is transformed from creative expression to a plantation industry for young artists; religiosity that is viewed voyeuristically and ill-understood; the (mis)appropriation of anything that looks and feels vaguely African as authentic and valid.

A key challenge for the African American community is to recognize and engage what health as a cultural production means in Black cultures, which are dynamic processes constantly interpreting and reinterpreting values, beliefs, norms, and practices — consciously and unconsciously. This also means that we must recognize that referring to Black culture in the singular is inaccurate. African American life is not a monolith. Black life in the United States is a tapestried reality. Geography, religion, ethnicity, gender, income, occupation, and other factors spark varieties of culture within African American life. There are strong common themes and challenges that help draw Blacks together, but there are equally compelling and necessarily differing paths that Black folk in the United States take toward our commonalities.

Given the richness of African American cultures and our awareness of health as a cultural production, it seems right to fully explore the health of Black folks before going on to advocate models of health care that are affordable and accessible for all of us in U.S. society. Such awareness, exploration, and advocacy are the stuff of genuine lament.

## Slave Culture

Regardless of where African Americans are on the socioeconomic ladder, health problems have a greater impact on Blacks than on other Americans. Two key reasons for this are genetic and environmental. Indeed, environment and its attendant living patterns can trigger the manifestation of the genetic potential for disease in any human being. Black folks have their own traditions, experiences, and health risks. Barbara Dixon notes that recent research is revealing that the rage and stress of living in a racist society are key factors as to why African Americans suffer from poor diet more than other groups. She believes that stress, a traditional U.S. diet that is high in fat and salt, and the Black genetic framework are a deadly combination.[2]

This combination has developed over time. During slavocracy, physicians had a range of deadly and inaccurate beliefs about Africans and African Americans despite the frequent use of slaves in highly questionable medical experiments. One particularly gruesome piece to this history is the "experiments" of J. Marion Sims, the so-called father of American gynecology. Sims conducted hundreds of surgical experiments on slave women in his backyard clinic from 1845 to 1849. He used a bent pewter spoon to pry open these women's labia (he is credited with inventing the speculum). He allowed the White, male medical professionals of his day, whom he invited to his "surgeries," a look into the vagina for the first time. Sims performed repeated, experimental, unanesthetized surgeries on dozens of slave women's vaginas in an attempt to correct vaginal fistulas, small tears between the vagina and urinary tract or bladder that can cause urine to leak. He succeeded in repairing a fistula on a slave named Anarcha in 1849 in the thirtieth operation she had undergone in four years.[3]

Physicians believed that black skin, big glands, big livers, and big kidneys were able to throw heat off more rapidly and that the hearts and brains of Blacks were smaller than Whites. Believing that Black nervous systems were less well developed led doctors to believe that this protected Blacks from fevers and accounted for their "childlike behavior and absolute dependence on whites."[4] They also were sure that Blacks had smaller lungs than Whites, saying that this explained the high incidence of pneumonia and tuberculosis among slaves. Dixon notes: "These physicians, who had no accurate knowledge of how diseases were contracted and spread, drew a scientific portrait of blacks as sluggish, dull in mind, weak in will. It was a portrait so deadly, and so economically useful, that it survives even to this day."[5] No word was spoken about an ongoing brutal environment or inhumane working conditions and treatment. Like any population, Africans had certain resistances and susceptibilities. Africans were genetically adapted to resist one or the more deadly strains of malaria. Today, nearly 100 percent of West Africans have red blood cells that contain a specific antigen that is resistant to one of the four strains of malaria.

Stereotypes revolving around heat and cold added to the victimization of African slaves. The belief that Africans could tolerate heat better than Europeans is somewhat suspect. Dixon notes that slaves probably suffered a *greater* heat load because deeply pigmented skin *absorbs* heat. Additionally, their intense workload would have increased the burden more. She suggests that Africans may have shown a higher *initial* tolerance to extreme humid heat because they were more accustomed to working in that environment. But other laborers probably adjusted to the heat and fared just as well as Africans.[6] She suggests that a physiological feature of Africans — the ability to retain vital body salts — may have helped Blacks balance the quicker absorption of heat by their bodies. Regarding the misconceptions about cold, modern studies of U.S. soldiers reveal that although Blacks may be more susceptible to cold injury at first, over time they acclimate.

Ironically, doctors did miss a deadly disease that involved skin color — rickets. Although dark skin provides protection against sun damage, it does not make as much vitamin D. This may well account for the high incidence of rickets in slave children.

The antebellum medical belief that Africans had small lungs was specious. In addition to the fact that Africans' lungs were no smaller or larger than anyone else's is the reality that pneumonia and tuberculosis ravaged both slaves and slave owners. The important twist is that slaves had a higher initial incidence of respiratory diseases and infections because they had never been exposed to those diseases; thus they had no immune system to fight them off. Slaves worked outdoors in all seasons and in all kinds of weather, and they came home to drafty, cramped cabins that did not protect them from dampness and cold. These kinds of deadly conditions combined with poor nutrition and the speedy spread of airborne infections among people living in close quarters. By failing to take into consideration these factors in the environment of slavery, science of the era was drawn to reach many false conclusions.

Comparative anatomy was not a part of the scientific tool kit of slavocracy. Although, as Dixon notes, there were dissections carried out on Black corpses, there is no recorded instance where their organs were systematically compared with those of Whites.[7] The grim reality of our communal lament is that environment and living conditions — not anatomy — were the factors that led to the greater susceptibility of Africans to certain diseases.

Most plantation owners expected slaves to report illnesses quickly. This was to guard against incapacitation or spreading infections to the White masters and their families and other workers. Midwives, herbologists, dentists, and barbers were used by planters and overseers to care for the health of the slave population. In reality, everyone living in the southern colonies battled infections and diseases. Primary among these were fever, respiratory diseases, and gastrointestinal parasites. However, children were hit especially hard. Slave children died frequently from diphtheria and whooping cough. Gastrointestinal parasites and rickets were joined by severe joint pains, chronic leg ulcers, and abdominal pains — the overt symptoms of sickle-cell disease. Many children died in infancy — born too small with a low birth-weight that led to their high morality rate (a condition that continues to plague Black babies today).

Southern doctors made heavy use of purging drugs, leeches, and lancets — all things that depleted the body of blood and nourishment. From our late twentieth-century vantage point, we can see how these only worsened the condition of a weakened patient. Slaves often became sicker after these treatments and often resisted White remedies. Slaves turned to older relatives rather than report their illnesses to the overseer. African remedies circulated secretly through the slave quarters and were passed from generation to generation in secret because slave owners usually forbade the use of African home cures.[8]

Disagreement remains about the nutrition of slaves, but there are some certainties. Their basic diet was corn and fatback or bacon that was distributed in weekly rations. Some slave owners provided rice instead of corn, and some added molasses and occasionally salted fish to the weekly rations. During hog-slaughtering season in the fall, lesser cuts such as chitlins (also known as chitterlings — intestines), maws (the stomach lining), and hocks (joints) would sometimes be given to slaves.

Meals were simple. A one-dish vegetable stew could last an entire week — the iron from the cast-iron pots providing an unintended dietary supplement. Some slaves hunted wild game and fished. They also introduced black-eyed peas, okra, peanuts, and sesame — all African staples — to the colonies. Dixon suggests that there is good historical evidence that slaves ate from a wide variety of goods with good nutritional value.[9]

For her, the question is whether or not slaves were able to *routinely* supplement their food rations. There were large differences in the daily diets of slaves. Dixon points to new research done on the coasts of South Carolina, Georgia, and northern Florida that shows that slaves were able to fully supplement their food rations. However, slaves away from the coastal plantations had a poorer diet, and hunger was common. Pellagra, a disease caused by a deficiency of niacin, was common. Symptoms began with diarrhea and vomiting. The person would become disoriented and begin to hallucinate and then finally die. Beriberi and "sore mouth" were also common among the slaves. These diseases were caused by deficiencies in vitamin A and many of the B vitamins. Many African slaves, like contemporary African Americans, were lactose-intolerant and therefore unable to digest milk sugar. This prevented many slaves from drinking milk when it was available. Instead of palm oil (as often used in West Africa) slaves had to use lard (that had far less nutritional value) to fry or flavor their food. From this mixed picture, a new culture that combined and mixed African and European colonial mores and customs took root. From these roots emerged the contemporary culture of health for African Americans and the larger U.S. society.

## Into the Twentieth Century

After the Civil War, food remained scarce and newly freed slaves experimented with wild vegetables like dockweed, dandelion greens, lamb's quarter, marsh marigold leaves, milkweed, pokeweed, and purslane. Varieties of pork cuts and salt pork remained the primary meats. Yet Black health continued to deteriorate with such a high death rate, especially in urban areas, that predictions of Black extinction became common. In urban areas, syphilis and tuberculosis overwhelmed the Black community. Children died of fits, seizures, convulsions, and tetanus. Rickets became so common that many African Americans thought that it was a normal stage of development for Black children.

The Black rural migration to the cities carried with it old medical myths that were transformed by centuries of slavery and devastating rural poverty. In what may well be a description of high blood pressure, Blacks thought "high blood" was caused by too much blood migrating to one part of the body, usually the head. They attributed this to consuming too many rich or red-colored foods and drinks such as beets, carrots, grape juice, red wine, and red meat.[10] "Low blood," what we now call anemia, was believed to be caused by eating too much garlic and acidic foods, such as vinegar and pickles, and not enough red meat.

## The Rise of Public Health

The formal health structure most Blacks encountered was that of public health. A 1920 definition of public health provided by Charles-Edward Emory, professor of public health at Yale University, helps highlight the problematics of public health in the United States:

> [Public health is] the science and art of preventing disease, prolonging life, and promoting physical health and efficiency through organized community efforts for the sanitation of the environment, the control of community infections, the education of the individual in principles of personal hygiene, the organization of medical and nursing service for the early diagnosis and preventive treatment of disease, and the development of the social machinery which will ensure to every individual in the community a standard of living adequate for the maintenance of health.[11]

Paul Starr, a social historian, suggests that this definition is an invitation to conflict because it crosses the boundaries between the practices of public health and private medicine and other private institutions such as religious groups and businesses.[12] The history of public health is one of struggle over the limits of its mandate. From religious groups, public health authorities encountered moral objections to state intervention on behalf of governmentally sponsored conceptions of health and hygiene. Businesses were concerned about the economic consequences of a public health policy. Most significantly, the medical profession believed that public health agencies were encroaching on, if not violating, their ability and right to practice medicine.

This somewhat adversarial relationship between private practitioners and public health officials shaped the development of local and state health departments. Organized health departments developed after the Civil War with Louisiana creating the first state board of health in 1855. Although the Louisiana board was ineffective, New York City (1866) and Massachusetts (1869) did establish the first effective city and state boards respectively. In 1870, the federal government centralized the direction of its Marine hospitals under a surgeon general in the Marine Hospital Service. After new outbreaks of cholera and yellow fever, Congress in April 1878 gave the Marine Hospital Service the authority to quarantine vessels that might be carrying the contagious diseases. But it also gave local authorities the power to override any quarantine decision.[13]

Repeatedly, the economic boundaries of public health were determined by the direct cost of public health to taxpayers and the indirect cost to business and the larger society. With the development of the field of bacteriology, public health efforts became more efficient and more cost-effective by doing away with ill-conceived and indiscriminate interventions by public health officials. This shift to more specific treatment, such as the regulation of the water or the milk supply, provided the basis for a less-adversarial relationship between public health and business.

Starr argues that a central element in this new relationship was a new conception of dirt.[14] Charles V. Chapin, health commissioner of Providence, Rhode Island, was a leading figure in public health. He saw that earlier public health legislation made "no distinction between dangerous dirt and dirt not dangerous, and warfare was waged against everything decaying and everything which smelled bad."[15] Chapin's views were a bit extreme in that he did not believe that dirt per se caused infectious disease, and he dismissed general measures for cleanliness. Crucial for African Americans and other folks surviving in unhealthy environments, Chapin believed that environmental sanitation was *not* a public health issue, stating, "I fail to see how poor housing in itself produces much disease."[16]

Chapin represented a shift in public health that began around 1910. In his 1917 popular book *How to Avoid Infection*, Chapin wrote that it was more important to remove adenoids from children than it was to remove ashes from the backyard. He believed that personal hygiene could replace public health activities. He advocated washing hands well before and after eating and always after the use of the toilet versus creating healthy environments for communities. Chapin also noted that personal hygiene was cheaper: "The introduction, or even the purification, of a municipal water supply may require millions. . . . To wash the hands before eating and after the toilet costs nothing."[17]

The 1910 shift also emphasized the use of the doctor as a force in prevention by using her or his knowledge to organize medical examinations of entire populations. This narrowing of public health objectives also made public health more politically acceptable. Starr suggests that the growth of medical professionalism, which also carried with it an emphasis on personal hygiene and medical examinations, caused a shift away from the broad advocacy of social reform to more narrow judgments that could be defended as the exercise of neutral authority.[18] This gave rise to the creation of clinics and an emphasis on individual health examinations. The development of individual health examinations helped foster the belief that we needed more medical care and health supervision because the exams almost uniformly showed that very few people were healthy and normal.[19]

By the 1920s, the promotion of health examinations became a major objective of public health organizations. In 1922, the American Medical Association (AMA) endorsed the idea of examinations of those "supposedly in health." The National Health Council called for a three-day period when the U.S. populace would go to their doctors for examinations. Ironically, public health sponsorship of preventive medical examinations became unpaid advertising for the medical profession because as diagnostic and educational services expanded under the guidance of public health, treatment was typically left to private physicians.

## Public Health and the Worlds of Black Folks

As the larger U.S. society experienced a concerted effort to increase its health, southern state and local public health directors did little to change the patterns of segregated, inadequate, and ill-diagnosed Black health care. Historian Edward H. Beardsley argues that these health directors failed their Black patrons far more than they failed other groups — a situation that continued until the infusion of federal money in the New Deal era.[20] Beardsley points out that this failure was not the responsibility of these directors alone. There were many instances of health officers who wanted to provide better care to Blacks but were blocked by state legislators and county commissioners who had never accepted the idea of substantial public taxation for social welfare — particularly if the major beneficiaries would be Black. In the White medical establishment, private doctors opposed — on economic grounds — any health program that appeared to or did encroach on their domain of curative medicine. They made sure that public programs did not venture beyond the circumscribed boundaries set for them.

In his 1909 study of Black social conditions, W. E. B. Du Bois looked at health care. This study shows that Blacks were as aggressive as the socio-economic and cultural milieu would permit when addressing their health needs. Du Bois found that although there were Black hospitals promoted and run by Blacks, the main support for these hospitals came from the state or from Whites. The scientific efforts of new Black doctors — who were cut off from clinical work in larger and better-equipped predominantly White hospitals — were joined with a philanthropic desire on the part of some Whites to help the sick after the Civil War.[21]

Du Bois found some hospitals — such as Freedmen's Hospital in Washington, D.C., which was supported by the federal government, and Lincoln Hospital and Home in New York City — that, though well-endowed and begun from a philanthropic impulse, did not permit Black doctors to practice in them, though they did take Black patients and trained Black nurses.[22] In southern cities, colored wards were maintained by aid societies like the Colored Women's Hospital Aid Society of the John Sealy Hospital in Galveston, Texas. This aid society had thirty active members who met monthly and contributed dues of ten cents. Their efforts supplied the hospital with six sanitary beds (at twelve dollars a piece) and the women patients with nineteen garments.[23] Often these colored wards became separate hospitals that were given city aid or survived by using subscriptions. Some of these hospitals — such as Good Samaritan in Charlotte, North Carolina, Lincoln in Durham, North Carolina, Lamar in Augusta, Georgia, and Roper in Charleston, South Carolina — became endowed.

Doctors and nurses also organized hospitals. Du Bois notes that Dr. Matilda A. Evans, the first licensed woman physician in South Carolina, founded a hospital and nurses' training school for colored people in Columbia.[24] Georgia had three such hospitals (Fair Haven Infirmary of Atlanta and McKane's and Charity Hospitals of Savannah), and Virginia had two (Richmond had the Richmond and Woman's Central League Hospitals).

These smaller hospitals helped set the stage for larger, well-equipped hospitals such as Provident Hospital and Training School of Chicago and Frederick Douglass Hospital of Philadelphia. In addition, some hospitals were connected to schools such as Hampton Institute in Hampton, Virginia, and Spelman College in Atlanta. Du Bois brings his report to a close noting that the First Baptist Church of West Washington, D.C., had a dispensary that treated 150 persons in its first three months of operation.[25]

Beardsley notes that southern health officers and a few socially conscious private doctors discovered the "Negro health problem" in the years just before World War I. The amalgam of southern states beginning to do serious collection of vital statistics in 1910, the instituting of full-time health officers, and the growing Black migration from the rural to the urban South helped to make this "problem" visible to the larger society. Black migration was a key factor in this equation as the invisible of the rural areas became visible in the urban centers. In rural areas, organized health work and statistical reporting were almost nonexistent. In the city, high rates of morbidity and mortality became matters of public notice, comment, and concern.[26] By 1920, southern health professionals were having to reflect on social and economic determinants of Black health such as housing, lifestyle, and preventive medical services.

At the 1914 American Public Health Association (APHA) meeting, Prudential Insurance statistician Frederick L. Hoffman stated that "in the struggle for race supremacy the black race is not holding its own."[27] Hoffman and other race fatalists thought that extinction would be the inevitable result of Blacks trying to live as free people. Although in a minority position, Hoffman and his ilk believed it to be wasteful to spend public funds for a race destined to die out, and at least one southern health administrator advocated neglect: "The ultimate extinction of the colored race was just a matter of time. Why seek to check the effect of the forces of nature?... [Leaving Blacks to their] predestined fate was a simple and effective method of solving a vexing question of race adjustment."[28]

Believing that the task was large and might require a generation, most at the convention recognized that proper sanitary, housing, and social policies would halt the decline in Black health. With racist assumptions providing the foundation for every discussion, many of this group believed that "negroes will not better themselves.... Their nature is such that benefits... have to be given to them, almost forced on them." Some, like a Kentucky official, argued that only stern policies would suffice: "Somebody must get behind the negro with authority and tell him that he must do so and so or 'git.'" And a Galveston health officer suggested draconian measures: "The vagrant negro... is a menace to white health and white security. He is nearly always a criminal degenerate of high or low degree. I believe he should be emasculated."[29]

In contrast to the discussions of the APHA, other public health physicians were looking beyond "negro traits" to physical environment as a more basic cause of black ill health. These doctors yoked environmental reform with health education and better nursing. In doing so, they stressed that the Black nurse was best equipped for the task. Further, all this could be made possible only if southern health officers took on the responsibility for stopping the decline of Black health. The degree of success in this was determined by whether these officers were willing and able to keep the topic of the health of the poor in the public consciousness and as a focus of private discussions.[30]

Indeed, meeting the needs of the Black and White poor was a precarious proposition during the economic depression of the 1930s, because the severity of the depression threatened to crush the South's entire public health structure. When the cotton economy collapsed from 1930 to 1933, private groups and governments defaulted on their financial obligations. This forced state legislatures to make drastic cuts in agency budgets. It also forced public health boards to cut projects initiated in the 1920s, and many considered gutting programs that were basic to public health.[31]

Southern boards were not alone in facing the devastation of the depression. The 1931 APHA reports from around the country revealed budget cuts and staff reductions. By 1931, two hundred local departments experienced moderate to severe appropriation cuts. But the southern experience was harshest because of the weaker economic base and more tenuous commitment to social programs.[32]

The Public Health Service (PHS) received its second congressional appropriation for local work combined with Rockefeller Foundation monies, these funds being available to all states. The restrictions on these monies, however, were such that in the end they were of little use to southern states. Small county health units of three persons or less and units that lacked the assurance of continuing local or state support were automatically excluded from assistance. Beardsley notes that the basic purpose of saving the best county organizations was laudable but self-defeating, for it decreed that only those departments that did not really need help could get it.[33]

From 1930 to 1933, public health work in the South followed the same course lined with stagnation and bankruptcy as U.S. businesses did. In 1933, the fear that the cutbacks in public health funding would lead to an upturn in mortality became a reality. At a time when more folks who had previously relied on private medicine now had to turn to public medicine, they faced a public health delivery system that had lost most of its ability to provide adequate care. For Blacks who had access to hospitals, these hospitals were all strained to the point of collapse.

Not surprisingly, the burden of increased death and sickness was carried by the poor; and among the poor, Blacks were disproportionately represented.[34] Beardsley notes that although Black migration to the cities continued its rapid pace in the 1930s, it was in the cities that Blacks were most endangered because it was there that they were least able to sustain themselves financially. In 1932, a writer for *Opportunity* magazine wrote that Blacks "are being forced off jobs to make places for unemployed white men — by intimidation, coercion and murder."[35]

The election of Franklin D. Roosevelt ushered in the beginning of large-scale federal aid for public health work. With this came a shift of control to the federal government from the states. Before 1933, the PHS and the Children's Bureau had almost always been active in an advisory capacity only in the various states. Now a new pattern emerged in which the federal government sustained state and local programs financially (up to 50 percent) and set the direction of these programs. Although regional emphasis was retained in this pattern, federal funding (with its attendant guidelines and regulations) provided the framework of the discussion and tended to make local health programs and procedures much more uniform across the South.

One of the social goals of the New Deal was improved public health. In March 1933, Congress included substantial funding for health relief in the law that created the Federal Emergency Relief Administration (FERA). To put this plan into operation, the PHS wanted to use state boards of health to take on part of the job of identifying the medically needy and arranging care for them so that they could then tap into FERA funds for their preventive programs. When state boards became nervous about becoming welfare offices, they suggested that FERA aid be used to expand existing programs in school health, home sanitation, and public health nursing. These programs could then be focused on indigents.

A compromise was reached when all parties agreed that part of FERA emergency medical fund monies would remain in the offices of state relief administrators and be paid directly to doctors and dentists who cared for FERA clients. Black medical leaders pressed the issue that Black doctors be given an equal chance to participate in medical relief work. However, FERA and its state offices made no effort to steer Black patients to these doctors, and many Black relief patients sought out White doctors as Black doctors continued to complain of discrimination by FERA.[36] The rest of FERA medical relief went to the PHS and state boards of health with the sole condition that nurses be sent into homes only on the orders of private doctors. Once again the split between private practice and public health emerged. In 1935, FERA was replaced by the more generously funded Works Progress Administration (WPA), and health projects of the earlier agency underwent sizable expansion.

## Contemporary Era

Although life expectancy has improved generally for everyone, Black life expectancy rates have always lagged behind. In 1900, a White infant could expect to live 47.6 years while other children could expect to live about 33 years.[37] In each successive decade, the numbers increased in parallel fashion until 1984 when the figures were 75.3 years for Whites and 69.7 years for African Americans. From 1984 to 1988, increased unemployment and poverty halted the parallel progress as White expectancy continued forward (75.6 years) while African Americans began to fall behind (69.2 years). The harsh reality was that African American men had a lower life expectancy rate (64.9 years) than any other racial-ethnic group in the United States.[38]

By 1991, the Health and Human Services Annual Report on U.S. health revealed some sobering statistics: the morality rate for African American and Native American infants was double that of Whites; the life expectancy for Blacks was six years less than Whites; the rate of strokes for Blacks was almost double that for Whites, and within this figure was the alarming statistic that for Blacks between thirty-five and fifty-four, the rate was four times higher; the leading cause of death for African American men between the ages of fifteen and twenty-four was homicide; Native Americans between fifteen and twenty-four had the nation's highest death rate from accidents — this was closely associated with alcohol consumption; the death rate for Native Americans from liver disease was 327 times higher than for other racial-ethnic groups; the prevalence of obesity was greater among Blacks, especially women, and increased with age — making diabetes, high cholesterol rates, and hypertension in young and middle-aged African Americans increased concerns; and HIV infection spread most rapidly between African Americans and Hispanics/Latinos.

Barbara Dixon points out that poverty is at the base of most of the health problems of African Americans. More important, she notes that there is more to poverty than low income. There is poor diet, poor housing, overcrowded clinics, and inadequate information about health and nutrition — all these help form the foundation for larger lament about Black (un)health.[39] However, an important caveat must be made in discussing and understanding African American health and health care. It is important to distinguish between the conditions of poverty that foster disease — such as lack of access to health care and fear and distrust of a biased health-care system — and genetic predisposition to disease as we consider options for medical research and practice as well as issues of accessibility and affordability.

This said, African Americans in the working poor and poor classes often lack education or marketable skills. When this is combined with institutional and structural racism, an endless cycle of poverty is passed on generationally. The high rate of poverty for African Americans (30 percent in 1990 alone) is a violent contributing factor to diseases that could be prevented or cured with commonplace therapy and that end up killing thousands of poor African Americans. Simply put, it is more difficult for the poor to get preventive care. Gordon Schiff, director of General Medicine at Cook County Hospital in Chicago, puts it most bluntly:

> We have 1000 people a day coming to see us. Half to two-thirds have to wait eight to 10 hours to be seen. So we need to decide who can safely wait and who we need to get in and see in an hour. . . . I think the kind of triage that is also occurring externally is causing these people to wash up on our shore.[40]

## Deadly Realities/Harsh Stereotypes

The preceding brief sociohistorical overview of African American health and health care helps set the context for understanding illness and disease within African American communities. An important place to begin this discussion is a reconsideration of the whole notion of race as distinct from genetics. What does it mean when I cite statistics such as 11.6 percent of volunteer organ donors are Black, or that far more African Americans than White Americans get breast, prostate, lung, colon, and esophageal cancer? What does it mean when Denise Ross — the medical director of Health Care Management Alternatives, a Medicaid managed-care program in Philadelphia with a 90 percent African American clientele — says that "African Americans are disproportionately represented in just about every disease category that exists"?[41]

Increasingly, scientists view race as a label of convenience.[42] Practically speaking, all human beings belong to the same species, *Homo sapiens*, with various environmental adaptations occurring relatively late in human history. As different groups of humans moved and merged, individual genes were carried and fused into thousands of generations living in many different environments. Races, as we tend to think of them in late twentieth-century life, arose as a result of spontaneous mutations.

When we use skin color to classify groups, this gives *one* gene supreme authority over the *millions* of other genes we all carry in our genetic makeup. Further, no discrete *package* of gene differences has ever been identified as belonging to a specific race. A quick survey of individuals in any given "race" reveals a great intraracial diversity that we have been trained to ignore or accept as normal (as opposed to different). Race cannot be equated with such characteristics as character, intelligence, or personality. Variations in mental capacity occur — from the genius to the very slow — in all groups.

Simply put, the human body is an evolutionary compromise, an "amalgam of trade-offs."[43] As we continue in this lament over health care, carrying with it the notion of health care as a cultural production, I now add the importance of *genetics*. What interests me are the ways in which *genes* are passed from parent to child — for diseases are connected to genes. Added to socioeconomic and cultural factors, genetics may well help all of us better understand the more intractable diseases that affect African Americans, such as the high incidence of low-birth-weight babies, hypertension, and diabetes.

Perhaps one of the best places to begin is with the genetic factors that affect vitamin and mineral intake and processing. Dixon points out that studies reveal that Blacks near the poverty level receive less than half the calcium and iron that Whites do. These African American diets are often low in vitamins A and C, magnesium, vitamin B complex, and protein.[44] She goes on to note that even when income increases, Blacks have a tendency to choose meats and other proteins before fresh fruits, vegetables, and whole-grain products. Sodium intake is high and even more so for those who rely on processed, packaged, or convenience foods.

Certain vitamin deficiencies affect Blacks at every income level.[45] Regardless of where African Americans are economically, it is hard for them to get enough vitamin D and calcium. This is due to the fact that because of pigmentation, Blacks receive one-third less ultraviolet light that triggers the body's production of vitamin D. Vitamin D is needed to help the body use calcium and magnesium — both minerals that are already low in the typical diet of most African Americans. Most folks in the United States get extra vitamin D from milk. But Blacks, who are often lactose-intolerant, tend to avoid fresh milk and milk products.

African Americans at all income levels also must deal with salt sensitivity. In the 1970s, researchers discovered that people differ in their tolerance for salt. Most people release excess sodium through sweat and urine. Many African Americans do the reverse — their kidneys retain salt. Salt retention helps the body conserve fluids, and it may well be that this was a beneficial genetic mutation that helped people living in the torrid African climate survive. It is also possible that this feature occurred during slavocracy to help Africans conserve fluids in the Middle Passage. This helpful genetic mechanism became a liability when people with this salt sensitivity began to eat more salt — particularly as we do today. The incidence of hypertension among African Americans is almost twice as high as among Whites.[46]

Closely linked with salt intake are issues of eating and weight. More than 30 percent of African Americans are overweight. About 45 percent of Black women are obese (20 percent above the ideal body weight for their height, frame, and age). A sobering reality is that 60 percent of Black women between the ages of forty-five and seventy-five weigh far more than they should.[47]

Although these statistics are alarming, they should not be taken without some questioning. There is good reason to question how weight and obesity are defined. Before 1990, doctors used information from insurance companies to measure the "ideal" body weight. These ideal weights were largely based on the insurance records of White men.[48] In 1990, the government updated the tables in its *Dietary Guidelines for Americans*. Nevertheless, Linda Villarosa, a health writer for *Essence* magazine, points out that the tables are still controversial because ideal weights are nearly impossible to estimate. Further, the guidelines still do not distinguish between men's and women's bodies. Villarosa suggests that it is best to pay attention to one's emotional and physical health to determine whether or not one needs or wants to lose weight. Once again genetics is a part of the equation. Lorraine Bonner, a physician in

Oakland, California, notes that African Americans *may* carry a specific gene inherited from African ancestors:

> There is evidence to suggest that the Africans who survived the Middle Passage to this country *were those who were best able to* utilize *and* retain the meager scraps of food they were fed. . . . People who are in an environment of famine maintain fat as a means of selective survival. I think it's safe to say that many African-Americans today have retained this genetic marker from their African ancestors who were brought here as slaves.[49]

Lest we rely too heavily on the inevitability of our genes, it is important to realize that the foods many Black folks consume also play a part in how large or small they are. A painful reality for Blacks is that the soul food tradition handed down through the generations is high in fat, sugar, and calories. Much of it is fried in grease and flavored with fatty pork parts. Dixon notes that even when Blacks and Whites have similar income and education, live in the same region, and eat much the same foods, there are still differences in their eating habits.[50]

Black folks, like the majority of people in the United States, are now eating lighter breakfasts and sandwiches at lunch. Dinner is eaten after work, and it has become the biggest meal of the day. But the pattern of snacking (cookies and candies are the foods of choice for this) remains unhealthy, compounding the effects of the soul food tradition.

Poverty is also a factor. Poor men and women are twice as likely to be overweight as those who are more affluent. Low-fat, low-calorie foods and fresh fruits and vegetables are often expensive or unavailable in poor communities. This leaves many poor folks with the high-fat, high-calorie, processed food in fast-food restaurants — these are the only foods they can afford or can find. These fast-food chains may be feeding into the crisis of poor nutrition, although many of the owners of these establishments say that their customers prefer the saltier, fattier selections and larger portions.[51]

In far too many stores in poorer neighborhoods, there are few if any nonfat and no-salt products. When these more healthy alternatives are available, they cost more than the regular brands. White bread, sugary snack cakes, alcohol, and cigarettes are aggressively marketed, but such is not the case for healthful foods. Store owners say that they cannot sell healthy products to customers who do not want them. These owners are clear that they need the help of major food manufacturers, nutritionists, and advertisers if there is to be any change in their customers' eating habits, because many inner-city residents believe that nutrition information is for rich White folks.[52] Put bluntly, the poor simply do not see themselves portrayed on television and billboards consuming healthy food products.

In addition to more research on the links between diet and health with an eye to race and income, it is important to note that in the inner city, many people eat to survive, and they try to get the biggest sandwich with the most calories in order to stay full longer. But there is an even more compelling factor that feeds into the attraction of quick-service restaurants — safety, cleanliness, and good lighting are strong draws in neighborhoods where the housing and the streets are dangerous.

Obesity is a factor in the high rate of diabetes — two to three times the rate of the general population — in the African American communities in this country. More than three million Blacks have the disease. Diabetes is prevalent in older Black women. Many Black folks do not even know they have this serious condition — it can lead to kidney disease, stroke, heart failure, and blindness.

A sobering lament for all of us is that heart disease, cancer, strokes, and diabetes are this nation's top killers. They are even more deadly among African Americans. The salvation in this is that these are, in large measure, preventable. Linda Villarosa points out that "if everyone would stop smoking, switch to healthier diets, and get out and exercise several times a week, the death rates from these diseases would drop dramatically."[53] She also points out that many Black folks fall victim to the "quicker and sicker" syndrome — early death because they are too busy or too busy taking care of everyone but themselves. African American women are notorious for this, as they often overlook preventive care for themselves.

Heart disease is the number one killer of all Americans. The rates of death from cardiovascular diseases among African Americans are among the highest in the industrialized world.[54] Much of this is due to the fact that Black folks have high rates of hypertension or high blood pressure — affecting one in three.[55]

Some of this may well be due to birthplace. In a study published in the *New England Journal of Medicine,* the researchers looked at death records from 1988 to 1992 and at 1990 census data from the Northeast. The researchers noted that for those they studied in the northeastern United States, the rates of deaths from cardiovascular disease for White men (285 per 100,000), as compared to Black men (299 per 100,000), and for White women (155 per 100,000), as compared to Black women (165 per 100,000), were similar.[56] But the researchers found that southern-born Black men and women both had mortality rates from cardiovascular disease that were substantially higher than that of their counterparts born in the Northeast.

Caribbean-born Blacks had rates substantially lower than those of their northeastern-born counterparts. This study shows that differences among the groups in the rates of death from coronary heart disease were greater than those for death due to stroke or hypertension. In each category defined by age and sex, Caribbean-born Blacks had significantly lower rates of death from coronary heart disease than did Whites. Additionally, Black men who were twenty-five to forty-four years of age and were born in the South had a rate of death from coronary heart disease that was 30 percent higher than that of northeastern-born Blacks, and four times that of Caribbean-born Blacks of the same sex and age.

Although this is one of the few studies of its kind and must be treated as such, it does bear watching as more studies may give us a clearer picture of the relationship between birthplace, genetics, diet, and environment. In a study of various poor Black areas, researchers from the University of Michigan found that Blacks living in the Black Belt of Alabama had the *lowest* mortality and the *highest* poverty rate. Harlem in New York City had the *highest* mortality rate and the *lowest* poverty rate. Adding to this increasingly complex picture is the fact that a 1980 study revealed that Black men living in Harlem had less chance surviving to sixty-five than men in Bangladesh — and the situation has grown worse since 1980. But interestingly, African Americans living in Queens and the Bronx had only slightly higher mortality rates than the national average.[57]

Hypertension has often been called the silent killer.[58] An estimated sixty million Americans have it, and only half of them know it. African Americans are at particular risk because one in four of them has it. Left unchecked, it can strain the heart and damage arteries — conditions that can trigger heart attacks, strokes, kidney failure, and loss of vision.

Researchers still debate the causes of hypertension, but most agree that a genetic predisposition is a key factor. James Reed, a professor at Morehouse School of Medicine in Atlanta, also points to the interrelationship of environment and genetics in this.[59] Indeed, reports continue to document lower blood pressures in Africans than in African Americans.[60]

African Americans are less responsive to beta-blockers than are White Americans. Beta-blockers are one of the four main groups of drugs used to treat hypertension. They work by blocking many of the effects of adrenaline in the body, thus causing the heart to beat more slowly. Diuretics increase the rate at which the body eliminates urine and salt and decreases fluid in blood vessels; calcium-channel-blockers block the entry of calcium into cells and decrease the tendency of small arteries to become narrow; and angiotensin-converting enzyme-inhibitors block the formation of the natural body-chemical angiotensin II, which allows the blood vessels to dilate. Rita Horn, head pharmacist at St. Francis Hospital in Miami, is clear that no one drug works or is good for everyone: "It more or less has to be examined on an individual basis. . . . Patient compliance is the main thing. It's hard for some people to change their behavior, but the drug won't do you any good if you don't take it."[61] Perhaps the best advice is common sense:

reduce salt intake, watch your weight, exercise regularly, manage stress, and see a health-care professional.

It is important to inject a lamentable reality at this point. In the United States, Blacks with heart problems get less-advanced treatment than Whites. A study of heart treatment in veterans' hospitals, where the patients' finances have less influence on the statistics, made clear that the problem is race. White patients were consistently more likely to receive advanced surgery for certain heart conditions.[62] The likelihood is that in situations where doctors have more choices in the different types of treatments, African Americans get less-advanced treatment than Whites.[63]

Cancer is the second most frequent cause of death for Black women, and Black men have the highest cancer rates in the nation. Cancer can strike many parts of the body, but three cancers are particularly common and lethal for African American women: lung, breast, and cervical.[64] Next to breast cancer, lung cancer is the leading cause of death among Black women. Villarosa notes that cigarette smoking is almost entirely to blame. She goes on to explain that African Americans smoke more than Whites, and although increasing numbers of Black men and women have quit smoking, the decline in smoking is substantially slower among Black women than among Black men.[65] Nonsmokers are at risk, especially those who have mates who smoke — and we all are exposed to the risk of lung cancer due to air pollution.

One in eight women in the United States will develop breast cancer, which is the leading cause of cancer deaths for African American women. Breast cancer strikes Black women at earlier ages and is less likely to be discovered early — leading to more deaths. Cervical cancer is more prevalent among Black women than among their White counterparts, and the death rates for it are higher as well.

Another disease of the immune system, lupus, affects Black women to an inordinate degree. Of the more than five hundred thousand people stricken with it, nine out of ten are women ages fifteen to forty-five, and of those, three out of five are Black. Researchers have found neither the cause nor the cure. Those who have it say that lupus "makes you feel lousy all of the time."[66] Symptoms include a red rash or color change on the face, often in the shape of a butterfly across the bridge of the nose; painful or swollen joints, usually accompanied by redness; unexplained, chronic fever; chest pain with breathing; unusual loss of hair; purple or pale fingers or toes from cold or stress; sensitivity to the sun; low blood count; nausea; vomiting; and abdominal pain.

Two other immune-system diseases that find a home among African Americans to an unusual degree are sarcoidosis and sickle-cell disease. In sarcoidosis, which strikes Black women from ages twenty to forty, the sufferer experiences weakness in her arms and legs and partial paralysis. Once again it has no known cause or cure, and there is sketchy information available about it. With sickle-cell disease, the sufferer has sickle-shaped, rather than round, blood cells, a condition that may have helped our Black ancestors survive malaria. But for contemporary African Americans, sickle-cell disease can be deadly. It also affects people in the Caribbean and those of Southeast Asian, East Indian, Latin American, and Mediterranean descent. But sickle-cell disease is primarily a disease of African-Americans — it strikes one out of twelve of us.[67]

Asthma is a vexing health problem for all of us in the United States. Nearly ten million Americans have asthma, including a disproportionate number of Blacks.[68] This disease is controllable with preventive steps and proper medication, and far too many Black people die of it. The asthma death rate is three times higher for Blacks than for Whites, and asthma is the number one chronic illness among Black children. When combined with poverty, it is especially dangerous and damaging to youngsters.

A variety of drug-related illnesses and addictions find homes in African American communities. Smoking is the top cause of preventable deaths in the United States. The Centers for Disease Control's report on smoking and health estimates that 434,000 people die of smoking-related diseases such as lung cancer, emphysema, and heart disease yearly.[69] This is twelve hundred deaths per day or fifty deaths an hour. As noted earlier, African Americans are more vulnerable to the health-related problems of smoking because Blacks smoke more than Whites and quit less often.

As HIV/AIDS, violent crime, and drugs consume a good deal of our attention, cigarette smoking goes on quietly killing Black folks. Reed Tuckson, the former commissioner of public health for the District of Columbia, notes that cigarette smoking accounts for nearly 40 percent of all deaths among adult Black men living in Washington.[70] It is important to keep in mind that six times as many people die of smoking as from automobile accidents; cigarette smoking is the number one cause of lung cancer (the number one cause of death by cancer in women); smoking also contributes to breast cancer and other cancers; cigarette smoking accounts for one-third of all deaths from heart disease; cigarette smoking is the major cause of emphysema and chronic bronchitis; and smoking during pregnancy increases the risk of spontaneous abortion, stillbirths, and infant death. Babies born to women who smoke during pregnancy weigh an average of nearly one-half pound less than babies born to nonsmokers.

Alcohol consumption leads to a number of serious health problems such as cirrhosis of the liver, sexual dysfunction, and fetal alcohol syndrome. Reports, including one from the Department of Health and Human Services, show that heavy drinking causes African Americans an inordinate amount of social problems such as violence, police encounters, high-risk sexual behavior, motor vehicle accidents, trouble at work, and spouse abuse. Of course, these social problems are not confined to the Black communities of the United States. However, due to skewed arrest, sentencing, and incarceration rates, these problems tend to take on a higher profile and have a deeper effect in many African American communities.

There are at least two important caveats to interject here. First, Black youths tend to drink at slightly lower rates than White youths. This leads Robert Staples, a sociologist, to conjecture that the young African American population has a lower rate of heavy drinkers and a larger population of abstainers.[71] Second, Staples's research shows that, in contrast to White families, in Black families fewer adult members drink or have friends who drink, and there is a greater level of closeness—even in families that do not fit the nuclear family model.[72]

As a nation, too many of us are medicating ourselves with cocaine, heroin, and prescription drugs to soften the rough edges of life. Cocaine and heroin first appeared in the United States at the turn of the century in the form of over-the-counter miracle cures and Coca-Cola. Then, no one dreamed that the heroin and cocaine traces found in these products could be addictive. The U.S. government outlawed both drugs in the 1920s after thousands were already seriously addicted.

African Americans did not begin using narcotics in large numbers until the 1950s when they became accessible and cheap. By the 1970s, a drug subculture had emerged in many Black communities that often brought with it crime, fractured family systems, and homicide. Then crack cocaine hit like a tidal wave on an unsuspecting community in the 1980s. Cocaine, an expensive drug, was born again in the very affordable form of crack. For many, one hit of this drug meant instant addiction. Crack dealers became familiar faces on many streets. Coinciding with this was a 150 percent increase in the prison population from 1980 to 1990, as presidents Ronald Reagan and George Bush oversaw a war on drugs.[73] Black people, particularly Black men, were overrepresented in these numbers. One marker for this was 1988 figures that showed that although African Americans make up roughly 12 percent of those who regularly use illicit drugs, Blacks accounted for more than 38 percent of all drug arrests.[74]

Crack cocaine addiction has exacerbated the ongoing problems of crime, poverty, unemployment, and racism. Drug-dealing children are increasingly taking over as heads of their families, largely because of their incomes from selling crack; young, pregnant mothers are risking their lives to secure the drug and, in some cases, exchanging sexual relations for it or the money to buy it; some adolescent girls are deserting their families and forming violent gangs to sell and buy crack; female addicts are exceeding male users for the first time in African American history in some communities; and the extended-family network in Black communities, which has traditionally absorbed needy children, is dealing with holes in its safety net because of the ravages of drugs.[75]

Drugs are exacting a heavy toll in many African American communities and in all our individual lives. It does not help that some of this overmedication is prescribed. In a five-year study, researchers from the University of California–Berkeley found that at least one-third of Blacks seeking care in three busy California psychiatric emergency wards received twice the dosage of a powerful antipsychotic drug that was given to patients of other racial-ethnic groups.[76] The researchers could not find any reason except race for why these dosages, *which were often higher than recommended,* were prescribed and administered.

As a nation we have a collective drug problem. In 1991, there were 1.8 million cocaine addicts and 700,000 heroin addicts — the highest addiction rates in our history.[77] Some experts estimate that between 5 and 6 million people in the United States are in need of serious drug treatment.

Lest we get too far down the path of hopelessness, there are some myths and stereotypes that must be addressed regarding African Americans and drugs. First, there is the myth that drugs are a Black, inner-city problem. The reality is that although drug use is higher in inner-city neighborhoods than in wealthier ones, in the country as a whole, African Americans account for just 12 percent of users while Whites account for 70 percent — statistics that come from a study by the National Institute on Drug Abuse.[78]

Socioeconomics and neighborhood type are better predictors of drug use than race. Poverty, despair, and drug use *are* natural dance partners. Regardless of race, the rate of drug use among the unemployed is more than twice that among the employed. Twenty-eight percent of unemployed Blacks and twenty-three percent of unemployed Whites use drugs. The homeless are the heaviest drug and alcohol users. This prompts the National Institute on Drug Abuse to state that "race/ethnicity was not a significant determinant" of drug use.[79]

A second myth about drugs is that crack is a "Black" drug that is running rampant in the African American community. Socioeconomics come into play as a more important factor than race with this as well. A study in the *Journal of the American Medical Association* found that crack use does not depend strongly on race-specific factors.[80] In fact, Blacks and Whites from similar neighborhoods are equally likely to smoke crack. The major thing to keep in mind is that due to the economics of our country, Blacks are more likely to live in a drug-infested neighborhood than Whites. However, the 1988 *National Household Survey on Drug Abuse* showed that the vast majority — more than 97 percent — of African Americans had never smoked crack.[81]

All this is not to deny the reality of the devastation of drugs on Black life in the United States. My aim is to put drug abuse into a much more realistic light, so that it can be accurately analyzed and understood.

African Americans have a significantly higher risk for almost every disease or addiction found in the United States, and we are much more likely to die of them than other groups. This has tremendous implications for our mortality rates. It begins with birth. The hopeful news is that Black infants now have a better chance of surviving to their first birthday than at any time in our history in this country. The troubling news is that the gap between infant mortality rates for Blacks and Whites is growing. In 1950, Black infants were 1.6 times more likely to die than Whites. In 1988, black infants were 2.1 times more likely to die than Whites.[82]

Black infant mortality hinges on low birth-weight. Low birth-weight can be caused by preterm labor and delivery, intrauterine growth retardation, or a combination of these. If babies are born too soon (before thirty-seven weeks) or too small (less than five and one-half pounds), they are at greater risk. The high incidence of Black low birth-weight is a precursor to high infant mortality weights. Although the low income of Black families is a frequently cited cause for Black infant mortality, it is only one of many factors. Strikingly, neonatal mortality for the highest income African Americans was approximately twice the rate for Whites at that same income stratum. Infants born to college-educated African American parents have higher infant mortality rates than for a comparable group of White infants.[83]

Poverty is not as dominating a factor in these dismal infant mortality rates as it is in the case of drug use and abuse. Black middle-class families suffer higher mortality rates than White middle-class families. The contributing factors to this are "a lifetime of shoddy medical care, lack of prenatal care and — most telling — the chronic stress of being black in America."[84] A recent study of the mortality rates among Blacks and Whites in the United States is quite revealing. The researchers note:

> When they were compared with the nationwide age-standardized annual death rate for whites, the death rates for both sexes in each of the poverty areas were excessive, especially among blacks (standardized mortality ratios for men and women in Harlem, 4.11 and 3.38; in Watts, 2.92 and 2.60; in central Detroit, 2.79 and 2.58; and in the Black Belt area of Alabama, 1.81 and 1.89). Boys in Harlem who reached the age of 15 had a 37 percent chance of surviving to the age of 65; for girls, the likelihood was 65 percent. Of the higher-income black areas studied, Queens-Bronx had the income level most similar to that of whites and the lowest standardized mortality ratios (men 1.18; women 1.08). Of the areas where poor whites were studied, Detroit had the highest

> standardized mortality ratios (men 2.01; women 1.90). On the Lower East Side of Manhattan, in Appalachia, and in Northeast Alabama, the ratios for whites were below the national average for blacks (men 1.90; women 1.95).[85]

The researchers conclude that differences in mortality rates before the age of sixty-five between the advantaged and the disadvantaged in the United States are sometimes great, and there are important differences among impoverished communities in patterns of excess mortality.

There are other health issues. According to the *New England Journal of Medicine,* Black patients tend to receive less-intensive hospital services and are less likely to be satisfied with the care they receive than White patients with similar health insurance coverage.[86] Other parts of this lament reveal that Blacks are more likely to suffer kidney failure, but less likely to get a transplant. Also, environmental racism takes a heavy toll. Sixty percent of the total Black population lives in communities with one or more uncontrolled toxic-waste sites.

## Black Health Care

In a September 12, 1996, editorial in the *New England Journal of Medicine,* H. Jack Geiger lamented that a research article in that same issue found that African Americans received deficient health care in the United States. He noted that the researchers, who drew on many different databases covering every type of acute-care hospital, including the hospitals in the Veterans Affairs system (which are free-care institutions),

> controlled for age, sex, Medicare and other insurance status, income, disease severity, concomitant morbid conditions, and underlying incidence and prevalence rates in the population subgroups under study. Yet the results have almost always pointed in the same direction. In one multihospitals study, [the researchers] found deficiencies in the most basic components of clinical care for black and poor patients as compared with patients who were white and more affluent, although all were Medicare beneficiaries.[87]

Geiger goes on to note that numerous studies have already revealed that African Americans are less likely to receive renal transplants, receive hip or total-knee replacements, and undergo gastrointestinal endoscopy or a host of other procedures. But Black folks are more likely to undergo hysterectomies and the amputation of a lower limb. Geiger is troubled by the repeated findings that Blacks with ischemic heart disease, even those who receive

Medicare or are in the free-care systems, are much less likely to undergo angiography, angioplasty, or coronary-artery bypass grafting.[88] He points to the studies in the Veterans Affairs system in which African Americans were 33 percent less likely to undergo cardiac catheterization, 44 percent less likely to undergo angioplasty, and 54 percent less likely to undergo coronary-artery bypass grafting than the Whites in the same study.

He notes that the provision of health insurance alone does not ensure equity. Further,

> with major confounding variables increasingly controlled and adjusted for, investigators tend to invoke unspecified cultural differences, undocumented patient preferences, or a lack of information about the need for care as reasons for the differences. The alternative explanation is racism — that is, racially discriminatory rationing by physicians and health-care institutions.[89]

He then retreats, suggests that there is not yet enough evidence to make this charge definitively, and states that "if racism is involved it is unlikely to be overt or even conscious." Then he offers a probing list of questions:

> What choices are black patients and white patients actually offered by their physicians? What do they hear? Do their physicians make specific recommendations? Do the patients participate fully in the decision-making process? What criteria do physicians use in making these clinical judgments? Are they applied equitably, or are they subtly influenced by racial stereotyping on the part of time-pressured physicians, reinforced both by institutional attitudes and by unwarranted assumptions about prevalences and outcomes?[90]

He is clear that the results of this study are alarming enough to take at least two steps now:

> Two steps would constitute a beginning. First, the routine and ongoing examination of racial disparities in the use of services and in the choices of diagnostic and therapeutic alternatives should be part of the quality assurance protocols of every hospital, every health maintenance organization, and every other system of care. Second, awareness of the dilemmas associated with race and health care should be part of every physician's training. In a 1994 survey of U.S. medical schools, only 13 of 78 responding institutions offered culturally-sensitivity courses designed to improve understanding of diverse ethnic groups, and all but one of those courses were elective.[91]

Geiger's at times pointed editorial reveals a medical health-care delivery system that is not structured to respond to the health-care needs of Black

America. In the mid-1980s, a report from the Department of Health and Human Services revealed that African Americans had seventy-five thousand more deaths per year than would be expected. By 1993, that figure rose to one hundred thousand.[92] This is a lament in that access to quality health for all persons, regardless of their ability to pay, should be a part of the humane fabric of any society.

This points to a need for trained and talented health-care providers in the African American communities across this nation. In 1994, of the almost sixty thousand medical school students in the United States, only four thousand were African Americans. Dentistry, nursing, pharmacology, and other health professions also had low numbers of Blacks.[93]

Leonard E. Lawrence, president of the National Medical Association (NMA), in 1994 spoke to this need.[94] He was clear that an increase in the number of Black health-care providers was necessary to begin to address the health-care needs of Black folks.[95] He also pointed out that although 75 percent of Black health providers already choose to practice only in racial-ethnic communities, that is hardly going to solve the problem — the practice must spread beyond Black medical personnel. Finally, he pointed out that racial-ethnic practitioners have a history of being reimbursed at lower rates and endure more rigorous review by external regulators.

The mission of the NMA is to promote the science and art of medicine and to better the public health and the quality of life of individuals and families.[96] The NMA voted in favor of instituting Medicaid and Medicare in 1965 before the American Medical Association; in 1992, lobbying by the NMA caused the National Institutes of Health to perform additional clinical trials on low-dose oral alpha interferon, which has proved to be an effective treatment for AIDS in large clinical studies in Kenya. The NMA recognizes domestic violence as a major public health issue, and it encourages doctors to routinely screen women and children for signs of abuse. In the area of HIV/AIDS education, prevention, and treatment, the NMA supports the distribution of condoms and sex education in public schools to reduce the risk of the spread of HIV/AIDS between adolescents, the education of prisoners on the proper use of condoms, and the distribution of condoms in prisons.[97]

Even as the NMA seeks to make inroads into Black health and health care, the rise of managed care has changed the nature of the debate dramatically. As HMOs emerged, many racial-ethnic providers were squeezed out of practices in areas where they had long ties. African American physician Randall C. Morgan Jr. suggests that managed care may ultimately help break down strong doctor-patient relationships as people change physicians, change plans, or see a number of physicians in the same plan rather than have their own doctor who may have generations of experience with the same family.[98]

Morgan is also concerned that there will be fewer doctors available who know the kinds of indicators that need to be monitored regarding culture and the specific illnesses and diseases that Black genetics can foster. It is possible, says Morgan, that Black physicians may "get outbid for the managed care contract of the patients that are in their practice if they can't compete, either price-wise or access-wise, with larger groups and organizations. This is due to the fact that many Black doctors are in solo practices or in small group practices."[99]

The world of managed care will make it extremely difficult for solo practitioners, the heart and soul of traditional Black health-care delivery, to survive. There is a rather grim possibility that we must face in this. As Morgan points out:

> [T]he system of managed care is really made to not include every physician that we have in America — it's made to be somewhat exclusive — there are a lot of criteria that are used to disqualify some physicians from being part of a managed care entity. One of them is board certification, another is malpractice insurance, but also malpractice judgments or activities in a practice in terms of how many malpractice suits or alleged suits there are. And other types of quality review issues from hospital staffs.... Racism cannot be discounted as a factor in preventing African American physicians from being a part of large managed care groups.[100]

Morgan is also pessimistic about the future of noninsured patients as the role of managed care in the United States increases, and he sees four problems that the African American community must address regarding managed care: a lack of Black doctors in managed-care programs, a lack of culturally sensitive care for patients, a lack of care for uninsured patients, and the (in)ability to develop a relationship with one primary doctor.

Yet as we approach managed care with some caution, we must also evaluate the ways in which the overall current health-care delivery system works or fails to work in the lives of many African Americans. First, Medicaid has never lived up to its promise to eliminate our two-tiered system of health care. The income restrictions have been and remain so tight that the program currently covers less than one-half of the poor. Although some of the recent changes in Medicaid mentioned in chapter 2 suggest a genuine attempt to address this, the majority of the working poor are excluded and remain uninsured.

An example of what this looks like comes from Illinois. In 1989, a single, elderly person could not have an income of more than $292 per month to qualify for Medicaid. He or she could not have assets of more than $2,000. These were known as Medicaid spend-down limits. These figures are appalling enough, but the additional hoops one had to jump through to get Medicaid were extraordinary. For example, one became eligible for a green card (i.e., access to care through Medicaid) on the day of the month that one's medical bills and receipts showed that one had met one's spend-down limits. What this meant for many was that if one met one's spend-down on the twentieth of the month, one qualified that day for the rest of the month — ten days. After that coverage expired, one had to apply again.[101]

Second, gaps in Medicare remain. During the first full year of Medicare, 1967, the rate at which parients were discharged was 29 percent lower among minority beneficiaries (most of whom were Black) than among White beneficiaries. By 1987, the rate among Blacks was 4 percent higher than among Whites.[102] In a study that looked at Medicare data on hospital discharges among those sixty-five years of age and older from 1986 to 1992, researchers found that African American beneficiaries received seventeen common procedures less often than White beneficiaries.[103] These included coronary-artery bypass surgery, percutaneous transluminal coronary angioplasty, and total hip replacement.

The researchers found that certain less-common surgical procedures, such as the amputation of all or part of a lower limb, were performed more frequently among African Americans (3.6 times as frequent). In 62 percent of amputations, the principal diagnosis was diabetes mellitus, which is only 1.7 times as prevalent in elderly Blacks as in Whites. Also, bilateral orchiectomy was 2.2 times as frequent among Black men as among Whites. In 90 percent of these cases, the principal diagnosis was prostate cancer, although the rate of prostate cancer among the elderly is only 1.3 times as high in Black men as in White men.

In a discussion of their research, the researchers note that African American beneficiaries in general and Black and White low-income beneficiaries have fewer doctor visits for ambulatory care, fewer mammograms, and fewer immunizations against influenza. They are hospitalized more often and have higher mortality rates. The researchers also suggest that these patterns indicate that Black folks and poor folks receive less primary and preventive care than either White or more affluent beneficiaries.

African American senior citizens are among the most vulnerable to the shifting sands of our current health-care debate and policies. Even in the face of high morbidity and mortality rates, the Black elderly make less use of health care, have more chronic diseases, and must contend with limited access to high-level acute care and long-term facilities. In large measure, these circumstances are due to the overrepresentation of the Black elderly in the lower socioeconomic groups. For older African American women, the poverty rate is nearly 55 percent (in contrast to 12 percent for the general elderly population).[104]

Finally, because of the dearth of primary-care services in poor neighborhoods, a tragic adversarial relationship has developed between public health and private medicine in poor communities across this nation. The long history of circumscribing and tight monetary control of these primary-care services has turned some neighborhoods in the United States into medical wastelands.

In 1995, several major cities announced their intention to sell, close, or drastically cut the services of public hospitals. A pattern of reductions in payments for the elderly and the poor from federal, state, and local governments places these hospitals at risk. In 1995, 30 percent of public hospitals were in the inner city; the remaining 70 percent were in suburban and rural areas. Most survived on the revenues from Medicare, Medicaid, and local governments, using those monies to provide direct services to patients.

In an editorial in a November 1995 issue of the *New England Journal of Medicine,* Jerome P. Kassirer noted that

> public hospitals are medical havens for the underinsured and the uninsurable. They have tried hard to provide culturally sensitive care to socially and economically underprivileged persons through multifaceted programs that include (among other things) social services, translators, security, transportation, and child protection.... To the extent that these hospitals manage ordinary conditions such as cancer, hypertension, and cardiac failure, they serve as community hospitals for their local neighborhoods.... Compared with private hospitals, however, they handle proportionately more patients with conditions that have considerable financial and social as well as medical impact, including drug addiction, alcoholism, abuse, trauma, tuberculosis, and AIDS.... They are an important site for the training of students and young physicians in the care of such patients. Many house the only special-care units — such as trauma centers, burn units, and neonatal intensive care units — in their regions.... Despite the austerity of their facilities, these institutions are the sites of substantial clinical and basic research.[105]

Kassirer went on to note that the then-impending changes in health-care delivery through changes in Medicare and Medicaid and the rise of managed care meant that public hospitals would be left with a "preponderance of indigent patients who have complex medical and social problems but no insurance." His predictions have begun to come true. He ended his editorial with a call to focus on the people who were being served by public hospitals — not the public hospitals themselves, their physicians, or their staffs. In Kassirer's words, "as state funds dry up and eligibility criteria for Medicaid tighten, even more people will become uninsured. Given this trend and the shrinking support for care for the indigent, the outlook for the poor and uninsured appears dismal."

*Part 2*

# EXPLORING HEALTH AND HEALTH CARE IN BLACK AMERICA

## Chapter 4

# "The Doctor Ain't Taking No Sticks"

*The Tuskegee Syphilis Study*

Many of the problematics found in chapters 2 and 3 are better illuminated when we focus on specific situations of the cultural production of Black health. I thus turn now to explore three specific cases involving African American health. The first is the Tuskegee Syphilis Study. I begin by setting various sociomedical contexts of the experiment. After laying out the basics of the experiment,[1] I then explore the theo-ethical implications of the experiment for our study of lament.

W. E. B. Du Bois once said that "being a problem is a strange experience." In an odd way, those words take on new and more deadly dimensions when we look at the events, ideologies, and rationales that intertwined to shape the Tuskegee Study. The men who were the subject of the study, their families, and their communities suffered through senseless disease, wracking illness, and early deaths. The men's only "crime" was that they were poor, had limited and often poor health care, were poorly educated, and were Black. Their story is one of lament and regret.

This is a story of what *may* happen when a community of the dispossessed meets a behemothic health-care system. The sobering tones of this lament remind us that, had it not been for some hard-fought intervention, the experiment might still be going on — after all, the ones who originally had the power to make the decision about the length of the study determined that it would end with the death of the last man. Six are still alive.

### The Sociomedical Context of Early Twentieth-Century Black Health

In 1900, the Black mortality rate was 29.6 deaths per 1,000 persons compared to 17.3 for Whites. The leading cause of death was tuberculosis (TB), which had a death rate for Blacks nearly triple that of Whites. The next four most frequent killers were pneumonia, diseases of the nervous system, typhoid fever, and malaria.[2] These troubling figures arose from a situation in which Blacks were having a difficult time tapping into the economic expansion going on in the United States at that time. By the 1920s, when the expansion was in full swing, most Blacks were not reaping the benefits of the boom.

Between 1920 and 1930, 824,000 Blacks moved from the South to the North. By 1930, there were 50,000 foreign-born Blacks in New York City alone. In the South, the Black urban population grew by one-third between 1920 and 1930 (reaching 2.6 million by 1930). Although over half of the country's Black population remained in the rural South in 1930, one in four Blacks lived in a southern city.[3]

A major occupational shift accompanied Black migration.[4] By 1930, more Black men held blue-collar jobs than worked in agriculture. Black female employment in industry increased although most northern Black women continued to work in White homes. Racial discrimination in industrial life was widespread, but as the northern Black population expanded, opportunities opened up for Black professionals and businesspeople. For decades there had been a small Black middle class that included lawyers, doctors, musicians, saloon keepers, and dressmakers. Their clientele was predominantly Whites. Joining this small elite was a growing Black lower middle class that provided services to Black folks. Ministers, newspaper people, hotel and drugstore owners, real estate and insurance agents, and funeral directors added complexity to the Black class structure.

After World War I, a new political militancy among Blacks arose. On the one hand, Black trade unionists were faced with White trade unionists who did not want any semblance of desegregation, let alone integration in the trade union movement. On the other, *both* Marcus Garvey and the disciples of Booker T. Washington were among those in the Black community discouraging Blacks from joining White-led unions because of the racism — indeed, they urged Black trade unionists to seek good relationships with their employers instead.

As New Deal programs began to alleviate the inordinately negative impact of the Depression, racism continued to play a heavy hand in Black life. President Roosevelt and his cabinet officers received hundreds of letters complaining of the discriminatory practices of local relief officials.[5] In a letter from Chicago, a writer stated: "We would like to know do the government insist on Jim Crow in the W.P.A. projects?" In another letter from Vicksburg, Mississippi: "The way they are treating the Darkies here is a Shame. They wont give them food nor Cloths nor Work too do[.] When they Ask for Anything they drive them away as they were dogs."

These overarching elements help us understand the ways in which the medical community approached Blacks and syphilis. Added to this were the limitations of earlier research tendencies that focused on the "syphilitic Negro concept." This concept was in place as the age of antibiotics came to the fore in U.S. medicine. Before the availability of antibiotics, syphilis was a devastating worldwide scourge. Western medicine created a separate specialization to study syphilis — syphilology. In addition, the diagnosis of syphilis centered on the variety of lesions it produced. This meant that dermatologists were those who most frequently made the diagnosis of syphilis. Therefore, syphilology became intertwined with dermatology. Early syphilology centered also on congenital syphilis.

The treatment for syphilis contained within it strong dermatological roots. But, most important, syphilis was seen as hereditary. These twin pillars provided the philosophical foundation for the tendency of U.S. medicine at the turn of the century to make racial interpretations of any Black-White discrepancies in syphilis incidence and mortality.[6]

David McBride, a historian, describes the ideas of the New York physician Howard Fox, who was one of the most active of the northern medical exponents of the racialist view.[7] In a 1912 journal article, Fox emphasized a new lesion phenomenon that needed to be added to several "dermatological peculiarities of the negro" and described the abnormal frequency of "annular forms of the papular syphilide . . . in the negro race." From there, Fox argued that this new lesion phenomenon should be included with keloid, elephantiasis, and fibroma "as affections that are especially characteristic of the negro." Fox, like his southern colleagues, drew universal conclusions about Blacks from observation of a specific set of patients.

These racialist explanations fueled an opposing intellectual movement by Black physicians and a small but growing group of social scientists and welfare workers. Other Black medical specialists saw the racialist theories as abstract conjectures that had little to do with their attempts to advance Black health and hygiene. McBride argues that these Black medical professionals knew they had scant clout in blunting or halting racialism in the medical profession. Their hope, along with those who actively opposed the racialist argument, was that the medical and public idea that Blacks were more racially susceptible to communicable diseases would die out. They focused on offering resources that would provide comfort for victims of disease *and* on remaining academically and politically active in their profession as they faced enormous pressure from the wider medical establishment to restrict the devastation of diseases in the Black community.

Black and White southerners had different responses to infectious diseases in urban Black communities. Black health professionals and civic leaders put together a network of small hospitals, infirmaries, colored wards, public-oriented professional associations, medical schools, and nurses' training schools. Also in this early period (from 1904 to 1912) the National Medical Association (NMA) grew from 50 members to 521. The NMA sought to "insure progressiveness in the profession" and "help improve living conditions among the Negro people by teaching them the simple rules of health."[8]

Joining this progressive spirit in Black medicine was a strong interest among educated Blacks in health campaigns or professional medical activities related to TB, venereal disease, or other major health problems in Black communities. Black churches, insurance companies, and colleges took the lead in organizing public health campaigns. One example of this was the Men's Sunday Club of Savannah, Georgia (founded in 1905). The club held regular meetings to hear local Black physicians on health matters and discuss ways of improving community health. The average attendance was nearly two hundred. These kinds of efforts were joined by enthusiastic financial and political support for local Black hospitals and nurses' training facilities (see chapter 2).

In the mid-1910s, Black medical professionals and other segments of the Black population worked vigorously to reduce the devastating effects of infectious diseases, preventable infant illnesses, and unsanitary living conditions. One example of this was the Health Improvement Week held in April, an event that Booker T. Washington began in 1915 and that lasted until the 1930s. Black leaders in education, health, and religion organized programs in Black communities designed to increase public awareness of health problems and self-improvement measures for communities, the home, and in schools.

McBride argues that these early community-based health programs were the foundation of future community-based health movements; however, there were basic weaknesses in the early programs that limited their effectiveness in dealing with health problems.[9] The first of these weaknesses was the "institutional and technical deficiencies of black hospitals" whose "primary focus was providing surgical services and opportunities for black physicians' and nurses' training, not preventive health care programs." The second limitation McBride notes is that the southern medical establishment was unsupportive of Black community-health institutions and the Black medical-professional hospitals and medical-school projects.

After World War I, Black communities mounted an aggressive campaign to improve health care. McBride credits the "fragmenting concentration of blacks in the rural South, the overflowing social problems within northern urban black communities that ensued, and the growing power of specialized medicine emerging primarily from the northeastern medical establishment" as the key factors for this drive.[10] Part of this shift involved a movement away from neighbor groups and local organizations like the church as the sites for health education and services, the control shifting to public health authorities, "liberal white and black social welfare experts, medical specialists pursuing the microbiological aspects of disease and influential philanthropists championing black medical training and disease control demonstrations."[11]

This shift also entailed reorienting toward clinical specialization and microbiological communicability and promoting hospitalization over home care. Finally, medical professionals *began* to see that basing medical procedures on "Negro race traits" was inadequate and flawed. Among public health authorities, infectious-disease researchers, progressive social scientists and welfare workers, and philanthropists, the environmentalist approach was preferred. The adherents to this approach recognized that although "it may be theoretically possible to delineate races using certain phenotypical or genotypical criteria, black and white Americans had essentially similar inborn immunity and susceptibility to disease, and medical treatment had basically the same effectiveness on patients regardless of race. Race, then, was only one index to possible disease susceptibility."[12]

During the 1920s, Black health care was lodged in city and county health departments, general hospital wards, neighborhood health centers (some with Black staffs), and public health campaigns and health-demonstration sites throughout the country sponsored by large philanthropic foundations — the Julius Rosenwald Fund being the chief among these. The small Black hospitals, infirmaries, and sanitariums, though important in training Black doctors and nurses, only reached a small proportion of Blacks — predominantly in the South. The large, urban, public hospitals (usually White-controlled) and municipal and private neighborhood health facilities became the primary sites for Black health care. McBride notes that Black public health professionals became the "first line of defense" in the drive for Black health.[13]

The Julius Rosenwald Fund, created in 1917 and administered by its founder, began a broad-based school building program from 1917 to 1927. This program, based in the southern states, yielded several thousand school buildings. In 1928, the fund expanded by adding projects in medical welfare, library services, social studies, and race-relations activities. A key interest in this was financing and developing Black colleges and professionals.[14]

Edwin Embree led the foundation and its health-care program in this second phase. Embree viewed tuberculosis, syphilis, and maternal and infant morality as the key scourges in Black communities. The fund divided its "Medical Program for Negroes" into four areas: studies and surveys, health problems, Negro physicians and hospitals, and Provident Hospital. The fund focused most of its energies on the latter two areas. McBride gives a summary of the philosophy of the fund at this time:

> Embree and the Rosenwald Fund viewed the problems of infectious disease and infant and maternal deaths among blacks as inseparable from the need for an adequate supply of black medical personnel and separate clinics and hospitals. Indeed, the black health professional strata that emerged during the 1920s and 1930s was primarily a result of this

> program. The Fund's black health program was a three-prong development. First, demonstration projects in TB and syphilis investigation and treatment were funded in cooperation with the Public Health Service throughout sites primarily in the South. Second, the Fund assisted a small number of black hospitals (about a dozen or so annually) to serve as training centers for black interns, physicians, nurses, and hospital administrators, while at the same time operating clinical services especially needed by these hospitals' particular clientele. Finally, its black medical program sponsored the employment of black medical professionals by local public health departments, especially those throughout the South.[15]

The medical community's increased focus on syphilis as the country's major disease problem also played a role in the reshaped focus of the Rosenwald Fund. The shift in reporting cases — from pre–World War I silence from private physicians to postwar public-health-agency reporting — yielded a steady rise in cases between 1919 and 1935. In 1919, 113.2 cases per 100,000 persons were reported. By 1935, the number of cases was 212.6 per 100,000 persons.[16]

Federal researchers began to study how and why the spread of syphilis differed in Blacks and Whites since World War I. The Rosenwald Fund did not see the epidemic threat of syphilis as being as pressing as the rise in tuberculosis. It seems that "Fund workers envisioned that venereal disease among blacks, no matter how allegedly rampant, would remain within the nation's black communities."[17] In addition, the research on the detection and treatment of syphilis was beyond the fund's financial means.

In 1929, the fund focused its support behind the syphilis research of Taliaferro Clark, the Public Health Service's (PHS) officer assigned to the fund. Clark traveled the South setting up syphilis studies in Black communities. For the officers of the fund, the long-term solution to Black health problems was to increase Black hospitals, clinics, and medical and nursing schools. Therefore, throughout the 1930s, the fund spent the bulk of the monies allotted to health in expanding buildings and equipment in Black hospitals to increase their quality and capacity to educate Black medical professionals.

One area in which the fund had particular success was its southern campaign to add Black public health nurses to state health departments. The fund offered to assume partial funding for these nurses. The fund had approached all the southern states with this offer by 1929. By 1930, there were nearly forty Black nurses fulfilling these duties.[18] Though relatively small in numbers, these Black public health nurses had a profound impact on local public health services. Frequently, these Black nurses were the only Black employees in their public health departments. They performed a variety of tasks and usually evoked mass community cooperation with White-controlled health-care projects and clinics.

The 1930s New Deal expansion of the PHS and its campaign to eliminate venereal disease also addressed the Black-White health and mortality differential. However, by the end of the 1930s, deficiencies in federal antidisease programs were evident. Outspoken Black doctors, nurses, and social workers led the challenge to the priorities and approaches PHS authorities used in their attempt to eliminate excess Black mortality from TB, syphilis, and other health problems.

McBride notes that the basis of this clash was conflicting philosophies. Federal health officials worked toward achieving their goals by placing a high priority on investigating specific diseases and their prevalence, improving specific medical care services for victims, and winning the support of the U.S. public and politicians. Black community-health activists placed Black health within the broader context of social problems that included impoverished living conditions, few modern medical resources, and a reliance on folk medicine.[19]

With the Depression came soaring rates in Black mortality. The 1920 death rate for Blacks was 48.4 percent higher than for Whites. By 1930, this had increased to 52.8 percent. Heart disease and TB, respectively, were the leading causes of death. Infant mortality rates were devastating, although national rates were dropping.[20] In the early 1930s, twenty-two thousand out of two hundred and fifty thousand Black infants died each year. Of those who died in their first year, over half died within thirty days of birth. The four leading causes of Black infant deaths were natal or prenatal — premature birth; congenital problems; injury at birth; and certain diseases: syphilis, respiratory diseases, gastrointestinal diseases, and communicable diseases. An important note in this is that Black infant morality was more common in the urban areas of the North and South than in the rural regions.

Preventable conditions and/or communicable diseases shortened the lives of adult Blacks. Public health officials and major insurance companies considered the ravages of syphilis disturbing.[21] In 1934, syphilis was diagnosed as the cause for 17,700 deaths. In addition, there were estimates of up to seven million persons with syphilis — one in ten adults would have the disease in her or his lifetime. Nearly five hundred thousand new cases were being added to the treatment roles annually, making syphilis the leading public health crisis of Black America and the nation.

Although, as noted previously, environmentalism was gaining strength in this era, public health officials still relied on a racialist ideology to form treatment plans for syphilis in the Black communities across the country. McBride suggests three reasons for this.[22] First, racialism did not die after World War I; it intertwined with segregationist ideologies. Second, the growing federal health bureaucracy moved more in the direction of laboratory and radiological research to explain the microbiological aspects of infectious diseases rather than in the direction of environmental or social behavioral factors. Finally, researchers believed that they had developed the capacity to investigate the microbiological and racial determinants of epidemic disease. An important element in this for understanding some of the horror of the Tuskegee Study is that they believed they could do this using large, presumably pure Black and White populations.

## Overview of the Tuskegee Syphilis Study

The events in Macon County, Alabama, are a microcosm of what *can* happen when an economically depressed, Black community encounters a skewed understanding of health care. The Great Depression had a devastating impact on the county. In the 1930s, most of the residents in the county lived below the poverty level. As recently as 1970, one-third lived in homes with no indoor plumbing. The typical house was a shack with a dirt floor, no screens, little furniture, a few rags for bedding, and a privy only when underbrush was nearby. Drinking water came from an uncovered, shallow well that was often unprotected from direct surface drainage.[23]

There were fifteen White and one Black private physicians in the county during the early 1930s. Tuskegee Institute (an area Black college) had five physicians, and the area where the government conducted the syphilis-control work had five more. However, their services did not have much impact on the health of Blacks in the area. Most went "from cradle to grave deprived of proper medical care."[24] One elderly Black resident, speaking in 1932, painted a disturbing picture of what health care was like for these folks:

> I ain't had a Dr. but once in my life and that was 'bout 15 yrs. ago. . . . The Dr. ain't taking sticks, you know; if you go to him, you better have money and if he comes to you, you better have it. So you see that makes a po' man do without a Dr. when he really needs him.[25]

The Tuskegee Syphilis Study conducted by the U.S. Public Health Service (PHS) involved four hundred southern Black men for forty years — 1932 to 1972. The PHS did not tell these men that they had syphilis, and the service did not treat them so that researchers could discover the "natural history" of the disease. The end-point of the study was death, at which time the researchers autopsied the men to see what havoc the disease had wrought on their internal organs. Medical personnel never warned the men that they could pass the disease to their sex partners or to their unborn children.

The experiment began as a 1930 Rosenwald Fund control demonstration in Macon County, Alabama, where federal epidemiologists did a syphilis-control survey that revealed that the infection rate was 35 to 40 percent among the nearly ten thousand Blacks surveyed. The initial protocol was to do a one-year treatment program by using a Black doctor and nurse. The testing and treatment began.

The PHS had to secure the support of Tuskegee Institute and the Rosenwald Fund. Officials realized that such high infection rates might cast doubt about the claims Tuskegee made that it was having a positive effect in the area. The fund was particularly protective of its work among Blacks and aggressive in quelling any information that cast Blacks in a negative light.

When Robert Moton, then principal of Tuskegee Institute, learned the actual infection rates in Macon County, he supported the project with the only caveat being that its findings be limited to medical journals so that it would not hurt the chances of the doctors and nurses being trained at Tuskegee in finding work in hospitals or clinics. He suggested that the program be expanded with the idea that "the information if properly used might aid us in getting more funds from the State to carry on a state wide program."[26] The PHS officials agreed to Moton's stipulation and never violated this agreement.

PHS officials ignored the principle of the patient's right to know and withheld information that was crucial to the program's ultimate goal of controlling syphilis in Macon County. Officials told folks that they were treating them for "bad blood," a southern euphemism for a whole range of illnesses. One study revealed that Blacks did not connect syphilis with sexual acts. Bad blood did not carry any social stigma and was "spoken of in about the same manner as one speaks of having a 'bad heart' or 'bad teeth.'"[27] An interviewer's report notes that only one person thought that bad blood was congenital:

> "I knowed I had bad blood 'cause my mamma had scrofula when I was born." Only one interviewee, a woman who had enormous sores on her breast and arm, was aware that bad blood might be contagious. As she was trying to nurse her baby, she stated, "Dese boils hurt so bad . . . dey's sore from de kernel." She treated her sores with sulfur and vaseline and said she needed to wean her infant "so de boils won't turn on it."

Using the euphemism of bad blood was effective because in a county as poor as Macon, practically everyone suffered from some illness that they believed was caused by bad blood. When health officials used the term, they were giving folks excellent cause to come out for tests and treatment because they believed that they would receive treatment for their ailments and had no reason to feel ashamed of participating in the program.

However, H. L. Harris Jr., a Black physician employed by the Rosenwald Fund to evaluate the earlier syphilis-control demonstrations, raised a pointed question:

> It would be interesting to discover the effect upon clinical attendance were the terminology bad blood replaced by a term which would identify this disease with the bad disease which the patients know under a variety of local names. The large Negro attendance is due in part to the fact that in the minds of these people there is nothing to suggest that syphilis is not entirely respectable.[28]

Harris's questions were not answered because, in part, the program had the relatively limited goal of proving to state and local health officers and private doctors that rural Blacks could be tested and treated for syphilis. As James Jones points out, "The Public Health Service's officers and the Fund's officials apparently decided that there was no room in their one-step-at-a-time approach to conduct social hygiene work among poorly educated blacks, or to lecture them on the prophylaxis of syphilis. The doctors wanted to get on with the work at hand."[29]

Harris made several trips to Macon County and filed reports to the Rosenwald Fund that raised troubling questions. Harris noted inadequate planning. He questioned whether everyone who needed help was being reached because doctors confined their efforts to areas near paved highways. He decried the effects of a demanding workload, primitive clinical conditions, and the absence of thorough physical examinations. All these concerns led him to question if treatment would be administered properly.

One older patient described the pill-distribution scene at a clinic: "They was just throwing 'em out in the crowd, not tell 'em how to take 'em and nothing and somebody asked how to take 'em and he yelled out, 'Three times a day with a little water,' and that all he said."[30] Another patient questioned the bedside manner and competence of the government doctor who treated him. "He lay our arm down like he guttin' a hog. . . . I told him he hurt me. . . . He told me 'I'm the doctor.' I told him all right but this my arm."

When Oliver C. Wenger, director of the PHS Venereal Disease Clinic in Hot Springs, Arkansas, read Harris's evaluation, he attempted to dismiss it as "an honest report made by a good observer on a subject he knew nothing about, after a bird's eye view of a few hours, on a group of his own people who are as foreign to him as so many Chinese."[31] He deferred final opinion of the demonstration until all the results were in. In a second pessimistic report, Harris suggested that the syphilis-control demonstration had accomplished all that it could, and he recommended that the fund not extend the program. He believed that the county needed a comprehensive health and social welfare program to address its needs.

Michael M. Davis, director of medical services for the Rosenwald Fund, accepted the Harris report and set up an outside review of the syphilis-control demonstrations by a team of syphilologists and a sociologist. Charles Johnson, chair of the Department of Social Science at Fisk University and a noted Black sociologist, was chosen because of his reputation and because he had already worked on earlier projects with the fund. His interviews with families involved in the demonstrations ended with his largely favorable review of the manner in which health officials conducted the program. Johnson's report was joined by equally positive reviews by the syphilologists, but they still did not answer Harris's concern that a more comprehensive program was called for.

Davis advocated that the fund's board of trustees continue the work in a much more comprehensive manner. But at its spring 1931 meeting, the board decided against continuing the syphilis-control program. The effects of the Depression did not leave the fund untouched. This, coupled with the southern states' inability to contribute financially and the enormous costs associated with such an undertaking, left the board little choice.

With financial support gone, the PHS decided that the best way to attract more money for the program was to continue it as a study of untreated syphilis, and it entitled the study "The Tuskegee Study of Untreated Syphilis in the Negro Male." This became the longest known nontherapeutic experiment on humans in medical history. Those in control of the study reasoned that poor, uneducated, isolated, rural Alabamians would not have access to treatment. The author of the idea, Taliaferro Clark (a senior PHS officer), saw an unparalleled opportunity to study the effect of untreated syphilis. This was in blatant disregard of the fact that the men *had* received treatment for syphilis under the Rosenwald Fund's demonstration project. After professional and political wrangling between public health officials and private doctors, Clark reached the compromise that he would find local sponsors for the study. This made Tuskegee Institute the most logical and effective choice in soothing professional rivalries and being able to reach into the Black community.

After securing the support of Eugene H. Dibble (the medical director of Tuskegee Institute and head of its Andrew Hospital) and Robert Moton (the principal of Tuskegee), the PHS began to assemble the staff for the project. Dibble volunteered the services of his interns and nurses to administer the syphilis treatments under the direction of Raymond A. Vonderlehr, the federal PHS officer in charge of the study. Dibble also loaned the staff an office, an examination room for conducting the clinical examinations and necessary lumbar punctures, and the use of the hospital's X-ray equipment and technicians. He was also willing to meet with the officials of the Macon County

Board of Health and private doctors to quell any misunderstandings and explain the nature and scope of the project.

Moton and Dibble saw an opportunity to help the school in its work for Black Americans. Indeed, Dibble supported the experiment, in part, because he thought that it might demonstrate that costly treatment was unnecessary for people who had latent or third-stage syphilis. This position echoed the position of the PHS. He encouraged Moton's support because Tuskegee Institute "would get credit for this piece of research work. . . . [The study would] add greatly to the educational advantages offered our interns and nurses as well as the added standing it will give the hospital."[32]

The medical protocol for the project was highly suspect. Clark asked Joseph Earle Moore, a noted syphilologist at the Johns Hopkins University School of Medicine, to recommend a protocol for the study. Moore recommended that women be excluded because it was impossible to get information on the date of infections. This was because women had a difficult time recognizing the early symptoms that could be easily mistaken for such problems as vaginal itching and burning. Although not recommended by Moore, men younger than thirty years old were included in the study. The researchers relied solely on the earlier syphilis tests done in the Rosenwald Fund demonstration project rather than also collecting accurate clinical histories. Moore warned against contaminating the experiment with those who had received treatment and recommended against lumbar punctures to diagnose neural syphilis — both of these recommendations went unheeded.[33]

The words of Moore sealed the fate of the experiment. As he reviewed the medical protocol and gave his opinion on what needed to be included, he ended with these words: "[The study] would be of immense value. . . . Syphilis in the negro is in many respects almost a different disease from syphilis in the white."[34] Jones's estimation of these words is profound:

> No statement from Dr. Moore could have had greater significance for the future of the study. By the 1930s science had settled the question of whether there were any racial differences in the disease's etiology with a resounding "No!" Similarly, clinicians agreed that treatment was the same for both races. But belief in the notion that syphilis developed differently in blacks and whites ran through every echelon of the medical profession. To have a syphilologist of Dr. Moore's stature make that statement lent scientific respectability to more than half a century of clinical speculation. The meaning was not lost on Dr. Wenger, who wrote Dr. Clark: "I am glad to see in print for the first time by a clinician of Doctor Moore's experience and reputation make the statement 'Syphilis in the negro is in many respects almost a different disease from syphilis in the white. . . . This study will emphasize the differences."[35]

This is a crucial point. The White physicians of the PHS were confident that there were racial differences that affected health and disease. They rejected, in large measure, any environmental explanation for the frequency of the disease in poor, rural, Black communities. These doctors expected that the Tuskegee Study would provide a useful racial comparison to an Oslo, Norway, study that also traced untreated syphilis. But there is an important fact that must be pressed here — the Oslo study was retrospective. That is, the researchers in that study examined previous case records of White people whose syphilis went untreated. This is wholly different from the Tuskegee Study, which deliberately withheld treatment and information from an entire poor, Black community. It is grotesque that Vonderlehr proposed that the researchers expand their study of untreated syphilis in other racial groups, suggesting that they could conduct a study with Native Americans.[36]

A trusted Black public health nurse from the community, Eunice Rivers, was hired to keep track of the men, and the PHS enlisted the cooperation of the nearby teaching hospital at Tuskegee Institute in examining the men annually and charting the progress of the disease. Rivers worked in the field of public health from 1923 to well after her retirement in 1965. She participated in the study because it gave her a job with income (a precious commodity for a Black woman of that era) and she believed that it would promote Black health. Like many Black professionals and educators at the time, she did not question the experiment because she, like others, did not find it problematic.

The experiment began in October 1932 with Rivers assisting the PHS in recruiting and testing rural Blacks in the county for syphilis so that doctors could identify candidates for the study. Rivers knew this work well because she had participated in the earlier Rosenwald demonstration project. The medical personnel were swamped with people coming to the sites to have their blood tested and to receive treatments. Men and women showed up at these sites, and attempts to segregate the men posed problems. Susan Smith quotes both Vonderlehr and Rivers:

> According to Dr. Vonderlehr, "In trying to get a larger number of men in the primary surveys during December we were accused in one community of examining prospective recruits for the Army." Rivers reported that some of the women, especially the wives of the men selected from the study, were mad that they were not included because "they were sick too." Some even told her, "Nurse Rivers, you just partial to the men."[37]

The people of Macon County cooperated because they needed and wanted medical attention for their ailments. The men received annual physical examinations, aspirin, free hot meals on the day of their examinations, transportation, and burial stipends. They also trusted Rivers. She was the only continuity in the experiment, as the doctors changed over the years. It seems doubtful that the experiment could have continued for forty years without her assistance and the status the experiment gave the participants by associating them with both Tuskegee Institute and the federal government. Such associations were things that men of their social class and caste rarely experienced in that era.

It seems that Rivers did know that the men were systematically denied treatment and was one of the authors (although it is not clear if she was an actual writer) of a 1953 paper about the study. When the press broke the news of the study in 1972, it was both confusing and heart-wrenching for Rivers. She defended her actions: "A lot of things that have been written have been unfair. A lot of things."[38] She believed that the effects of the experiment were benign because it did not include people who had early syphilis. Those with latent syphilis were not seen as dangerous because the possibility of transmitting the disease to their partners was less. She explained, "Syphilis had done its damage with most of the people."[39] But historian Allan Brandt notes that "every major textbook of syphilis at the time of the Tuskegee Study's inception strongly advocated treating syphilis even in its latent stages."[40]

Rivers also believed that the study had scientific merit and ascribed to the racialist argument of the PHS that syphilis affected Blacks and Whites differently. She further believed that the benefits of the study outweighed the risks because of the poor health care the men would have received normally. She consistently insisted that the men received good medical care, although that care was diagnostic, not curative: "[T]hey'd get all kinds of extra things, cardiograms and . . . some of the things that I had never heard of. This is the thing that really hurt me about the unfair publicity. Those people had been given better care than some of us who could afford it."[41]

Six years after the study began, the federal government joined forces with some southern state health officials in a syphilis *treatment* program for Blacks. In this program, the government involved Black preachers who announced the times of blood-testing clinics (often Sundays) and rallied congregations. Officials also sent those who came in for testing an official-looking letter that invited them to return to the clinic for another visit. Health officials made heavy use of letters because they were convinced that Blacks "like to receive letters, just as we all do and particularly in a large and official looking envelope. They show it to their friends. They carry it around with them for weeks."[42]

By 1938, the Georgia project had tested 80 percent of the Blacks in the area. For those with positive tests, 77 percent were convinced to begin long chemotherapy, which was the cure for syphilis at the time. One problem that arose was convincing patients to keep taking treatments that could last as long as eighteen months. However, the staff was persistent, and 68 percent of lapsed patients returned when threatened with quarantine or jail. This project was successful. The October 1940 physicals showed a 40 percent drop from the 1937 infection rates, and the rate of stillbirths attributed to syphilis fell by 50 percent.

As the results and treatment plan of the Georgia project show, the protocol for the Tuskegee Study was suspect just six years into the study. The researchers refused to use long chemotherapy in 1938. And they later failed to follow suit when, following the introduction of penicillin after World War II, southern states began concentrating patients in rapid treatment centers to treat Blacks quickly. Writing about these new treatment plans, Beardsley notes:

> For the first time in memory, millions of young Southerners of both races received medical and dental care, housing, clothing, and food of first quality. Not only were they the more healthy for it, but their war experience accustomed them to regard such care and living standards as a norm, which they would expect their communities to continue after the war.[43]

As one reviews the rationales used by the federal researchers to continue the study, it almost seems that they knew of no other alternatives and thought no other funding was available or possible. Such was not the case. A 1937 report published by the Metropolitan Life Insurance Company, a study of its policyholders from 1911 to 1935, ended the section detailing syphilis among its policyholders with the following:

> The disease is almost wholly preventable and practically always curable if aggressively treated in its early stages. The crux of the problem is to overcome the present tendency toward concealment, so that persons who have been exposed to the infection will promptly seek proper medical attention. The campaign to stamp out syphilis must be directed toward correcting the public attitude toward this disease; and its ultimate control must be based upon the widespread provision of facilities adequate for early diagnosis, and prompt and sustained treatment.[44]

In addition, the LaFollette-Bulwinkle Act of 1938 earmarked $7 million annually to fund state venereal-disease control.

Yet the experiment continued. Questionable medical opinions about the peculiar incidence of cardiovascular syphilis were presented as fact. When physical examinations did not yield *any* of the expected evidence of higher rates of central nervous system syphilis, it was blamed on the behavior of lower-class Blacks obscuring these clinical manifestations of the disease.

Vonderlehr decided to delay the lumbar punctures to the end because he knew they would be the least pleasant part of the experiment. Jones writes that Vonderlehr "decided on a policy of bald deceit" by assembling the men at the various field clinics and "then transport[ing] them by automobile at a rate of twenty a day to Andrew Hospital, where the spinal taps would be performed and the men would be kept overnight for observation in case of adverse reactions."[45] Vonderlehr wrote to Clark:

> My idea in bringing them in large groups is to get the procedure completed in a given area before the negro population has been able to find out just what is going on. Individual patients would be told that they are coming in for an examination but they would remain all night after we had them here, and the details of the puncture techniques should also be kept from them as far as possible.[46]

Clark was concerned not about the deceit but about the financial costs of Vonderlehr's plan. He reminded Vonderlehr that the PHS did not have the funds to pay for such a plan and that the hospital would have to absorb the costs of hospitalization. He later justified the ruse in a letter to Moore, saying: "These negroes are very ignorant and easily influenced by things that would be of minor significance in a more intelligent group."[47]

Vonderlehr's form letter to the men inviting them to the hospital was constructed to impress them. It invoked the names of all the organizations that the men would associate with medical authority, but *no mention was made of lumbar punctures.* Instead, the letter began:

> Some time ago you were given a thorough examination and since that time we hope you have gotten a great deal of treatment for bad blood. You will now be given your last chance to get a second examination. This examination is a very special one and after it is finished you will be given a special treatment if it is believed you are in a condition to stand it.[48]

The letter also warned that the men might have to spend one night in the hospital, again avoiding any mention of the lumbar puncture and instead saying:

> You will remember that you had to wait for some time when you had your last good examination, and we wish to let you know that because we expect to be so busy it may be necessary for you to remain in the hospital over one night. If this is necessary you will be furnished your meals and a bed, as well as the examination and treatment without cost.

The letter worked, and the spinal taps began in May. The doctors continued to hide the fact that they were performing diagnostic rather than therapeutic procedures by telling the men that they were receiving spinal shots. These "spinal shots" — though dismissed by Wenger as "nothing serious," and most of the men were able to return to work after twenty-four hours — were cruel. Rivers's memories of the punctures are pointed.[49] She described them as "crude, very crude at that particular time," because "the technique was not smooth," and "a lot of them were stuck two or three times." The punctures were "very painful," and many of the men suffered "severe headaches." She noted the hard effects of the ride home over rutted roads and thought the lumbar punctures were "really dangerous because [there were] very few of the men who didn't have some complaint after." She also described the terror the men experienced as they "were scared to death" thinking of something "going into the spinal column or cord." She was also clear that her supervisors thought that she was "too sympathetic with the patients, and I was. I was concerned about the patients 'cause I had to live here after he [Wenger] was gone."

The men's accounts are striking. "It knocked me out. I tell [you] I thought I wasn't going to make it. I fainted, I fainted you know. Just paralyzed for a day or two. Just couldn't do nothing." Another man described the severity of a stiff neck, saying, "I thought several times I would ease around and get off the bed but I'd have to hold my neck [back]... and just crawl along on my knees."[50]

The spinal tap was to mark the end of the study in terms of clinical contact with the men. However, when Vonderlehr succeeded Clark as director of the Division of Venereal Diseases at the PHS, he kept the study alive. Over the next forty years, the position of director of the Division of Venereal Diseases was filled by a man who had worked on the study, thus insuring that the study would continue. Vonderlehr was convinced that the study would eventually reveal important information about the effects of syphilis on the cardiovascular system of Blacks. He, and many others after him, consistently ignored the major flaw of the study — it had been contaminated by the treatment the men had received in the earlier Rosenwald study.

As the years passed, the men in the study were systematically denied treatment — at times this violated public health statues; at other times, the experiments were exempted from national legislation mandating testing and treatment for tuberculosis and syphilis. The study even survived the PHS program of administering penicillin to syphilitic patients in 1943. In a grotesque piece of reasoning, the PHS officials concluded that improved health programs and the discovery of penicillin were reasons for *continuing* the experiment. This made the experiment an opportunity that could never be repeated again.

The atrocities revealed in the Nuremberg trials had no effect. PHS officials did not see experimentation on Jews as being similar to experimentation on a group of poor Black men in the South. John R. Heller, then director of the Division of Venereal Diseases, saw no connection. In a later interview, he said, "I, like most everybody else, was horrified at the things that were practiced upon these Jewish people, such as doing experiments while the patients were not only alive but doing such things as would cause their deaths. All these sorts of things were horrendous to me and I, like most everyone else, deplored them." He made no connections to the Tuskegee Study "because to me there was no similarity at all between them."[51]

Directors of the Division of Venereal Diseases consistently rebuffed any attempts, internally or externally, to question or halt the experiment. A comprehensive review of the procedures of the study in 1951 yielded substantial changes in protocol, but the issue of contamination and the ethical merits of the study were not addressed. Instead, PHS officials reasoned that the study could be useful in looking at aging. In 1957, the Centers for Disease Control (CDC) took control of the study from the PHS. As time wore on, it was assumed that the study would end only when the last subject died.

This gruesome "experiment" did not stop until 1972, when a PHS whistle blower leaked the story to the media. Before that date, the only member of the medical profession to voice opposition to the study was Irwin J. Schatz, a staff member of the Henry Ford Hospital in Detroit. In June 1965, after reading one of the published reports of the study, he wrote to the primary author:

> I am utterly astounded by the fact that physicians allow patients with a potentially fatal disease to remain untreated when effective therapy is available. I assume you feel that the information which is extracted from observations of this untreated group is worth their sacrifice. If this is the case, then I suggest that the United States Public Health Service and those physicians associated with it need to reevaluate their moral judgments in this regard.[52]

Jones notes that the letter was not answered and that a note written by Anne Q. Yobs, coeditor of the report, was stapled to it: "This is the first letter of this type we have received. I do not plan to answer this letter."

One year later, Peter Buxtun, a venereal-disease interviewer and investigator for the PHS in San Francisco, sent a letter to William J. Brown, then director of the Division of Venereal Diseases, raising questions about the nature and scope of the study and about its ethics. After a heated confrontation with his superiors, he resigned voluntarily from the PHS and enrolled in law school. Buxtun would not allow the matter to rest and pointed out that the volatile nature of U.S. society at that time could blow open the case and that contemporary society would not accept the rationales for continuing a study such as this.

This letter convinced the PHS to convene a panel of physicians to discuss the Tuskegee Study. These participants had no training in medical ethics, and none were Black. The panelists voted to continue the experiment and then turned their attention to protecting the PHS. After some discussion, the panel decided it best to update the local doctors and the Macon County Health Department on the experiment. Although the racial and gender composition of the Macon County Health Department had changed, the PHS once again prevailed in its 1969 meeting with officials. Most disturbing is the complicity of the Black doctors at this point. These doctors agreed to the study and told the PHS officials that if they had a list of the participants in the study, they would not give them antibiotics but refer them to the local health department. The doctors received the list.[53] The PHS also reestablished a limited working relationship with Andrew Hospital. Once again, no one questioned the ethics of the experiment.

Buxtun's pointed questions and increased objections from other doctors did instill uneasiness in the PHS officials. Although they saw no moral problems with the study, they did fear what might happen if the experiment came under media and public scrutiny. In late 1970, James B. Lucas, assistant chief of the Venereal Disease Branch, was the first high official to admit that the experiment was inconsistent with the goals of the PHS and bad science because it contained those who had been treated. "Nothing learned will prevent, find, or cure a single case of infectious syphilis or bring us closer to our basic mission of controlling venereal disease in the United States."[54] This said, Lucas still supported the continuation of the study.

It was Buxtun's unwillingness to let the matter drop that led him to talk with Jean Heller, a reporter working for the research bureau of the Associated Press in Washington, D.C. Heller broke the story on July 25, 1972.

When the federal government bowed to public opposition to an internal review, it appointed a nine-member citizens panel to investigate the experiment. The panel included five Blacks and was headed by Broadus Nathaniel Butler, president of Dillard University in New Orleans.

In a calculated move to allay public fears of cover-up, Merlin K. Duval, assistant secretary for health and scientific affairs of the Department of Health, Education, and Welfare (HEW), stated, "I wanted a panel that would be sympathetic to the public point of view, so I loaded it with angry blacks. My purpose was an exercise in self-flagellation if you will. I knew we should take the whole penalty — that way there could be no criticism."[55] This said, Duval limited the scope of the inquiry by restricting the panel's mandate to concentrate on the issue of informed consent and the decision to withhold penicillin. He did not ask the panel to consider the initial decision to withhold the treatment that was available in 1932, salvarsan and bismuth, and he did not charge the panel with considering how racism or classism played a role in limiting the study to poor Black men.

Not surprisingly, the panel recommended that the experiment should be terminated immediately with the remaining men receiving whatever care they needed. It took months before this was implemented as federal health officials and lawyers debated whether or not the government had the authority to provide comprehensive health care for the surviving men. This was not resolved until the panel appealed directly to the secretary of HEW, Casper Weinberger, who announced that he had instructed the PHS to provide the necessary care. In an ironic twist, the only way that Weinberger could do this legally was to reopen the experiment so that the men could receive health care as part of the official study.[56]

The panel deemed the experiment ethically unjustified in 1932 because researchers did not obtain the informed consent of the participants. Also, the panel found that penicillin therapy should have been made available to the men as of 1953 when it became available to the general public; further, the panel implied that salvarsan and bismuth should have been used earlier. Its final conclusion was that existing protections for human subjects of experiments were severely lacking, and it offered procedural and substantive recommendations for safeguarding subjects.

In 1974, the federal government paid a $10 million settlement to the six thousand victims of the Tuskegee Study and their heirs in an out-of-court settlement of a class action suit. In 1997, almost twenty-five years after Buxtun turned over his files to the press, President Bill Clinton issued a formal apology to the survivors of the study and their families and to the surviving family members of those men who had died.

## When You Got No Sticks

A myriad of things make this "experiment" appalling. The men and their families were victims of classism and racism. They were politically impotent, had the most hated disease of their day, and lived in a culture that daily emphasized their worthlessness. As Bill Jenkins, an epidemiology professor at Morehouse School of Medicine, notes, it is extremely doubtful that this study would have been performed on middle- or upper-class Blacks.[57]

To better understand this point, let us begin with the late 1920s. At that time, the Public Health Service (PHS) was pursuing three avenues of syphilis research. One, the Cooperative Clinical Study, involved five sites. At the University of Michigan site, Udo J. Wile bored holes in the skulls of mentally ill patients with general paresis and aspirated their brain tissue to then inject the tissue into rabbits to show that the tissue could transmit syphilis to the animals. This procedure was doubly appalling because it had no diagnostic or therapeutic benefit, and the patients were not competent to give their consent. Wile did not ask their families for consent, and when the public outcry became intense, his response was imperious: "You may quote me as having absolutely no interest in the matter, whatever people may wish to think regarding the experiment."[58]

The general conclusion from all the sites of the PHS research was that the effectiveness of arsphenamine in treating syphilis was indisputable. When treated with arsphenamine, 77 percent of the patients had negative serology and remission of their symptoms. Yet when the PHS years later had to defend its decision to withhold treatment of the men in the Tuskegee Study, it claimed that arsphenamine was ineffective and would have been of little value in the experiment.

A 1934 evaluation of serological tests for syphilis conducted by the PHS found serious discrepancies in the clinical reports on the Tuskegee men that were not dealt with in a serious manner. Although the reports from Tuskegee revealed a high rate of cardiovascular disease among the subjects, there was no evidence that this was caused by syphilis. The researchers simply implied that the syphilitic condition of the Black men was the cause of the cardiovascular and other problems. There was clinical evidence of neurological impairment in some patients, but none of the men developed any sign of the complications associated with neurosyphilis. As Benjamin Roy points out, the rate for neurosyphilis was less than that of the earlier Cooperative Clinical Study.[59] Interestingly, the writers of the clinical reports found reasons not to make any comparison between the Tuskegee men and the Oslo study or earlier Tuskegee reports. These discrepancies were caught by Norwegian researchers who criticized the reports before they were published. Yet the PHS continued to claim that the disease complications they found in the Tuskegee men were syphilitic. Additionally, the racialist assumptions concerning syphilitic cardiovascular disease in Blacks were not borne out in the 1934 evaluation. The pathological reports showed an equivalent incidence between Blacks and Whites when using data from a study done at Yale University.

Consistently, the specious clinical and pathological papers from the study were tolerated because those who read them largely accepted the researchers' claim that the biological differences between Blacks and Whites led to different biological outcomes regarding the disease. Irrespective of the facts, Blacks were deemed more syphilitic than Whites, and any data that suggested the contrary were attributed to Blacks who had syphilis that had escaped detection until better means of diagnosis were available.

The fact that the experiment was not a secret study — many of its reports appeared in medical journals and were openly discussed at professional meetings over the years — makes it even more disturbing. One PHS official told reporters that more than a dozen articles from the study had appeared in some of the nation's best medical journals during the time period of the study. These articles described the basic procedures of the study to a combined readership of more than a hundred thousand physicians. These articles merit a closer look.

From 1936 to 1973, thirteen articles appeared in major medical journals that clearly explained the nature of the study and its crushing consequences on the men. The thirty-seven-year silence from virtually all segments of the medical community gives one pause. The medical establishment knew well that untreated syphilis often led to blindness, deep skin lesions, insanity, heart disease, and early death.

In a probing study of the rhetoric involved in the articles related to the study, linguist Martha Solomon notes that the disease is described as a "dynamic agent" bent on destroying its "host" through the cardiovascular and central nervous systems.[60] In this, the patient is reduced to the scene in and on which the disease operates. In the initial report in 1936 read at the American Medical Association convention before it appeared in the journal *Venereal Disease Information,* a depiction of the disease emerges that persists throughout all the articles from the study: the agent is syphilis, whose effect is "the production of morbid processes involving the various systems of the body" and "disability in the early years of adult life." Researchers sought a "more detailed analysis of the material [in which] attempts will be made to describe and evaluate specific changes brought about by the disease in the infected individual with particular reference to the cardiovascular system."[61]

In subsequent reports, the emphasis is on the action of the disease as a dynamic agent. Solomon suggests that using this kind of rhetoric minimizes the role and significance of the observer because events are recorded by a "neutral, detached observer who sees them as they exist." This kind of realism emphasizes the objectivity and detachment of the observer and conveniently removes the observer from any consideration that he or she could or should intervene in the events that are being reported.[62]

Solomon goes on to note that the true agents in the study are the PHS doctors whose credentials, affiliations with the PHS, and prestigious titles are listed in the authors' information in each article. They are also described as a dedicated, self-sacrificing team. From the 1955 report:

> The contribution of time, thoughts, and energy of many individuals with the full knowledge that the fruits of their efforts would not mature until years later, and in other hands, has been vital. As in all such

> lifetime studies the devotion of these scientists and public health workers to the search for knowledge for the sake of knowledge and with selflessness must here be acknowledged.[63]

The action of these agents is passive, not dynamic, as they "follow" and "survey" the patients. The only dynamic acts that Solomon detected involved conducting tests or autopsies. In this, the guiding purpose of these doctors was the pursuit of knowledge that could benefit all humanity. The men of the study were the means through which these doctors could achieve their higher purpose. The men were reduced to subjects. As such, they could be dehumanized, at times literally: "The shortening of life expectancy observed in man [has] a counterpart in the white mouse, in which it has been shown by Rosahn that a syphilitic group has a significantly lessened life expectancy."[64]

The articles display a detached, if not condescending, attitude toward the men. Articles from 1953 and 1954 discuss the nonmedical aspects of the study and environmental factors respectively.[65] From the 1953 report, Solomon points to the following passage:

> Incentives for maximum cooperation of the patients must be kept in mind. What appears to be a real incentive to an outsider's way of thinking may have little appeal for the patient. In our case, free hot meals mean more to the men than $50 worth of free medical examination.

And from the 1954 article:

> [There is a] nonchalant attitude of the patients toward calendars and time-reckonings. . . . [T]hese men like relatively few dishes. As a rule they were interested only in meat (pork or chicken, never beef) and bread, and would select vegetables only upon the suggestion they do so.

The articles and the whole protocol of the study harbor assumptions about the low educational status of the majority of the patients, racialist assumptions about the nature of Black health, and a generally superior and paternalistic stance of the PHS and CDC doctors. These attitudes combined to prevent the doctors from considering appealing to the Tuskegee men from a purely scientific stance.

Solomon states that "reducing patients to scene and agency is common in reports of non-therapeutic projects."[66] The focus is on observing the disease and cataloging its effects rather than on the flesh and blood, the humanity, of those who are being "studied." As so many of the events of the experiment show, a myopic worldview emerges that in this case was ringed with paternalism and racialist ideologies. The doctors saw the Tuskegee men's Black skin as a sign of inferiority, as separating the men from the doctors. This happened to the degree that race (read color, poverty, rural lack of sophistication, poor health, poor education) became the determinative factor in continuing this awful experiment on human life. Few, Black or White, raised questions about the validity of racial and class stereotypes when considering the merits of the study.

The absolute value became knowledge, not human lives. The doctors of the Tuskegee Study represented a relatively liberal mind-set in relation to prevailing attitudes of the era, but the craving for knowledge, the need for sera (fluids drawn from the men), racialist assumptions, and classist attitudes prevented them from seeing that rather than being a noble and valuable study, the experiment was a tribute to inhumanity, bad medicine, and flawed scientific methods.

The kind of societal myopia that ran rampant in the PHS and the CDC is a call to lament — for the PHS, and later the CDC, did not act alone. This was a cooperative effort of the Alabama State Department of Health, the Tuskegee Institute, the Tuskegee Medical Society, and the Macon County Health Department.

In a 1972 press release, Tuskegee Institute acknowledged that the facilities at Andrew Hospital and its personnel had been used in the study, but only in the 1930s when the surgeon general of the United States had requested their participation as part of a larger treatment program. This press release referred to the men as "voluntary participants" in a study "to develop new and more effective treatment programs" with procedures that were "acceptable under the clinical conditions prevailing 40 years ago, when the drugs available for treatments . . . were dangerous and their long-term effectiveness had not been established."[67]

Tuskegee officials went on to state that the institute had lost contact with the experiment by the time penicillin became available and that both the treatment program and the study of untreated syphilis had been moved from Tuskegee to the Macon County Health Department by 1946. The press release also stated that "there has been no active medical program at Tuskegee Institute's John A. Andrew Hospital connected with this USPHS study." Jones points out that this is true technically, but it obscures the fact that Tuskegee lent its tacit approval as it permitted the use of its facilities and personnel. The administrator of Andrew Hospital told reporters that the men had been X-rayed at the hospital two years earlier (that is, in 1970), but reasoned that this was not direct involvement because the hospital's X-ray facilities were available to all.[68]

The other collaborating agencies made similar statements in distancing themselves from the study. In each case, individuals and agencies failed to be completely forthcoming about their roles in failing to halt or question the study when opportunities arose. This was true from the pathologist who performed some of the autopsies, to the Alabama State Board of Health (its director saw the controversy over the study as "trying to make a mountain out of a molehill"), to the Macon County Health Department, to the Macon County Medical Society.

The numerous attempts to justify the study compound its onerousness. One doctor who served as director of the Division of Venereal Diseases between 1943 and 1948 declared: "There was nothing in the experiment that was unethical or unscientific."[69] This is in direct contradiction to the facts of the experiment. Men who were presumed positive, but turned out to be negative either because of treatment or by seroconversion, were deleted from the study. Likewise, men who were presumed negative, but tested positive, were moved into the syphilitic group.[70] This cooking of the numbers maintained the "credibility" of the positive and negative control groups.

What PHS and CDC officials failed to acknowledge to the public was that the men's sera made them valuable as well. Serological tests for syphilis were lucrative in the commercial market. In the United States alone, syphilis testing increased from two million in 1936 to twenty-eight million in 1943 and remained at a steady twelve million annually into the 1960s.[71] This volume was assured by the laws requiring syphilis testing for marriage certificates, newborns, military recruits, industrial physical examinations, and admissions to hospitals. Although there can be no direct causal link established, it is interesting to note that the U.S. dominance in syphilis serology lessened after the Tuskegee Study was ended.

The Tuskegee sera enabled the PHS to exercise its lawmaking power to regulate syphilis serodiagnosis, which had become an industry in its own right. It is important to recognize the importance of this move given the long history of adversarial relations between private physicians and public health physicians and workers. When the Tuskegee men had their yearly samples drawn, it was for the "sole purpose of providing sera for regulatory and standardization purposes unrelated to research."[72]

The National Venereal Disease Act of 1938 centralized and even broadened the administrative legal and police power of the PHS. Most important, it allowed greater latitude in pursing human research and made the Tuskegee Study legal. From 1936 to 1946 there were no clinical reports on the Tuskegee men. This gap was due to the need to train a new field physician and to officials trying to decide what to do with the fact that some of the patients had received treatment. When PHS officials decided to add new untreated syphilitics to the study, this violated the *clinical* part of the study, but it did meet the needs of the *serodiagnostic* component of it. In a valid clinical study, participants cannot be added or deleted without compromising and invalidating the results.

Officials from the PHS and CDC justified the study and the withholding of penicillin as medically justifiable. CDC spokespersons consistently presented the Tuskegee Study as a medical matter involving *clinical* decisions that may or may not have been valid. The fact that data abounded that contradicted decisions to continue the study was ignored. In an odd, unscientific twist, the PHS and CDC refused to seriously evaluate why their assumptions were not being borne out, and they consistently attempted to fix the problems by assuming that the reasons for them lay in yet undiscovered or unrealized relationships between their fixed set of deadly presumptions. They engaged in the worst kind of positivist reordering of the universe to have the data fit their racialist ideologies.

Ethics took a back seat. The decision to withhold treatment was the immoral foundation of this experiment. Once a new and improved form of treatment was developed for the disease, justifying its continuation demanded casuistry of the highest order. Even when the story broke in 1972, the PHS and the CDC — reacting to the indignation of the press and public and many in the medical community — avoided dealing with the core issue of the scientific merits of the experiment.

Many physicians went so far as to defend the study, pointing out that there had been only one study dealing with the effects of untreated syphilis before the Tuskegee Study. One physician from Vanderbilt University's School of Medicine pointed not only to this, but also to the argument that penicillin would not have benefited the men. However, this doctor went one step further and asserted that *the men* were responsible for the illnesses and deaths they sustained from syphilis. He held *them* responsible for not seeking treatment for a disease that went unnamed for them. The Hippocratic Oath to prevent harm and heal the sick whenever possible was not a part of his argument.

Perhaps the final note in this sad, sad lament is not so much shocking as it is sobering. The original contract between the PHS and the Alabama Department of Health to initiate the study contained a patent agreement that made any invention that derived from the study the sole property of the U.S. federal government.

## Chapter 5

# It's Not Always Just in Her Head

## *African American Women, Health, and Health Care*

The worlds of women and health care have their own peculiar vexations in the United States. The same kind of arrogance, ignorance, and stereotyping that gave rise to racialist medical theories also spawned sexist medical theories. In the early 1800s, those who were more conservative cited scripture to prove women's inferiority. Appeals to Adam's rib and the travail of childbirth abounded as proofs of women's more subservient role in society.

In the mid-1800s, challenges to these assumptions by women's rights advocates and political liberals prompted biologists to measure the size of women's skulls, the length of their bones, the rate of their breathing, and the number of blood cells they had. These studies led biologists to conclude that women were the weaker sex.[1] Physicians joined this ideology and became convinced that the true nature of a woman was to be sickly and that she was at the mercy of her reproductive system because a woman's regular monthly cycle irritated her "delicate nervous system and her sensitive, small, weak brain."[2] Women were thought to be particularly vulnerable to nervous conditions, and this became a way to refute any argument from the rising middle class of women who sought the right to vote, attain an education, or have professional careers. This understanding of the delicacy of womanhood did not extend to slave, or working-class, or poor women.

Also emerging at this time was the perception that class was a natural and biological distinction. Originating from earlier views that saw social caste and class divisions to be divinely ordained, the nineteenth-century view of class was that it was determined by innate, inherited ability. With Marxist thought challenging such assumptions, on one hand, and social Darwinism reifying these assumptions, on the other, physicians were confronted with a choice.

Briefly stated, social Darwinism suggested that the new social inequalities emerging in U.S. society due to the industrial revolution reflected natural law. It is important to note that this theory, a perversion of Darwin's original theory of the "struggle for survival," was developed in the middle of the economic depression of the 1870s. This was a time rife with labor struggles, union organizing, and early socialist calls for the reorganization of the political order.

Many social Darwinists justified social inequality by arguing that the social elite must be the "most fit" because they survived so well, which then meant that social hierarchies reflected real biological differences. Poor health was a sign, if not proof, of biological inferiority. By the late 1800s, social Darwinist ideologies of race, gender, and class inequality provided the scientific basis for social policy.

As these views entered the early twentieth century, they joined other biological explanations of sex differences in disease and in social roles. The notion that gender was a fundamental biological trait that was built into the genetic constitution of our bodies was fueled by the discovery of the sex chromosomes in 1905.[3] In that same year, the term "hormone" was introduced. By the mid-1920s, researchers had identified several hormones related to reproduction and popularized the term "sex hormones." Sex chromosomes and hormones became the focus of research seeking to understand breast and uterine cancer and other sex-linked diseases. Environmental links were downplayed. Employers used these discoveries to dictate which jobs were suitable for women.

Much like the way racialist ideology focused on race as the key determinant of health and illness, sexist ideology was riveted to reproductive biology. These views also entered into the field of public health. More generally in medicine, women's health was confined to obstetrics and gynecology. In public health, women's health needs were concentrated in maternal and child health programs. Little attention was given to occupational health because women were considered as temporary workers — their true work was to be wives and mothers. Because reproduction was so central to women's existence, any nonreproductive health issues were left unaddressed or subsumed under men's bodies and men's diseases.

## Clinical Trials and Research

In 1983, the assistant secretary of health of the Public Health Service (PHS) commissioned a task force to study the status of women and health. Their 1985 report, *The Women's Health Report of the Public Health Service Task Force on Women's Health Issues,* found that there was gender bias in health-care research and delivery. This bias had, in turn, generated significant holes in knowledge about women's health.

In response to this report, the National Institutes of Health (NIH) warned any grant applicants that if women were not included in their study populations, the NIH needed scientific rationale for this exclusion.[4] This proved to be, at best, a vain hope. The General Accounting Office (GAO) audited the NIH and found that it was continuing to grant monies for research that excluded women. In testimony before the House panel reviewing the GAO report, House members learned that the NIH had not adequately explained its new policy on women to the research community, who did not understand it. As it turns out, many of those in the NIH also lacked knowledge of the policy.

The NIH took almost three years to issue detailed guidelines to its staff members, and the grant application booklet researchers were to use to draw up their funding requests was not rewritten to reflect the new guidelines. This meant that funding continued as usual, and women were excluded from programs funded by NIH grants. The revised booklet did not appear until 1990, more than four years after the NIH first introduced the policy.

A second marker is an Institute of Medicine report that revealed that in 1986 and 1987, only 1.8 percent of the NIH extramural funds were awarded to support research in obstetric and gynecology departments.[5] This low rate is not surprising given that at that time the NIH had only three obstetrician-gynecologists on permanent staff.

Another marker is June 18, 1990. On this date a U.S. House panel learned from the GAO that women were being systematically excluded from medical research studies, therefore putting their health at risk. Part of the vexation at that hearing was over the fact that a GAO investigator had found that some senior-level male researchers at the NIH considered policies designed to include women in medical studies to be politically motivated and without scientific merit.[6]

Women make 60 to 70 percent of all visits to doctors' offices and undergo more complex procedures, more examinations, more laboratory tests, and more blood pressure checks than men. Women receive more prescriptions and take more medications, spend more time in hospitals, and suffer more age-related disabling conditions than men. And women pay half the taxes that provide the financial base for the multibillion dollar NIH annual budget.[7] All this while being excluded, in large measure, from medical research studies designed to enhance the life of us all.

There is lament in the fact that when the NIH sponsored a five-year study showing that taking one aspirin every other day could reduce the incidence of heart attacks, those studied included 22,071 men and no women. This, although heart disease is the single most important cause of death in postmenopausal women — killing half a million women a year in the United States alone.[8]

There is lament in the sample of the "Mr. Fit" study that looked at the relationship between heart disease, cholesterol, and lifestyle — it included fifteen thousand men and no women.[9]

There is lament in a nationally funded long-term study about health and aging that studied only men during its first twenty years, although two-thirds of those over age sixty-five are women.[10]

There is lament in a major study that showed a heavy coffee intake does not increase the risk of stroke or heart attack — 45,589 men and no women were studied.[11]

There is lament that the active ingredient in many over-the-counter appetite suppressants was tested primarily on young men, although those who use these diet aids are overwhelmingly women.[12]

There is lament in the fact that a Rockefeller University project that explored the impact of obesity on the development of breast or endometrial cancer used only men.[13]

Perhaps we could assuage part of the sting of this lament if it were not for the fact that more than seventy years ago congressional hearings revealed that there was more money being spent on hog cholera research than on safe childbirth and prenatal care.[14]

Until recently, and to the detriment of the very women health advocacy has sought to speak for, the focus on women's health has been too narrow — the primary concern has been on reproductive health and how women are treated in the examining room, rather than on how women are treated in the laboratory and in the highly politicized arena of funding research.

I suspect that it seems obvious to many that women ought to be included in research designed to enhance women's health. Unfortunately, the tenor of many medical researchers' thinking is that women's monthly hormonal fluctuations complicate research and increase costs; there is worry about the risk to a fetus (and potential liability); women can become pregnant during a clinical trial; and finding enough women to make study results valuable is too hard.[15]

I am not sure whether it is a matter of irony or lament or both when the same researchers who cite these complicating factors in including women then assert that women are "just like men anyway," so they can draw up diagnostic plans and prescribe treatments based on the results of all-male studies.

If we place ourselves in the position of the researcher, there *is* an enormous advantage to having a homogeneous sample. Interpreting data is simpler; limiting studies to White males helps eliminate variables such as hormonal changes, race, and age that must be accounted for. In an odd way, many researchers see White males as "generic humans," which by default makes women of all racial-ethnic groups and men of color deviations from the norm.[16] As ethics professor Rebecca Dresser of Case Western University Medical School states: "Physical differences between males and females or between Whites and people of color are unacknowledged or irrelevant in this world view."[17]

However, the White-men-as-generic-humans argument is too simplistic. It ignores the fact that when researchers began to standardize methods for clinical and epidemiological research, racialist and sexist assumptions were so firmly entrenched that Whites and non-Whites, men and women were rarely studied together.[18] The harsh reality is that most researchers and physicians were, until painfully recently, interested only in the health status of Whites and in the reproductive health of women. White men have traditionally been the research subjects of choice for all health conditions other than women's reproductive health. The history of research in the United States is that the health of racial-ethnic men and women and the nonreproductive health of White women have been largely ignored. Rather than assuming that researchers are collapsing all of humanity under a White male gloss, we should understand that this is about the politics of difference.

This is a deadly lament for women. Excluding women because of their menstrual cycle makes no moral or ethical sense to me — it is not an anomaly for most women's bodies. To virtually ignore 52 percent of the population is disgraceful. Fear of harming the fetus only makes sense if we will *never* give the drugs and treatments being tested to pregnant women. Not all women are at equal risk for pregnancy. Excluding women from studies because of recruitment difficulties is specious.

There *are* unique female and male characteristics. What damage are we doing when physicians often prescribe fast walking as an exercise to strengthen bones in the elderly although women's musculoskeletal systems are often weakened by the decline of estrogen levels following menopause? What evil lurks when most drug trials have an underrepresentation of women although 60 percent of prescriptions are for women?[19]

The risk we run is that testing drug effectiveness only in men may eliminate drugs that might have worked better for women. This early exclusion may explain why antidepressants work better for men than women, although women suffer from depression twice as often as men.[20] It may well be that doses that work well in men, who are generally larger than women, may be different from those that work well for women.

## Health as Cultural Production

This lament is framed under the strong influence of the biomedical model in Western medicine. In this model health and disease are explained through an engineering metaphor in which the body is seen as a series of separate, interdependent systems. Ill health is seen as the mechanical failure of some part of one or more of these systems. The task of medicine, then, is to repair the damage.

The troubling thing about this model is that often the relationship between the mind and body is not explored with great rigor and individuals and groups are separated from their social and cultural contexts. Yet this model *has* been very successful in aiding our knowledge of various diseases and their treatment. It has aided in the discovery and the use of things like anesthesia and antibiotics. What has been missing, however, is the realization that health is a cultural production and that an extreme concentration on a curative model that "explains" the causes of diseases and explores the different ways in which we experience illness is too limited.

As both the preceding discussion of the Tuskegee Study and the following discussion of the impact of HIV/AIDS in chapter 6 reveal, there is more to poor health than disease. Understanding health as a cultural production pushes us not only to focus on the biomedical model, but to consider the ways in which *how* we are influences, if not forms, our healthiness or lack of it. This becomes important when looking at the ways in which sex and gender influence our health. It is even more so when we add race and class.

It is sobering that the Office of Research on Women's Health and the first Office for Minority Health Affairs were established in 1990 and 1991 respectively. In 1994, the NIH published guidelines on the inclusion of women and minorities in research involving human subjects. These recent dates indicate the slowness with which the federal government officially recognized that the majority of the population in the United States must be included in research along with White males.

Racism and sexism have combined to yield little research that is helpful or reliable in determining the frequency and causes of disease in racial-ethnic women. As Sue V. Rosser points out, some complications of racism and sexism have "effectively invalidated" some research of this type, in part because the phrase "women of color" is often seen as referring to "a coherent group when in fact it includes women of extremely diverse racial and ethnic backgrounds who are not related to each other genetically or culturally."[21] In fact, women of color may well differ from each other more than they do from White women.

This overarching phrase, "women of color," can mask the diversity that exists within a racial-ethnic group. Consider the Census Bureau's category of Asians/Pacific Islanders. This actually includes more than twenty-five groups including Chinese, Filipinos, Japanese, Indians, Koreans, Vietnamese, Hawaiians, Samoans, Burmese, Cambodians, Laotians, and Thais. Although these groups share a common origin in Asia and the Pacific Islands, they represent different cultures, languages, and somewhat different gene pools. The same comparisons and contrasts can be made for Hispanics/Latinos and Native Americans/Alaskans.

To date, there have been few clinical trials in which racial-ethnic women have been the focus of the research. The results have not produced an adequate body of information about health and disease processes in these women. In some of the worst scenarios, women have been used as guinea pigs in clinical trials of unsafe drugs or for experiments to document the possible biological bases of social ills.[22]

There have been, however, many studies that have identified access to health care as a controlling factor for health and disease in racial-ethnic women. Diseases like hypertension, cardiovascular disease, alcoholism, some cancers, and diabetes join increased homicide rates and maternal and infant mortality rates to decrease the life expectancy of racial-ethnic women when compared to White women.

It appears that genetics, environment, and inadequate access to health care combine in deadly ways in the lives of far too many racial-ethnic women. Compounding this problem is the fact that there have been virtually no controlled clinical trials to discover the degree and scope of the contribution of genetics, environment (e.g., diet, smoking, exercise, and living near toxic or polluted sites), and medication to decreased mortality rates for racial-ethnic women.[23]

Rosser cites the rising rate of cancer among African American women as an example of this.[24] Although this rise is often attributed to the stress that Black folk experience, as of 1994 there was no well-controlled study that examined the various factors that would lead to such a conclusion. Such a study would have to consider the interstructuring of race, gender, and class with family history of cancer and commonly understood stressful lifestyle factors such as the death of a spouse or partner, divorce, moving, substance abuse, and homosexuality. These factors would also need to be compared between women of the same class, with similar family histories of cancer and similar levels of stress, and across racial groups.

Although the lament litany that began this chapter indicates the dearth of women as participants in clinical trials, it does not reveal the gross underrepresentation of racial-ethnic women in clinical trials. When White women are the only participants in experiments and the data are extrapolated to all females, this invites inaccurate, if not deadly, treatment plans that do not account for the different frequencies and manifestations of a condition or disease that can and do occur in racial-ethnic populations.

For example, using the mammograms of a 50/50 population of White and African American women who are fifty-five years old to determine the frequency of breast cancer in women in the United States could result in underestimating the frequency in the total female population because Black women exhibit lower incidences of breast cancer than White women. This could then skew funding initiatives because the study would be based on data that have an overinflated population of African American women — Black women are only 12 percent of the population, not 50 percent.

However, there is another scenario in this mammogram example. A 1997 North Carolina study revealed that doctors are less likely to recommend breast cancer screening to African American women than to White women.[25] This nine-year study found that the doctors for about 25 percent of the Black women had them take a mammogram. This compared to 52 percent of White women. Nationally, there remains a gap, but it is closing. This might not be so troubling if it were not for the fact that although Black women do have decreased rates of breast cancer, they are more likely to die of it.

The North Carolina study did not account for the race of the doctors, and it is not clear what role, if any, racism may play in the discrepancy. There is a strong possibility that economics may be a controlling factor in this.

The complexities of the preceding example help highlight the fact that when women are grouped together as a monolith, the frequency of certain genes in different racial and ethnic groups goes unrecognized. This can and often does lead to biased results. Again, an example helps draw this out. Consider a study that looked at the effectiveness of drinking milk as compared to taking calcium tablets in preventing osteoporosis; the study included only White and Asian women because the researchers were aware of data that suggested African American and Native American women have lower rates of osteoporosis, which led the researchers to exclude them from the study. If the researchers did not recognize and factor into the study that a high rate of a type of glucose deficiency in the Asian population can mean that it is possible that a substantial number of the Asian women in the study were unable to tolerate drinking milk and therefore lost the benefit from calcium in the milk, then that oversight would make the data flawed. The result may have biased the whole study toward calcium pills.

It seems that racial-ethnic women are the focus for particular aspects of women's health research that often represent social problems of some kind. This is a new melding of racialist and sexist thinking that can lead to deadly conclusions and misguided diagnoses not unlike those found in the Tuskegee Study. We must look, with an analytical and critical eye, at why racial-ethnic females are the focus of studies on teenage pregnancy and substance abuse during pregnancy.[26]

Efforts to study and prevent Black teenage pregnancy have received considerable funding, although the frequency of pregnancy among African American teenagers has declined.[27] The rates that have increased are among White teenagers and among Black and White *unmarried* teenage women. This is a much more complex situation than the media and common perception lead us to believe. It is true that overall, birth rates remain highest among Black teenagers. However, it is important to note that rates in the late 1980s rose 25 percent for Hispanics/Latinas, 19 percent for Whites, and 12 percent for African Americans.

Identifying teenage pregnancy with blackness masks the realities of other racial and ethnic groups. It also tempts us to see teenage pregnancy as only a medical problem, one that can be solved by increasing research dollars and developing protocols that educate the public about prenatal care, inappropriate nutrition, and the dangers of low birth-weight. These are very real and potentially death-dealing medical issues that should not be ignored or dismissed. However, to the degree that we concentrate on the medical aspects of teenage pregnancy and do not address social issues such as societal perceptions of beauty and how this affects young girls' self-image, access to jobs, and educational options — also factors in discussing teenage pregnancy — we fail to address in a systematic manner the high costs that come when children birth children.

In addition to often being the preferred study population for social-problem research, racial-ethnic women have often been the targets for high-risk clinical trials in which there was a danger that the drug being studied would produce dangerous side effects.[28] For instance, 132 women in Puerto Rico were the subjects of the initial testing of the birth control pill. This first pill contained high doses of estrogen, and it was unclear what these high levels might do to women's bodies. Further, there were no controls for the genetic differences that might occur. In the end, the pill was not marketed on the U.S. mainland until it was considered safe.

Like the men of Tuskegee, some racial-ethnic women have been used as experimental subjects without first having given consent based on a full disclosure of information. Many of these cases involve sterilization. In a sobering statistic, more than one-third of the women of childbearing age in Puerto Rico were sterilized between 1940 and 1970 without their consent.[29] African American, Native American, and some lower-income and poor White women have been forced to take birth control pills or to be sterilized to receive government support for their children.[30]

## The Worlds of Black Womenfolks

The 1990 census found that 16.4 million of the 31 million African Americans in the United States are females. In other words, more than half the Black folks in the country are women. With regard to Blacks in the United States, health conditions that are thought to or do have a genetic basis receive more public attention and resources than conditions that stem from behavioral choices. For example, research on health conditions arising from substance abuse or environmentally caused illnesses receives less attention and support than research focused on sickle-cell anemia.[31]

Given this, our behavior becomes important, for it may be our primary means of survival in a health-care system such as this. It is important to take advantage of preventive tests such as Pap smears and breast examinations. Many Black women fail to do so. This is deadly given the fact that the incidence of cervical cancer among Black women is twice that among Whites.

Prenatal care is vital in helping bring healthy children into this world. In 1992, only 64 percent of African American mothers received early care. Those who received late or no prenatal care were more likely to be poor, adolescent, unmarried, rural residents, or more than forty years old. These are the same categories that are considered high risk for pregnancy.

In the 1977 National Medical Care Expenditure Survey, only 46 percent of African Americans stated that they usually received care in their doctor's office. By 1993, the percentage had risen to only 48 percent.[32] In this 1993 study, 21 percent of African Americans revealed that the outpatient department was their usual place of contact with a doctor. The outpatient department includes the outpatient clinic and the emergency room. One reason for this is related to health insurance. Those Blacks who do not have health insurance are more likely to seek care infrequently — this may be compounded if they are poor. Another reason may be the hours of operation for the outpatient departments. If one is in an hourly wage job, making and keeping appointments in the nine-to-five workday may mean a loss of precious income. Those working the graveyard shift or shifts with irregular hours are also affected. Both of these wage-earning types of job are more likely to be held by lower-income and poor people.

There have been some gains for Black women. Between 1950 and 1981 the death rate for African American women from heart disease decreased by 45 percent and from cerebrovascular disease (strokes) by 63 percent. The vexing news in this is that in both 1985 and 1992, Black women were still dying at rates that were two times higher than the national norm.[33] In addition, a greater number of Black women suffer nonfatal strokes than the national average. There remains little research that considers socioeconomics, environment, and gender as risk factors for cardiovascular disease. It is also not clear what role hormones play in these figures, but it is clear that there is a significant increase of heart attacks in postmenopausal women. Further, there is growing evidence that women of every age group who use estrogen have lower rates of cardiovascular disease than those who do not use estrogen.[34]

Cancer is second only to heart disease as a cause of death for U.S. women. There are five leading sites for cancer in Black women (in order of prevalence): breast, colon, rectum, lung, uterus, and pancreas. Although White women have higher incidences of most types of cancers than African

American women, Black women have higher death rates and lower five-year survival rates for most types of cancer.[35] The typical diagnosis of cancer for Black women comes at later stages, making treatment less effective.

Diabetes affects about fourteen million people in the United States. It was relatively uncommon among Blacks at the turn of this century but is now the third leading cause of death among African Americans.[36] In fact, it increased fourfold from 1963 (228,000) to 1985 (1 million). The estimates are that another 500,000 Black folks have undiagnosed diabetes. The rate of noninsulin dependent diabetes is 95 percent higher in Blacks than Whites. In addition, 500,000 Black elderly have diabetes, with the greatest incidence occurring before age sixty-five.

Some term the prevalence of diabetes among African American women an epidemic.[37] Black women have an incidence of diabetes that is twice higher than that among White women, and Black women are more likely to die of its complications. One in four Black women who are older than fifty-five have diabetes. The disease is often associated with obesity, and about 83 percent of diabetic African American women between the ages of twenty and seventy-four are obese.[38] In addition, to be diabetic during pregnancy is more dangerous for Black women than for Whites. Surrounding all these grim statistics are genetics, race and racism, socioeconomics, environment, and behavioral choices.

Compounding this litany of lament is a study by the Institute for Women's Policy Research that revealed that racial-ethnic women have a more difficult time gaining health insurance than White women, and they are disproportionately represented in the ranks of the uninsured.[39] In this study, racial-ethnic women were 40 percent (4.6 million) of 11.7 million uninsured women. Hispanics/Latinas were almost three times less likely to have health insurance than White women, and African American women were twice as unlikely.

This becomes crucial information when we also add the fact that private health care in the United States is shifting from a fee-for-service system to one based on managed care. Hospital staff layoffs and bed reductions are markers of this change as hospitals must move into the world of health care as business and become both competitive and profitable. Medicare and Medicaid often do not reach the health-care needs of the urban and rural poor. Patients are being discharged sooner; there is more outpatient surgery; underused facilities are closing; and executive staff jobs are being cut.

Within this new world of managed care, Black women are more likely to have conditions that are diagnosed as untreatable, given limited treatment options, and denied hospital admission entirely. Along with poor men and women of all backgrounds, and racial-ethnic men, African American women are more likely to be deprived of radiation or chemotherapy for cancer, dialysis for kidney failure, and bypass or balloon surgery and pacemakers for heart disease cases.[40]

As managed care continues to increasingly pervade health care, it is important to ask who (and in what combinations and at what levels of authority and power) is making the decision about treatment or its denial. Is it individual health-care specialists, insurance companies, managed-care guidelines and procedures, or the patient?

This is a mixed bag.[41] More than one-quarter of African American women work in the public sector and are as likely as White women to be covered through their employers because there remains a high rate of insurance coverage in these jobs. Black women are more likely than other groups of women to work in firms that provide health insurance because they tend to work for larger companies (those with one hundred or more employees). The decline in coverage comes when access to indirect coverage (i.e., coverage through the policy of a spouse) is factored in. This is where racial-ethnic women are less likely to receive health insurance coverage — in part because of the high number of single Black women. In addition, racial-ethnic women are less likely to marry men with insurance policies that include coverage for dependents. However, Black women are more likely to use public insurance (Medicare or Medicaid) than Hispanics/Latinas, Asians/Pacific Islanders, and other racial-ethnic women. This is because Black women are more likely to be unmarried. Married women are less likely to be eligible for Medicaid.

Breaking these broad figures down into different categories can better help us to understand what is happening to racial-ethnic women. We begin with family type and the presence of children. Unmarried women with no children have the lowest rates of health insurance coverage. Women in two-parent families have the highest degree of coverage — except for Latinas. However, these statistics have their own internal complexity. Although a childless, unmarried woman is more likely to be uninsured, she is in a group that has higher rates of *direct* coverage (i.e., coverage through her own policy) than single mothers. Among racial-ethnic single mothers, African Americans and Latinas rely on public health coverage at similar rates. What pushes Black women to higher rates, overall, in relying on public health is their higher rates of nonmarriage. If married, a racial-ethnic woman is less likely to be covered by her spouse's insurance plan because racial-ethnic men are less likely to hold jobs that have insurance plans that extend to their families. These jobs are more likely to be manual labor (except for Asian Americans) rather than managerial and professional (which often carry more extensive family insurance plans).

When we look at work, it should be no surprise that women in better-paying jobs are more likely to be insured than women in lower-paying ones. However, for racial-ethnic women, the disparities in access to health insurance are greater among workers who earn less than among higher-paid workers. Once again, direct employer-based coverage has an impact — women in higher-paying jobs tend to have similar levels of coverage. Also, if a racial-ethnic woman's personal earnings are lower, she is less likely than a White woman to rely on coverage through her spouse's plan. And among these women, Latinas are the least likely to have access to health-care coverage.

The size of the company a woman works for makes a difference. Across the board, racial-ethnic women workers have higher rates of being uninsured than White women. Those who are working in small companies are the least likely to have health insurance. Many Latinas and African American women work for small companies (less than twenty-five employees) in industries that do not have a history or pattern of providing generous health benefits to employees — retail trade and personal services. For Black women in these smaller companies, nearly half are uninsured. For Latinas, more than half are uninsured. White women in these jobs have much more access to health insurance, probably due to their spouse's employer plan.

We may well be in a time of postmodern social Darwinism. There is an element within managed care that has the ring of the survival of the fittest. I do not believe this is the intent, but it may well become the reality for African American cultures, communities, and individuals unless *we* begin to place an emphasis on prevention and begin to do those things that are well within our grasp that help us become advocates for our own health. We must do so wisely. Willa Mae Hemmons provides a helpful example of this for us. She describes a community-service billboard in an inner city that "proclaimed that health is threatened by certain 'preventable factors': obesity, smoking, stress, lack of exercise, substance abuse and poor diet." She goes on to note that

> the assertion that these factors are within the control of the individual is ominous for the Black woman. It takes generations to effectuate certain lifestyle and cultural behaviors. Unremitting social pressures aren't totally, or even sometimes partially, within the discretion of the recipient. Such assertions also reject the idea that substance abuse is a disease. Folk wisdom acknowledges that most programs to lose weight are unsuccessful even when attempted by highly educated, highly motivated people who lead relatively stress free lives. The individual responsibility approach minimizes the role of physical environment on health.[42]

We cannot fight for our lives in isolation — our health is a cultural production in which we all participate. As such, we must recognize the biological, social, environmental, and economic conditions that surround us and have profound impacts on our health. We also address our moralities, our value systems, that are guiding us as individuals and as communities to make choices, or not, about what is good for us. If our communal lament is genuine, then we must face the harsh realties rimming our lives as well as the promises of salvation that are there as well.

We know parts of our lament well:

- Black women live fewer years than White women.
- Our breast cancer is caught later, and we are more likely to die of it.
- The majority of women and children infected with HIV disease are Black.
- Our children are more likely to be born small, and they die more frequently before reaching one year of age.
- We have heart disease at younger ages; a heart attack is more likely to prove fatal; and we have twice as many cases of high blood pressure as Whites.
- Nearly 50 percent of us are overweight.
- We are more likely to smoke, and we are less likely to quit than White women.
- We have higher rates of sexually transmitted infection and pelvic inflammatory disease.
- Over half of us have been beaten, been raped, or survived incest.

# Chapter 6

# And All the Colored Folks Is Cursed

## *The Impact of HIV/AIDS on African Americans*

We know the principle on which it was based: at the periphery, an annular building; at the centre, a tower; this tower is pierced with wide windows that open onto the inner side of the ring; the peripheric building is divided into cells, each of which extends the whole width of the building; they have two windows, one on the inside, corresponding to the windows of the tower; the other, on the outside, allows the light to cross the cell from one end to the other. All that is needed, then, is to place a supervisor in a central tower and to shut up in each cell a madman, a patient, a condemned man, a worker or a schoolboy. By the effect of backlighting, one can observe from the tower, standing out precisely against the light, the small captive shadows in the cells of the periphery. They are like so many cages, so many small theatres, in which each actor is alone, perfectly individualized and constantly visible. The panoptic mechanism arranges spatial unities that make it possible to see constantly and to recognize immediately. In short, it reverses the principle of the dungeon; or rather of its three functions — to enclose, to deprive of light and to hide — it preserves only the first and eliminates the other two. Full lighting and the eye of a supervisor capture better than darkness, which ultimately protected. Visibility is a trap.

To begin with, this made it possible — as a negative effect — to avoid those compact, swarming, howling masses that were to be found in places of confinement, those painted by Goya or described by Howard. Each individual, in his place, is securely confined to a cell from which he is seen from the front by the supervisor; but the side walls prevent him from coming into contact with his companions. He is seen, but he does not see; he is the object of information, never a subject in communication.

—Michel Foucault, *Discipline and Punish*

> Then she say: Tell me what your God look like, Celie.
>
> Aw naw, I say. I'm too shame. Nobody ever ast me this before, so I'm sort of took by surprise. Besides, when I think about it, it don't seem quite right. But it all I got. I decide to stick up for him, just to see what Shug say.
>
> Okay, I say. He big and old and tall and graybearded and white. He wear white robes and go barefooted.
>
> Blue eyes? she ast.
>
> Sort of bluish-gray. Cool. Big though. White lashes, I say.
>
> She laugh.
>
> Why you laugh? I ast. I don't think it so funny. What you expect him to look like, Mr.?
>
> That wouldn't be no improvement, she say. Then she tell me this old white man is the same God she used to see when she prayed. If you wait to find God in church, Celie, she say, that's who is bound to show up, cause that's where he live.
>
> How come? I ast.
>
> Cause that's the one that's in the white folks' white bible.
>
> Shug! I say. God wrote the bible, white folks had nothing to do with it.
>
> How come he look just like them, then? she say. Only bigger? And a heap more hair. How come the bible just like everything else they make, all about them doing one thing and another, and all the colored folks doing is getting cursed?
>
> —Alice Walker, *The Color Purple*

Yet another part of our communal lament is that the Black body has long been a site of contention.[1] Herodotus spread rumors that certain parts of Africa were inhabited by a race of monstrous-looking humans. Medieval art often represented Blacks as grotesque figures with thick lips, large noses, receding chins, prominent cheekbones, and curly hair. Although by the eighteenth century some European artists and intellectuals began to recognize the subjectivity of their own standards of beauty, the Black female body remained an icon for Black sexuality broadly considered, and Black men and women were icons for deviant sexuality. This was played out to the degree that only certain body parts, not the whole female, were displayed in the salons of Paris.

Sander L. Gilman suggests that the Black presence in early North American society allowed Whites to sexualize their world by projecting onto Blacks sexuality that was dissociated from whiteness. Sarah Bartmann's body exemplified this spectacle of female body parts. Bartmann was dubbed the "Hottentot Venus," and her naked body was repeatedly displayed over a period of five years. When she died — literally from overexposure — at the age of twenty-five, she was dissected by her admirers in the name of science. As bell hooks considers Bartmann's story, she notes that the audience who paid to see her buttocks (that held special fascination for the spectators) and fantasize about the uniqueness of genitalia in life could now examine both in death.

As icon, the Black body in the West has a legacy that contains a grim aesthetic that often includes a sacrilegious ideology that demeans and devalues the body. As cultural production, the Black body often falls victim to the ideology found within Jeremy Bentham's panopticon. The health of the Black body as cultural production, then, becomes extremely problematic.

Bentham's panopticon — a scheme of thorough observation and control of inmates — is amazing and awful. Its intent is to induce in the inmate a state of consciousness and permanent visibility that assures that power will function automatically. Bentham sought to create an atmosphere of permanent surveillance — even if there is no one watching. The inmate spends a life under the tall outline of the central tower. But the inmate can never be sure when the tower is occupied or if someone is looking.

What an awful display of power and surveillance! One is totally seen without ever seeing. The one or ones in power see everything without ever being seen. It is not the person who controls — that we know and can live with. It is the situation — the distributions of bodies, surfaces, lights, and gazes — that dominates and controls.

It is a laboratory of power because it penetrates into human behavior. It can reduce the number of those who exercise it, while increasing the number of those on whom it is exercised. It is possible to intervene at any moment. Architecture and geometry control and give power of mind over mind.

This is an amazing display of power, for it does not come from the outside. It is insidious, subtle. For the panopticon is arranged so that an observer can observe — at a glance — so many individuals. It also enables everyone to come and observe any of the observers doing their work of control.

## Mama Might Be Better Off Dead

The preceding discussion of the Black body as icon and the panopticon of Jeremy Bentham provides both a sobering introduction to and a methodologically rich framework for the many dimensions of HIV/AIDS in the African American communities across the United States. The preceding helps provide the multilayered context I believe necessary for a rigorous discussion of HIV/AIDS in U.S. cultures and societies *and* for understanding the particular ways this discussion must be held in the Black communities of the United States.

Perhaps no other contemporary medical issue points more directly to the dilemmas and to the possibilities of Black health as a cultural production than the impact of HIV/AIDS. Part of the sobering reality for far too many African Americans is that their bodies have and continue to be treated as icons and cursed. One recent example is the decapitation and burning of Garnett Paul "G.P." Johnson in the small community of Elk Creek, in southwest Virginia.[2] When police arrived at the home of a local White man, they found the badly burned and headless body of Johnson in the yard. Johnson's death was not a crime of anonymity — he was well known in the small community and knew the two men charged with the crime well.

African Americans live in a culture in which we are under constant surveillance. And this surveillance is not confined to the urban core. It is difficult for a person of color to move about any geography in this land without drawing attention to her or himself. In the city, the community watches itself, sometimes in fear. The police watch and confine us to specific regions. In the suburbs we are watched as we enter stores and restaurants and gas stations. In the rural areas we may not be plentiful, and we are noticed — often most blatantly by children who have not been taught that staring is rude. For many African Americans, just surviving puts a strain on their health. That is why we have higher rates of heart disease and stress-related illnesses. Just making it through the day can take its toll on us. Surviving a week can be a major accomplishment. Growing old is often a sign of God's grace.

On a larger scale, we are a nation that is, in large measure, troubled by our health care or lack of it. At a time when more than two million people lose their health coverage each month, we are increasingly uneasy, although many will get their coverage back within a few weeks or months.[3] We are uneasy because there are still 42 million of us who go without, and of this number at least 9.5 million are children.

Those who do not have coverage are a lot like you and me. Eighty-five percent belong to families that include an employed adult. It is difficult for part-time workers or the self-employed to obtain group insurance. Some are in jobs they dare not leave because of their health benefits, and many people on welfare remain so because they can receive health benefits that they could not obtain if they were employed in minimum-wage jobs.

We have tried, as a nation, to fill the gaps. But community health centers, public health clinics, clinics for migrant workers, and public hospitals can only provide a patchwork of services for specific populations. All have their funding and staffing woes; all are stretched thin on their resources; all are struggling mightily. But we still fall short of meeting the need for reliable and secure health coverage for our fellow citizens. This leaves folks like Laurie Kaye Abraham frustrated. In her book *Mama Might Be Better Off Dead: The Failure of Health Care in Urban America* (1993), Abraham suggests that "perhaps the only time the uninsured have a good chance of getting timely, quality care is when they are near death."[4]

Even Medicaid fails folks in that the income restrictions are so tight that the program covers less than half the poor. Most working poor are excluded and remain uninsured, though some of their children are being progressively added to the program under reforms that began in the late 1980s. Sadly, those who do receive Medicaid often struggle to find decent, compassionate doctors. This is particularly true for the urban poor — more so if the person is Black or Hispanic/Latino.

Doctors perceive the urban poor as difficult patients. And often the urban poor *are* difficult cases because their ailments have been made worse by delays in getting care. These folks may show up at doctors' offices with more of what one physician calls "sociomas" — social problems that range from not having a ride to the doctor's office, to drug addiction, to homelessness, to despair.

The tragedy of health care for the poor, and by extension for large numbers of African Americans, sets up a deadly dynamic that makes it difficult to sort through the massive issues, stereotypes, phobias, and outright bigotry and hatred that accompany any discussion of AIDS in the Black community. The colored folks are cursed with a dread disease that finds one of its homes in a community that already suffers from poor health and poor health care. This is the lament and the tragedy of viewing the Black body as an icon, for an icon, an image, can be set aside without having to deal with the blood and heart of the person or the people. Even worse, the Black community can work against itself in trying to combat the rising tide of HIV inflections and AIDS that visits our homes on a daily basis.

## The Repercussions of Tuskegee

Stephen B. Thomas, director of minority health research at the University of Maryland Department of Health Education, believes that the Black community's reluctance to acknowledge AIDS is in part a tragic result of mistrust generated by the Tuskegee Study.[5] Because of the persistence of structured social inequality and its attendant stereotypes, phobias, and hatreds, many African Americans see a conspiracy against Black life that is lodged not only in individual acts of terror and hatred, but also within governmental structures. These conspiracy theories run a chilling gamut — from the belief that the government promotes drug abuse in African American communities to the belief that HIV/AIDS is a human-made weapon of racial warfare.[6] From the Nation of Islam to the popular Black television show *Tony Brown's Jour-*

*nal* to *Essence* magazine, the word "genocide" is often linked with HIV/AIDS in the Black community. In the September 1990 issue of *Essence*, in an article entitled "AIDS: Is It Genocide?" a New York City physician, Barbara Justice, suggested that "there is a possibility that the virus was produced to limit the number of African people and people of color in the world who are no longer needed."[7]

African Americans' serious and abiding fears about HIV/AIDS do not necessarily begin with stereotypes about gay men and prostitutes. They are also fueled by the overwhelming repercussions of the Tuskegee Study and the fact that the Public Health Service (PHS) chose not to educate the participants of the study or treat them once medicines for combating syphilis were developed and found effective. This is the groundwork for the continuing distrust that many African Americans have of public health officials. And these same public health officials are engaged in HIV/AIDS programs that are designed to reach out into communities of the dispossessed.

In his 1990 testimony before the National Commission on AIDS, Mark Smith, from the School of Medicine at Johns Hopkins University, described the African American community as "already alienated from the health care system and the government and . . . somewhat cynical about the motives of those who arrive in their communities to help them." For Smith, the Tuskegee Study "provides validation for common suspicions about the ethical even-handedness in the medical research establishment and in the federal government, in particular, when it comes to Black people."[8]

The strategies for HIV education and AIDS risk-reduction programs are similar to those used by the PHS to recruit and retain participants in the Tuskegee Study.[9] Once again, the PHS serves as the lead agency that is joined by a group of cooperating agencies at the state and local levels. Once again, trusted local institutions and individuals are being enlisted to help disseminate information and provide treatment. Once again, there is an attempt to use a culturally sensitive grassroots approach to guarantee the involvement of the participants. Once again, Black church leaders are being asked to help spread the word and let their churches be used as places for testing and providing meals and as bases to offer other necessities such as transportation, home-health-care, and emotional and spiritual support.

Although the Tuskegee Study was immoral, the PHS developed a model for its implementation that was culturally sensitive (to a degree), politically astute, and collaborative. It is a serious miscalculation to think that a study that was ended nearly thirty years ago (after running for forty years) has no enduring impact on the perceptions and beliefs of African Americans. This is a part of the context in which many African Americans interpret HIV/AIDS as a disease, as a form of genocide, as something that is combatible, as something that is avoidable, as something that is unavoidable.

Stephen Thomas and Sandra Quinn argue that the "failure of public health professionals to comprehensively discuss the study contributes to its use as a source of misinformation and helps to maintain a barrier between the Black community and health care service providers."[10] A Black health educator with the Dallas Urban League made a similar statement before the National Commission on AIDS: "So many African American people that I work with do not trust hospitals or any of the other community health care service providers because of that Tuskegee Study. It is like . . . if they did it then they will do it again." The two statements taken together help explain the fact that many Blacks see HIV/AIDS as a form of genocide.

Thomas and Quinn argue that public health officials must deal with the ongoing impact of the Tuskegee Study if they wish to make a significant and systemic impact on the growth of HIV/AIDS in African American life. Public health workers will have to address the fear many Blacks have of HIV/AIDS and genocide. Ernest Hopkins, director of health and treatment for the National Association of People with AIDS (NAPWA), notes:

> There are African Americans today who believe there are two forms of AZT, one for blacks that causes severe side effects and another with milder side effects for whites. This notion is tied to the days when AZT was given to everyone in high doses and lots of people had intolerable side effects. But some people thought blacks were being given a potentially lethal dose.[11]

The horrors of the sterilizations of poor Black women during the 1960s and 1970s without their consent or informed consent also form part of the suspicions many Blacks hold. One of the few attempts to gauge the extent of Black suspicion about AIDS was a 1990 survey of 1,056 Black church members conducted by the Southern Christian Leadership Conference.[12] The survey was conducted in Atlanta, Charlotte, Detroit, Kansas City, and Tuscaloosa, Alabama. Better than one-third of those surveyed believed that AIDS is a form of genocide, and one-third were unsure. Nearly half the respondents said that the government was not telling the truth, and 35 percent were unsure. Almost one-third believed that AIDS was a human-made virus, and nearly half were unsure. These are overwhelming figures, but not surprising ones when we realize that there is a history of medical investigators using Blacks as guinea pigs in some wretched scenarios.

It is lamentable that it seems that a great many of the colored folks *is* cursed. But the troubled history of health care for Black Americans is not the only element we must deal with in this arena of HIV/AIDS and Black folk. We need to look at issues of sexuality as well. As I have argued earlier in *In a Blaze of Glory: Womanist Spirituality as Social Witness*, understanding how Black bodies are seen and treated as icons opens a window on the reality that we live in a sexually repressive culture, despite the conventional wisdom that argues that we are, in large measure, a promiscuous culture and society. We are sexually repressed in that we make countless compromises regarding our sexuality to survive in both the larger culture and our respective religious homes. We are a sexually repressive culture because our fears and phobias about our bodies, the sexuality and sensuality found in them, keep us from exploring and understanding the ways in which we work, biologically. This lack of knowledge continues into our attempts at intimacy and commitment to such a degree that we confuse sex and pure lust with love and genuine commitment.

## Small, Captive Shadows

The 1992 report from the president's National Commission on AIDS alarmed many. The idea that 21 percent of the total population accounted for 46 percent of the people in the United States with AIDS caught many off guard.[13] In 1992, African Americans constituted 12 percent of the U.S. population and nearly 30 percent of AIDS cases. Hispanics/Latinos constituted 9 percent of the population and 17 percent of the AIDS cases. The 1997 midyear numbers continued to rise with Blacks and Hispanics/Latinos accounting for 53 percent of the number of cumulatively reported AIDS cases.[14] The numbers were: Blacks, 35 percent; Hispanics/Latinos, 18 percent. Even more alarming is the reported number of new AIDS cases between July 1996 and June 1997. In those figures, African Americans and Hispanics/Latinos constituted 63 percent of the cases.

The 1989 age-adjusted HIV-related death rate among Black males was three times that of White males. In 1994, it was six times the rate. African American females were nine times more likely to die of HIV than White females. The president's commission believed that the trends suggested that this disproportionate impact was likely to continue, and the 1997 figures bore this out. The cumulatively reported HIV cases for Blacks and Hispanics/Latinos constituted 58 percent of the total.[15] Once again, however, the reported cases from July 1996 through June 1997 sounded an ominous warning. For this period, the number of cases reported for Blacks and Hispanics/Latinos was 62 percent (up from 59 percent in the previous year).[16]

The African American community is the most disproportionately represented with respect to HIV/AIDS. The disease is growing faster in that community than in any other racial-ethnic group in the United States. From 1993 to 1995 alone, the number of new AIDS cases among Blacks reported to the Centers for Disease Control (CDC) increased by 52 percent (sixty thousand). During this same period, African Americans were six times more likely to have AIDS than Whites. There may be a physiological cause for the high infection rates for Blacks. African Americans seem to miss a mutated gene with a shrunken protein that prevents HIV from entering cells. No one with two copies of this mutated gene has ever contracted HIV, and when one gene is present, HIV progresses at a slower rate. It is estimated that 1 percent of all Whites have two copies of this gene and 20 percent have one copy. Thus far, there have been no African Americans found to have two copies of this gene, and only 3 percent have one copy.[17]

Beginning in 1990, AIDS became the leading cause of death for Black men between the ages of thirty-five and forty-four and the second leading cause of death for Black men and women between the ages of twenty-five and thirty-six. By 1996, AIDS was the number one killer of Blacks between the ages of twenty-five and forty-four.[18] Of the 1996 AIDS cases, 74 percent (1993 — 78 percent) were adult men (thirteen years or older); 23 percent (1993 — 19 percent) were adult women; and 2 percent were children (younger than thirteen years). Nearly 75 percent of African American AIDS cases fall between the ages of twenty and thirty-nine. More than 18 percent were among Blacks between the ages of twenty and twenty-nine. Many in this group were infected in their teens. The cumulative increase for adult women was 18 percent (from 43,301 cases to 51,410 cases) from June 1996 to June 1997. From December 1994 to June 1995, the increase in reported cases for adult women was "only" 11 percent.

It was in 1994 that Black and Latino/Hispanic adult males first accounted for a majority of the newly reported male cases: 53 percent. In 1997, this had risen to 58 percent, although the cumulative figures continue to show White men in the majority. For African American men, homosexual contact accounted for 32 percent (1993 — 43 percent) of the cases; injection drug use accounted for 31 percent (1993 — 36 percent); men who had sex with men and also injected drugs were 5 percent (1993 — 7 percent); heterosexual contact was the source of 10 percent; and for 23 percent the risk was not reported or identified.

The 1997 HIV infection cases also present a sobering picture for African American men. Homosexual contact accounted for 29 percent of the newly reported cases; injection drug use accounted for 17 percent; men who had sex with men and injected drugs made up 3 percent; heterosexual contact accounted for 9 percent; and for 41 percent, the risk was not reported or identified.

Black women accounted for 57 percent of the newly reported AIDS cases among adult females. Thirty-two percent (1993 — 53 percent) of these cases resulted from injection drug use. Heterosexual contact accounted for 38 percent — with sex with an HIV-infected person being 66 percent of this figure. It is important to note that the 1994 figures for this category revealed that sex with an injecting drug user was 50 percent of the total. This is a shift that will receive more attention later in this chapter. The risk-not-reported or risk-not-identified category was 28 percent. It is important to note that from 1991 through 1995, the number of women in all racial-ethnic categories diagnosed with AIDS increased by 63 percent. For his same period, the figure for all men was 12.8 percent.

A staggering 68 percent of the newly reported cases of HIV infection are among Black women. Within these figures, injecting drug use accounted for 18 percent, heterosexual contact was 35 percent, and risk not reported or identified was 48 percent.

Globally and nationally, children are extremely hard hit. On an international scale, nearly 1.5 million children tested HIV-positive by late 1994.[19] More than 75 percent of them are in sub-Saharan Africa and developing countries in the Americas. In the United States, there was an 18 percent increase of the reported cases from 1993 to 1994. It has slowed to 13 percent from 1994 to the present. In general, 90 percent of all infected children received the disease through perinatal transmission. In 1997, Black children accounted for 58 percent of all the reported pediatric AIDS cases in the nation. Ninety percent have been due to perinatal transmissions from mothers infected with HIV. Zero percent have been due to hemophilia-related blood products or the receipt of an HIV-contaminated blood transfusion. The mode of the remaining 9 percent cannot be determined.

The numbers for pediatric HIV-infection cases in Black children are also grim. Three percent are from hemophilia-related blood products or the receipt of an HIV-contaminated blood transfusion. Ninety percent were due to perinatal transmission, and the remaining 7 percent could not be determined. One in every four of all new HIV infections in the United States is found in youth between the ages of thirteen and twenty (this constitutes between ten thousand and twenty thousand cases).[20] Some fear that the infection rate among youth may be dramatically underestimated because youth do not get tested for HIV. For those between the ages of thirteen and nineteen, 28 percent are due to hemophilia-related blood products or the receipt of an HIV-contaminated blood transfusion; 25 percent are due to homosexual activity; and 20 percent are due to heterosexual activity; the cause of the remaining cases is unidentified.[21]

Those youths most likely to contract HIV are gay and bisexual males and hemophiliacs. Within this group, many, but by no means all, have been neglected and/or physically or sexually abused, are from low-income homes, are racial-ethnic (Blacks account for 44 percent, and Hispanics/Latinos are 19 percent), and have low self-esteem.[22] However, it is not only these at-risk youth who are susceptible to contracting the HIV virus. One high school teacher puts it well, "I worry about the typical high school students who go to football games and the prom. They're not protecting themselves. Many of my students don't think they are at risk for AIDS because they don't abuse drugs and they're not promiscuous."[23] The kinds of race, gender, and class stereotypes that stigmatize at-risk youth also permit far too many of us to believe that "nice" youth do not have premarital sex, do not use drugs, and are not homosexuals.

As the level of HIV/AIDS education available to youth declines due to a conservative backlash, some school districts, such as New York, have stopped talking about condoms. The Office of National AIDS Policy offers an alternative to this trend.[24] It advocates providing access to accurate information about HIV and prevention; providing information that is relevant for age, culture, lifestyles, and values to the variety of groups that make up our youth population; offering viable alternative choices and opportunities to practice new behaviors such as abstinence or safer sex; and making sure that all prevention education include efforts to build self-esteem.

The ongoing heterosexism in our communities continues to allow too many to believe that if they are not gay men, then they do not have to worry. This attitude persists in spite of the fact that the highest levels of knowledge about HIV/AIDS among Black folks were found in the younger groups and in those with the most education. Television, newspapers, magazines, and radio are helpful resources for the African American community. It is not that we do not know how AIDS is transmitted; as a community, we do. But this contrasts with the fact that only 14 percent of African Americans have been tested.

Added to this conundrum is a fact that public health workers in the African American community have noted — the attitudes of many clergy are not helpful in the fight against HIV/AIDS. The lead story in *Catalyst*, a publication of the AIDS Council of Greater Kansas City, notes that "because homosexuality has negative connotations in the Black community, some gay Black men masquerade as straight."[25] Injecting drugs, unprotected sex, and sex among unmarried heterosexuals — all high-risk behaviors that make people vulnerable to HIV and AIDS — are also subjects that are often shunned. Meaningful discussions about these behaviors have not taken place within many African American communities. Therefore, it is extremely difficult to have substantive conversations about HIV/AIDS.

Although many Blacks are well aware of the dangers of HIV/AIDS, there is still a deep-rooted ignorance about it. A case in point is Marilyn, who did not use condoms before or for several years after she was diagnosed as HIV positive. Her story is not one of willful neglect; it is one of ignorance, tragedy, and lament. It is also one that is repeated countless times by men and women in the African American community. She reflects, "It never occurred to me that someone got AIDS from heterosexual sex. I had used drugs years before my diagnosis, so I figured it must have something to do with that.... No one told me I was putting other people at risk. The only thing I got from the HIV testing site was a sheet of paper with doctors who treated AIDS patients on one side and a list of funeral homes on the other. A man I used to date is not HIV+."[26] She had no one to talk to at the time of her diagnosis to help her understand the ways in which she must now change her behavior to keep from infecting others and also the things she could do to live a healthier lifestyle.

As a culture, we are sexually repressed and sexually active, and we are getting ourselves in trouble. Many HIV-infected African Americans are not diagnosed until they experience serious symptoms. This can often be five or more years into the disease. Like others, many Blacks do not think they are infected or they do not want to know if they have a disease that has no known cure. The fears of Tuskegee can join with a fear of rejection. This fear of rejection is not without basis — some African Americans have been shunned and ostracized for being HIV positive or for having full-blown AIDS.

For African American men and women, the typical age at diagnosis for AIDS is between twenty-five and forty-four.[27] For HIV infection the typical age at diagnosis is between twenty and forty-four for men and twenty and thirty-nine for women.[28] This has enormous implications for the future generations of African Americans. It is a bitter irony that among high school students, 60 percent of the African American males and 20 percent of the females reported having had four or more sex partners. Yet only 55 percent of the males and 37 percent of the females reported having used a condom during their most recent intercourse. In a survey of sixteen- to nineteen-year-olds, only 28 percent reported always using a condom. This, even though the 1993 CDC figures showed that the number of AIDS cases increased most rapidly among heterosexuals — especially young people and Black and Hispanic/Latina women. In 1996, this increase was nearly 372 percent more than 1992: 4,045 to 15,054.[29] The increase is greater among women than among men and is higher among Blacks and Hispanics/Latinos than among Whites. The largest increases were among teenagers and young adults — primarily through heterosexual transmission.

Meanwhile, there is still no systematic, structural, and effective antidrug program in communities of the dispossessed in this nation. The colored folks are laboring under a mighty curse that is larger than HIV/AIDS. African Americans as a group receive lower levels of routine and preventive health services than other racial-ethnic groups.[30] When poverty is added to this mix, it becomes even more lethal. Poor folks have higher rates of HIV infection than middle-class and wealthy folks. When resources are scarce, poor folks may not have the money to purchase protection. And this becomes more than simply a matter of abstinence at this point. Framing this discussion within the context of health as cultural production can help us to understand the complexity of this issue: a plethora of gender codes and roles and issues of self-esteem are here at work in a system of structured social inequality. Many women, whatever their racial-ethnic or class location or age, are reluctant to insist that the men in their lives wear condoms. Kenneth Snow, an HIV/AIDS educator at Swope Parkway Health Clinic in Kansas City, Missouri, believes that poor Black men may be working on issues of self-esteem. Snow notes that they are "still trying to prove their manhood by having lots of sex partners and by refusing to wear condoms. They don't think they're at risk because they're not gay."[31] Any discussion of how to treat HIV/AIDS must take these realities into account.

The latter part of 1996 saw the first significant drop in the number of deaths due to complications from AIDS since the epidemic was first recognized in 1981. In 1997, this decline continued at 19 percent.[32] The expectation is that this decline will continue, due in large measure to greater access to medical care and the development of new drug therapies for the HIV virus and all the opportunistic illnesses associated with AIDS that can lead to death. Encouraging news is that the death rates for women dropped for the first time. Yet in an epidemic that is one of contrasts, it is also true that globally AIDS cases and deaths are increasing and in greater proportions than previously realized. In addition, the AIDS infection rate in the United States continues to rise among women — especially those living in the South.

The director for the various AIDS programs of the CDC, Helene D. Gayle, notes that the decline in the United States began before the first protease inhibitor drug hit the market in December 1995.[33] However, there is a disproportionate rate of decline in AIDS deaths among men, women, and racial-ethnic groups. Deaths of women decreased by 7 percent (22 percent for men), and death rates for Whites decreased 28 percent (10 percent for Blacks, 16 percent for Hispanics/Latinos).[34]

A warning bell is sounding concerning the knowledge many racial-ethnic people have concerning the newer forms of drug therapies such as protease inhibitors and their access to them. The CDC estimates that there are from six hundred thousand to nine hundred thousand infected people in the United States. To date, the average cost of the newer drug therapies can be $15,000 a year. This does not include the costs of lab tests or medical care that supports these therapies. Given these realities, it is not surprising that many health officials and activists working in this area have called for an increase in the federal budget for HIV drug therapy. Before protease inhibitors were available, sixty-five thousand people received support from the $207 million AIDS Drug Assistance Program. In 1996, this had risen to eighty thousand persons receiving support with a budget of $385 million. These new programs prove to be cost-effective for insurers (saving $190 million yearly) and allow more AIDS patients to stay out of the hospital. However, these savings were not put back into outpatient care in significant ways, therefore hampering many medical providers' ability to provide this care.

Many HIV-positive African Americans who have avoided the health-care system previously are seeking access to protease inhibitors. However, the cost of protease inhibitors has forced many communities to make choices that could deny those currently outside the system access to it. The result is that many doctors who are serving low-income and poor folks do not prescribe protease inhibitors.[35] People with private insurance may be able to afford this treatment, but for those on Medicaid, there is a monthly cap on drug expenses. Many HMOs restrict drug benefits to an average of $3,000 a year. Drug companies provide free drugs to some, but the demand far outstrips the availability of such programs.

For those not poor enough to qualify for Medicaid, nearly $200 million in federal and state AIDS Drug Assistance Programs (ADAP) are available, but this may cover only one-half of those who need this assistance.[36] Added to this is the fact that the availability of protease inhibitors varies by state. Where New York and California have extensive programs, only 10 percent of the HIV-positive folks in Florida qualify, and Kansas has a waiting list for those who need assistance and treatment.

As effective as protease inhibitors are, their success requires that patients follow a complicated schedule for taking the drugs; if not taken on schedule or if the patient is given a problematic prescription, he or she can develop a resistance to the drugs. Issues of class and race abound at this point as some in the medical community argue "that if the poor and homeless are given protease inhibitors and are noncompliant, they many spread drug-resistant strains of HIV to others."[37] This seems to be a concern that should be raised about anyone who takes protease inhibitors, not just the poor and homeless. A member of the Harvard AIDS Institute's International Advisory Council, Mario Cooper, states: "Doctors are selecting people out because of racial issues. Some won't even offer drug abusers the option of taking these drugs."[38] M. Keith Rawlings, co-chair of the infectious diseases division of the National Medical Association, adds these pointed words: "This whole notion that because a patient is poor, homeless or a drug abuser he [or she] is by definition noncompliant is an erroneous one. Compliance will be good if doctors are willing to take the time to educate them."[39]

## It Would Be Too Cumbersome

This looks like a curse, like a lament, but it is not only visited upon Black folk. It is a curse that can and does affect all of us. With over one-half million people in this country now reported having AIDS, it is no longer an us-them equation. By 2000, AIDS will have cost the global economy up to $514 billion.[40] Statistics from 1997 revealed that 30.6 million people (1 in every 100) are HIV positive. AIDS is having a tremendous impact on businesses around the world because it most frequently strikes adults at the peak of their productivity. In the United States alone, we will have lost between $81 billion and $107 billion from the economy.[41] Between $3 billion and $6 billion is spent on new infections annually on a global scale, and $75 billion has already been spent to date globally.[42] Throughout the world, two-thirds of companies with twenty-five hundred to five thousand workers and one in twelve small businesses have had an employee with HIV or AIDS.[43] The effect of the disease on these businesses adds up to about $32,000 annually for each infected employee.[44]

With these kinds of staggering financial statistics and projections, it is perplexing that significant research on the ways AIDS affects the lives of women did not begin until 1991. An additional frustrating fact is that AIDS became the fourth leading cause of death among women from the ages of twenty-four to forty-four in 1996. This lag follows the general pattern of medical research in the United States. Men, predominantly White men, are usually the key focus of research and statistical studies in medicine. Only after significant research has been done on this group (which is not numerically the largest research pool in the United States) does the medical and scientific community cast a wider net. However, this is done with the assumed or conscious control group being White males. Unlike the adult and adolescent male population, the vast majority of women who are HIV-positive or have AIDS are African American. Black women constitute 55 percent of those who have AIDS and 67 percent of those who are HIV-positive among women.[45] Most of these women are young and poor, and many are single parents. Young women are in the high-risk category for HIV/AIDS, and the age at infection is dropping (from thirty in the early 1980s to twenty-five in 1991).[46]

In short, HIV infections are escalating among women. Between July 1994 and June 1995, there was a 17 percent increase of reported cases to the CDC.[47] However, during this same period, new HIV cases fell 9 percent among White gay men and 3 percent among all men. In the past, the majority of HIV/AIDS cases in women were linked to injecting drug use. Now more women are contracting HIV/AIDS from heterosexual sex. A woman is two to four times more likely to contract AIDS during heterosexual intercourse than a man because the vagina is often slightly torn during intercourse, which then can expose a woman's bloodstream to the large concentration of HIV found in the semen of men who are infected.[48]

As noted previously, the interstructuring of race, gender, and class plays a crucial role here. Many Black women do not feel that they can or should insist on condoms or other protection in their sexual relationships. As Deeta Hamilton, an HIV counselor/educator for the Samuel U. Rodgers Community Health Center in Kansas City, Missouri, notes:

> With so many men in the black community either in prison or dead as a result of violence, there's a lot of competition among black women for the black men who are available. Because the demand for them is great, black men may have multiple partners. Even if a black woman knows her man may be involved with other women, she's reluctant to insist that he use a condom if he doesn't want to.[49]

Until 1991, women were rarely recruited for the clinical investigations into AIDS. According to an unpublished report by Harvard University AIDS researcher Deborah Cotton, as of 1990, there were only 801 women out of a total of 12,084 subjects enrolled in the federal government's extensive AIDS clinical trial group studies.[50] Women thus made up 6 percent of this study population, although women at that time made up 12 percent of all people with AIDS in the United States. Cotton's research found that nothing was known about the effects of oral contraception on HIV infection, although it was found that IUD users were at higher risk of developing pelvic infections that were (and continue to be) more aggressive and deadlier for HIV positive women. The Bronx, New York, and Newark, New Jersey, have concentrations of HIV-positive women, but these were not sites chosen for research studies. Finally, Cotton's study revealed that there were no efforts being made to provide transportation or childcare — things that are essentials for women who often have children and limited funds for transportation — so that women could be part of the studies.

Chapter 5 lamented the lack of women in medical clinical trials. A similar lament can be voiced over AIDS research for women. Far too much of the testing for HIV/AIDS has used White men as subjects, the research findings then being extrapolated to women. This means that little is known about the risk factors and unique expressions of this disease in women. It was only in 1992 that women began to be included in studies that looked at the ways in which HIV/AIDS affects and destroy the body.

Early on, the definition for HIV and AIDS ignored the biological differences between the sexes. For example, many women experience vaginal yeast infections and other gynecological diseases as early signs of HIV infection, but when studies were limited to men, this fact could not emerge. Although men and women share many common opportunistic illnesses and infections related to HIV, there are some significant differences as well. Women are more likely to experience bacterial pneumonia, endocarditis (inflammation of the membrane lining the heart), and septicemia (blood poisoning) than men, who often develop Karposi's sarcoma.

When researchers failed to include women's unique biological makeup in the early tests and diagnoses for the disease, it fed into the myth that women were not dying of AIDS. This myth, believed by many in the medical community and by women, may have created for us today a public health monstrosity. Like Marilyn, quoted earlier in this chapter, many women did not know they could contract the disease and did not alter their high-risk behavior. It meant that they did not know they could spread the disease. Ignorance kills. When Vivian Torres, a heroin addict and prostitute, learned from a prison doctor that she was HIV positive in 1988, she did not know how she contracted it. Her description of her meeting with the doctor is chilling:

> He said, "You've got six months to live. Whatever you know how to do best when you're on the street, go out and do it. Enjoy." And when I got out, I did exactly what he told me to do. Sometimes I wonder how many people I infected because I followed his advice.[51]

Another area of lament is the research on the drug azidothymidine (AZT). This research was done almost exclusively on White men, and then the findings were applied to women and racial-ethnic men. AZT has been used to treat AIDS since 1987, but it was not until late 1991 that federal researchers announced that using AZT in the early stages of treatment increased the survival rates in women and racial-ethnic men. In 1989, Brown University researchers considered how doctors decided which of their patients would receive AZT.[52] At that time, AZT was the only drug available that could prolong lives. After controlling for biological history, type of medical care, race, symptoms, health insurance, intravenous drug use, sexuality, and the question "Has your doctor ever suggested you take AZT?" the researchers found that White male patients with health insurance were 50 percent more likely to be given AZT than minority patients, intravenous drug users, and the uninsured. Men were three times more likely to get AZT than any of the women in the study. The researchers explored the possible rationales of the physicians. One possible one they considered echoes Tuskegee:

> The doctors were practicing a form of social Darwinism along with medicine, deciding who would get the drug based on the perceived "social worth" of their patients. On that value scale, women, who are also disproportionately represented among minority, drug-using, and uninsured groups, weren't seen as "worthy" of treatment that might keep them alive longer.[53]

It is important to note that at the time of the Brown study, many clinicians believed that AIDS was more deadly to women than to men. At that time women were not receiving treatment as early as men because of delays in diagnosis. This meant that men were living for years with AIDS while women were dying within a month of diagnosis. Yet the Brown researchers found enough warrant from their interviews to raise social Darwinism as a valid possibility for why traditionally dispossessed and disenfranchised groups were receiving poorer treatment.

As research continues to unfold concerning AZT, there is new evidence that mice whose mothers were given high doses of AZT during pregnancy are at risk for cancer.[54] However, health officials have still advocated the use of AZT for infected pregnant women because it seems to reduce the transmission of HIV to infants. They also point out that the doses used in the experiment with mice were much higher than the ones pregnant women take, and there have been no reported cases of cancer in the children of mothers who took AZT while pregnant.

When this situation is viewed through the lens of health as cultural production, even more issues arise. The study ACTG 076, begun in 1991, is an attempt to determine whether AZT might prevent the transmission of the virus from mother to child. While this is a tremendous step forward in looking at the peculiar effects of HIV/AIDS in women, it does raise some questions. AZT is highly toxic. When taken over long periods of time, it tends to lose its effectiveness in stopping the spread of the disease. Some researchers and critics see this study being more concerned about the well-being of the fetus than the health of the woman. Again Deborah Cotton notes: "Women have not been included in trials until all of a sudden people want to look at whether a drug will interrupt fetal transmission. All of a sudden it's fine to include women. You have to ask yourself why."[55]

ACTG 076 was originally a pediatric study of babies born to HIV-infected mothers. Cotton notes that the study changed to a prenatal one when "pediatric researchers decided it might be more efficacious if the drug 'was on board when [the babies are] born.'... They'll deny that now, but I heard them say things like that. But nowhere in this equation were people thinking whether this was good for the woman or not."[56] To date, much of the research concerning women and HIV/AIDS has at its core the assumption of women as caretakers and mothers rather than as autonomous human beings.

Considering the impact of HIV/AIDS in terms of health as cultural production helps widen the discussion to the very nature of the ways in which testing is now discussed in relation to women. The rationales run from punitive (mandatory testing for women prostitutes) to compassionate (make testing available to all on a voluntary basis). In 1988, the CDC completed a two-year study on the potential risks posed by female prostitutes to the heterosexual community. At one point, the suggestion was made that all prostitutes be required to undergo mandatory testing for HIV. Sociologist Carole Campbell pointed out that this would assure customers that the prostitutes were safe, but no similar assurances were offered on behalf of the prostitutes. As later research has shown, prostitutes are at greater risk than their male customers.

The mandatory testing argument has not been confined to prostitutes; it has been extended to all pregnant women. The stated purpose is to identify HIV-infected women as early as possible during pregnancy so that they will have the option of using an AZT treatment program that can substantially reduce the transmission of HIV to unborn infants. CDC and public health officials nationwide are vocal critics of such mandatory testing. They believe that women will avoid the test by delaying or not seeking prenatal care. In the African American community, where infant mortality is already high, introducing this type of systemic reason to avoid prenatal care could be genocidal.

It is true that, overall, gay men account for 44 percent of the AIDS cases in the United States, and men, in general, constitute 84 percent of reported AIDS cases among adults/adolescents in the country.[57] However, women now make up 18 percent of the total. But it is important to underscore that the proportion of cases for women have increased steadily for the last ten years. Most women are infected with HIV through injecting drugs (36 percent) or heterosexual contact with a man who is at risk for or has HIV infection or AIDS (37 percent). In other words, 97,396 women in this country who are HIV-positive *or* have AIDS are confronting a medical community that does not really understand how HIV affects women because the bulk of the research has focused on men. This may have a devastating impact on future generations.

Beginning in 1993, heterosexual transmission accounted for the largest proportionate increase in AIDS cases in the United States.[58] This trend has continued. AIDS is no longer a disease that we can associate with a small group of folks. It is now, and really has always been, *our* disease. Each and every one of us can lull ourselves into believing that "AIDS won't affect me because . . ." But the reality is, it can, does, and will. In 1985, heterosexual transmission accounted for only 1.9 percent of total AIDS cases. Now it is 8 percent. This is a frightening increase in twelve years.

## Humming a Hymn

Until recently, the Black community has remained invisible and powerless in this crisis. Denial, refusal to disclose one's infection, misfocused leadership, and condemnation or stony silence from the church have all gone into an evil stew of neglect. The Black Church has lagged behind with its refusal to acknowledge HIV/AIDS and its effects on congregations. The Black Church, like the White, is reluctant to address AIDS because of questions raised about transmission of the disease through premarital sex, homosexual activity, and intravenous drug use. Our sexual repression will kill us and kill others if we do not begin to grapple with the *reality* of HIV/AIDS. And it is a sad commentary on the witness and nurture of the Black Church that secular Black organizations are doing the historic work of the church in their ministries to the sick and dying.

There are growing numbers in the Black community and outside of it who refuse to bow down before this latest onslaught against the health of Black folks in the United States. Michael Ellner, president of the Health Education AIDS Liaison (HEAL) of New York City, cautions that if one receives a positive test, one should take six months to educate oneself about all the issues surrounding HIV and avoid taking any medicine, because it may do more harm than good. His warning is explicit: "No one would take any of the drugs prescribed for HIV if they only took the time to read the inserts that talk about the side effects of the medications."[59] William Richardson of the Atlanta Clinic of Preventive Medicine believes that people who are HIV positive and living with AIDS should have the primary say in what type of care they receive. Overall, the message is this: Get plenty of sleep and exercise; eat a well-balanced diet; avoid cigarettes, alcohol, and other drugs; and avoid or reduce stress.[60]

These cautions are being issued from many quarters because the HIV test remains problematic — there are still a high number of false-positive results. This is one of the reasons those who receive an initial positive test result are tested again after waiting six months. Some project the test to be wrong as much as 50 percent of the time. In general, the test reveals if one is antibody-positive. Any antibody in our bloodstream can produce a positive test result. This means that a cold, the flu, or prescribed antibiotics can yield a positive test result.

Richardson's Atlanta clinic has treated more than one hundred patients with HIV and AIDS. Some choose to take the various HIV/AIDS medicines; others refuse this treatment and try more natural remedies. But for Richardson, treatment must be holistic:

> We don't just concentrate on the body, but we also consider how things are going spiritually and psychologically as well as physically. [Our patients are] buying new houses, taking vacations and working like hell to keep their immune systems up and to psychologically balance and love themselves.[61]

Youth workers advocate peer education by using skits, miniplays, and other dramatic presentations about young people contracting HIV. Many workers who deal with high-risk youth are incorporating HIV/AIDS education in youth activities as a part of their general educational philosophy.

Dana Washington, the HIV/AIDS coordinator for the American Red Cross of Wyandotte County, Kansas, and Betsy Topper, the executive director of the AIDS Council of Kansas City, are clear that repetition is key for dealing with HIV/AIDS in the African American community — or any community.[62] Washington states:

> No matter how culturally relevant your message is, if it's based on a one-time, one-hour presentation it won't have much impact. Prevention programs that change high-risk behaviors take a lot of time. I will go to the same laundromat every week for months so I can build trust with the women who do their laundry there. The first time you talk to a woman about negotiating with her man over condom use, she may think to herself, yeah, that's a good idea. But she's not ready to do it yet. But every time we meet, I bring the subject up again. Eventually, she'll be ready to experiment with a new behavior.

And Topper explains:

> We still don't know exactly which prevention strategies work best for different populations, lifestyles and situations. We do know, however, how to create the kind of synergy that allows an at-risk population to really take in and respond to a prevention message. That involves repeating the message consistently in a variety of communication mediums, from one-to-one and group interactions to billboard advertisements and radio and TV spots.

The necessary science, technology, and experience already exist to help African American communities develop and implement effective community-based HIV/AIDS educational programs that are ethnically and culturally acceptable, accurate, and sensitive. The keys are to use program staff indigenous to the community, to use incentives, and to deliver health services within the targeted community.[63] It is true that all these strategies were used with Tuskegee, but public health professionals like Thomas and Quinn argue that the value of these strategies for today's programs should not be dismissed and discounted because of their association with some of the protocols used in the Tuskegee Study. For them, successful HIV/AIDS programs require a long-term commitment and collaboration with federal, state, and local agencies, health departments, community-based organizations, private industry, philanthropic organizations, and institutions of higher learning.[64] They argue that the lead group in this kind of coalition must be African American community-based organizations. Although these organizations have access to the community and credibility, they often lack the kind of administrative infrastructure needed to address the long-term advocacy, treatment, and research needed to address the impact of HIV/AIDS in Black communities. Therefore it is important that consistent technical assistance and long-range funding come from government and private agencies.

The reality is that Black health is a cultural production, and the impact of HIV/AIDS in African American communities must be treated as such. Public health research and practice as well as health research and practice in general operate in culture. This means that social values and political ideologies help form the fabric of how all of us in the United States determine how we will or will not address HIV/AIDS. Because of the moralisms found within any discussion concerning HIV/AIDS, I would be remiss if I did not end with the role of the church in this conversation. I will pick up the role of the Black Church again in chapter 7.

The Reverend Carl Bean tells this story:

> I went to see a client at UCLA [Hospital], and I'll never forget this little old black cleaning lady I saw there. If she hadn't come to clean that man's room, he would never have gotten his food. The lady picked up his tray from outside the room, brought it to his bed and began to feed him. She was not a technician from the dietary department, she was the cleaning lady. Some of the food had gotten cold and she even heated it in a microwave. I felt like here was one of my people that really was supposed to be mopping and emptying trash, but who stopped doing that to help someone. She didn't know about AIDS either, whether she could catch it or not. But her heart, her true commitment propelled her beyond whether she could catch it. She was humming a hymn.[65]

Humming a hymn may not sound like radical activity at first glance. But don't forget that humming and singing hymns have a rich tradition of justice and protest in the African American community. Slaves made it through the day by humming the spirituals. The civil rights movement was fired by the power of the spirituals and the hymns of the church. So this old Black cleaning lady knew what she was doing when she called on the power of a hymn to help her respond to human need.

There are people of faith in the Black community who are reaching out to live that faith. The Annual Black Church National Day of Prayer for the Healing of AIDS is held in several cities and in our nation's capital in February, and every year, support groups are forming in a growing number of African American churches.

Elliot Riviera, a community program planner in the New York City Department of Health, trains priests and priestesses of the Afro-Cuban religion Santeria to serve as AIDS counselors. Santeria, which is derived from the religion of the Yoruba people of Nigeria, is followed by many Blacks and Hispanics/Latinos in the inner city. Its practitioners are often better able to convey HIV/AIDS information than government workers or members of the medical profession.

"The African American Clergy's Declaration of War on HIV/AIDS" points the way for the Christian church. Its points are simple. The mission of the church is to minister love and support by forsaking no one. This battle must be fought from the pulpit and through all the institutions of the church. The church must develop a comprehensive AIDS awareness and education program regardless of sexual orientation, drug dependency, or lifestyle choices. The church must work with grassroots organizations to combat AIDS and act as an advocate on behalf of the whole community. The call is for compassion, nurture, and advocacy.

As churches like Glide Memorial United Methodist Church in San Francisco, Allen Temple Baptist Church in Oakland, California, City of Refuge Church in San Francisco, and Calvary Temple Baptist Church in Kansas City, Missouri, work with the community, a major priority is advocating increased support for community-based primary care to ensure delivery of prevention and care services for the entire range of health issues, including those for HIV/AIDS.

The Reverend D. Mark Wilson, pastor of McGee Avenue Baptist Church in Oakland, California, states it best:

> In many church communities, including African American, I have often heard fellow clergy say that it's not important how one gets HIV/AIDS, and that may be true. However, if we are saying this to ignore the suffering and the oppression we place on sexual minorities in our congregations, then it's already too late to help them and ourselves in our effort to heal the many wounds of AIDS. As Black churches have taken the Bible and reread and reinterpreted passages of Scripture which once taught that black skin was a curse and an abomination, and as they heard for themselves the empowering voice of God's love and justice, I hope that African Americans and others of good will, will again reread and reinterpret the Scriptures and hear the voices of those within our community... that cry out not only to be healed, but more importantly to be free.[66]

Of course the greatest hope is that a cure will be found soon and that this conversation will be the stuff of history books. When Shug explains to Celie the nature of God and the White folks' Bible, she points, in part, to a reality. But there *is* more for us as people of color. There is the ability to hum tunes while we do the work of justice, while we refuse to submit to the panopticon.

Shug goes on as she talks with Celie:

> God is inside you and inside everybody else. You come into the world with God. But only them that search for it inside find it. And sometimes it just manifest itself even if you not looking, or don't know what you looking for. Trouble do it for most folks, Sorrow, lord. Feeling like shit.
>
> It? I ast.
>
> Yeah, It. God ain't a he or a she, but a It.
>
> But what do it look like? I ast.
>
> Don't look like nothing, she say. It ain't a picture show. It ain't something you can look at apart from anything else, including yourself. I believe God is everything, say Shug. Everything that is or ever was or ever will be. And when you can feel that, you be happy to feel that, you've found It.[67]

It is time to sanctify a fast, call a solemn assembly, and gather the people — all of the people. For when there is genuine communal lament, a rich and faith-filled rending of the heart, there is also the possibility that God will hear our cries and work with us into salvation. The heart-breaking and anger-invoking and frustration-producing realities of Tuskegee, HIV/AIDS, and Black women's health do not stand alone. There are the voices of protest and dissent and outright fury who refused and continue to refuse to allow inhumanity to have the final say. It is to this hope, this salvation, that I turn in the final part of this book.

*Part 3*

# COMMUNAL REPENTANCE

# Chapter 7

# Wounded in the House of a Friend

## *Models of Care in the African American Community*

Between thirty-five and fifty million Americans have no health insurance at any given time. Many of these folks are unemployed or dependent workers or are working in jobs that pay below the subsistence level. The majority of the uninsured people are women, children, and working families below or near the poverty level. Some cannot afford insurance; others are uninsurable due to preexisting medical conditions. These grim realities do not take place in a vacuum.

In 1990, Black folks were 12 percent of the U.S. population of 258 million people. However, the media coverage of Blacks is disproportionately high in relation to that figure. Some of the media images of Blacks are positive, some negative. On one hand, we have a cavalcade of successful African American journalists, actors, musicians, athletes, and talk-show hosts. On the other hand, we also have a steady diet of criminals, Black poverty, drugs, homelessness, and violence given to us by way of the media.

These images are problematic given that a 1990 Gallup Poll revealed that the average American thought that America is 32 percent Black, 21 percent Hispanic, and 18 percent Jewish.[1] Actually, the real figure for Hispanics was 8 percent and for Jews was less than 3 percent. We do not know or fully understand who we are and how we are as a nation.

The incongruity of these figures (and the stereotypes, images, and attitudes they entail) with the actual lives of so many African Americans moves us beyond the ironic to the burlesque. The infant mortality rate for Blacks in the United States is 17.7 deaths per 1,000 births, compared with 8.2 deaths for White babies.[2] African American babies born to college-educated mothers have an 80 percent higher risk of dying in their first year than White babies born to college-educated mothers. Poverty and poor diet, health care, and housing make survival problematic for many Black infants. A 1993 UN Children's Fund report notes that among industrialized nations, "the United States has by far the highest percentage of children living in poverty: 20 percent, which represents a 21 percent increase since 1970."[3]

African American children are nearly three times as likely to be poor as White children. In 1993, 46 percent of Black children were living in poverty compared with 17 percent of White children. Sixty-three percent of African American youth grow up in single-parent homes compared with 30 percent for all U.S. families.[4] The problem here is *not* that the home is single-parent; the problem, in part, is that in today's economy, having only one income earner in a family increases the chances that the children will be poor. Too often these children may drop out of school or end up in foster care, group homes, and juvenile-justice facilities. However, let me stress the "may" in my previous sentence. *All* Black children from single-parent homes will not end up on drugs, in gangs, as dropouts, and on welfare. Many single-parent children survive and thrive among African Americans.

Homicide is the leading cause of death for African American males between the ages of sixteen to twenty-four. The life expectancy rate for Black men is 64.6 years compared with 73.8 for Black women, 72.9 for White men, and 79.6 for White women.[5] It is troubling that the UN, in its quality-of-life index, ranked African Americans number thirty-one, about the same as some Third World nations, while White Americans were number one.[6]

These figures take place in a larger social arena where obtaining mortgages and business loans is more difficult for African American families. Blacks face "steering" in real estate, insurance and job discrimination, higher unemployment and underemployment. Affirmative action, an idea we have never seriously tried in this nation, is under attack, an attack that threatens to reduce the chances for far too many African Americans to get into college and enhance the possibilities for a job with an income above the poverty level.

African Americans are urban, suburban, and rural dwellers. Although 73 percent of the rural poor are White, the poverty rates for rural Blacks and Hispanics are at least double that of rural Whites.[7] The rates are higher or at least equal to rates for members of these same groups living in inner cities. Many rural Blacks live in areas that have been poverty-stricken. Available educational resources fail to prepare rural Blacks for the current job market. Discrimination and rigid social structures also come into play, and the high incidence of female-headed households (59 percent) also increases the likelihood of poverty.

All this is not good for our health.

However true these facts may be, they only represent one part of African American health and life. It is important to note that, in 1994, 21 percent of Black families were husband-wife units in which both spouses contributed to family earnings.[8] This represents 1.7 million African American middle-class households with a median income of $44,990 (88 percent of the income comparable to Whites; outside the South the median income for Black families in this category was 96 percent of comparable Whites).

As Farai Chideya points out in her book *Don't Believe the Hype: Fighting Cultural Misinformation about African-Americans,* "there are many more black accountants than there are Black athletes, many more young Black men in college than in prison, vastly more self-supporting African-American mothers than ones on welfare."[9] In 1992, 47 percent of Black families were married couples; 46 percent were female-headed; and 7 percent were male-headed. For Whites, the figures were 82 percent, 14 percent, and 4 percent respectively.[10]

In 1992, 68 percent of Blacks twenty-five years old and over had a high school diploma. This contrasts with 51 percent in 1980. In 1992, 12 percent of Blacks and 22 percent of Whites had at least a bachelors degree. This compares with the 1980 figures that were 8 and 18 percent respectively.[11] In 1993, the Census Bureau estimated that there were 396,000 (209,000 men and 187,000 women) Blacks who were college-educated and working full-time in managerial positions. Overall, 600,000 college-educated Black men and women worked as professionals. Professional African American men earned an average of $47,000, and professional African American women earned an average of $40,494.[12] Neoconservative critics such as Dinesh D'Souza maintain that Black educational gains and increased enrollment in colleges were solely the result of affirmative action in college admissions. However, a 1994 Brookings Institution study found that it was only at elite public and private institutions that race was a "substantial plus" in admissions.[13] The reality is that 85 percent of African American students go to colleges that do not factor in race as a substantial component in reviewing applications.

A 1990 survey of high school students found that Black and White students were equally likely to state that they would obtain a college degree. This study found no racial difference in the dropout rate when controlled for family circumstances. There were equal rates between Black and White students for cutting class or missing school days. African American parents participated in meetings and asked questions of teachers and administrators at rates equal to Whites. Also, Black students who achieved an A in math courses or were invited to join high school honor societies did not feel any less popular because of their accomplishments.[14]

Blacks have made gains and suffered losses when it comes to income. The Black upper class has been rising; the Black middle class has remained stable; but many in the working class have become poor. In short, we are a much more stratified community than we have been in the past when it comes to economics. We are not solely a community of the poor, nor do our numbers represent the majority of those who are poor in this country. We are, in short, a much more complex people than the media or our collective perceptions as a nation lead us to believe.

The 1991 National Urban League annual convention highlighted the complexity of the tapestry of Black life in the United States. Five hundred and fifty corporations, nonprofit organizations, and government units purchased booths at the convention. It is doubtful that these various groups were there to make a political statement — they were there to enhance their visibility and therefore their business. Those corporations paid more than $750,000 for their booth space. Companies from Apple Computers to General Motors marketed their products and were responding to another reality of African American life — Blacks earn and spend enough to make the difference between profit and loss for many companies.

It is true that one in three Black families is poor. However, one in seven Black families has an income greater than $50,000 per year. There are still few Black CEOs, and some exhibitors at the Urban League's convention have less than admirable records on fair employment. However, the realities of economics were not lost on the CEO of Coca Cola, Donald Keough: "We must open the doors to embrace our diversity. One, . . . because it is right. Two, . . . because it makes good sense. It is in our self-interest as a nation."[15] Realistically speaking, how can any business afford to ignore a sixth of the population? This would be ignoring a significant revenue base and not paying close attention to the bottom line.

Connections between relative wealth and poverty were also evident at this convention. Corporate exhibitors paid a hefty fee for space, but local African American vendors were allowed free space and exposure. Convention delegates could look at new cars and computers, but anyone could pick up food samples in the exhibit hall.

While tangible, though limited, progress can be made in an Urban League convention, there are still companies like Mercedes Benz, Porsche, and Fiat that rarely, if ever, advertise in traditional Black magazines such as *Ebony, Essence, Jet,* or *Black Enterprise.*

We all are living in complex and sometimes scary times. Perhaps a conversation between Juilianne Malveaux — an economist, columnist, and television/radio commentator — and an unnamed White male illustrates some texture of the terror:

> I asked [him] once, what it was that he wanted. "My fair share," the White man said, without batting an eye. "What I have is my fair share. I worked hard for it, and now you are asking that I take less."
>
> "You have more than 90 percent of the city contracts, more than 80 percent of the police and fire employees. You dominate far more than you should. What else could you possibly want?" I asked in frustration. Without missing a beat the man responded, "All of it."[16]

Whether the man was an exception to the rule or not is not what I want to underscore here. What troubles me about this conversation is what the sense of entitlement can and often does do to us all. Those who start life with a sense of entitlement or gain that sense later in life have a hard time giving entitlement up. They think who they are — be the marker gender, skin color, age, geography, or income and buying power — gives them special privileges.

Amitai Etzioni also notes this deadly sense of entitlement that permeates far too much of U.S. society. In his words, this sense leads to the demand that the "community provide more services and strongly uphold rights — coupled with a rather weak sense of obligation to the local and national community."[17] Another understanding of this entitlement comes from Alan Keith-Lucas. Keith-Lucas notes that we have two contradictory desires: we want to be treated like everyone else, *and* we want to have our individual situations taken into account.[18]

Malveaux, Etzioni, and Keith-Lucas highlight the sense in which we have lost our appreciation and understanding of community and cooperation. We have disengaged from communal lament because we have lost a sense of genuine community as a nation. We move back and forth between rights and privileges as it benefits our personal agendas and desires. We make this even more deadly when we claim rights without a willingness to assume our concomitant responsibilities. This moral failure is due, in large measure, to a rampant individualism that emerged (again) in the 1980s. We grew, as a nation, to celebrate the self to such a degree that it became a moral good, a virtue.

This misbegotten celebration has spawned an increasingly dismal 1990s.[19] In the 1990s, one in seven children has lost her or his virginity by the age of thirteen. Almost half of U.S. citizens report chronic procrastination at work and calling in false sick reports. One-sixth of those surveyed admitted they abuse drugs or alcohol at work. Fifty-nine percent of us admit using physical force against another — only forty-five percent regret it. Twenty-five percent admit they would abandon their families for money, and seven percent freely admit they would kill someone if they were offered enough money.

We are in need of a communal lament, and we have forgotten how to cry out against the plague of locusts that visits us hourly. The careless drive toward entitlement without responsibility has made the United States an extremely unhealthy place to live if one is unable to afford to purchase such privilege. We, as people of faith, must recapture the spirit of community and profess that we believe in the worth of *all* of creation. Just as the whole community of Judah must lament, so all of us are in this together.

## Cultural Empowerment and Health

At this point, after painting such a disturbing picture concerning our health, it is instructive to return to the work of Collins Airhihenbuwa. He points out that health is a process of adaptation to a socially created reality. Rather than being purely instinctual beings, we are autonomous people(s) who create cultural responses to health and disease.[20] Thus, health is a cultural production. How we respond to the various environments around us determines much about our health. However, we cannot lose sight of the fact that we must examine and understand the environments in which we live. These two factors, our environments and our response to them, are key in understanding pathways to health and healing.

Far too many of the traditional ways in which health-care programs are discussed and implemented in African American communities assume a Western paradigm. A great gift of growing up African American in this culture is that part of our heritage comes from African kinship structures. So much of the statistics around single-parents come from the assumption of the nuclear family as the norm for all peoples. Additionally, when the term "extended family" is used, it suggests that the Westernized (and fairly recent) nuclear family is the norm. What happens when the extended family is used as the norm? The traditional nuclear family becomes abnormal, constricted. As this brief illustration points out, language and paying attention to language are imperative as we explore the nature of health as a cultural production.

Airhihenbuwa argues that developing culturally appropriate programs that adapt preventive-health programs to fit the needs of the community and its cultural contexts is an effective way to improve health care in a community. He posits that the cultural-empowerment method of health promotion and education has the most promise in attaining this goal.[21] He rejects the preventive-medical model — which focuses on the role of individual decisions and their impact on adopting positive health behaviors — because it has a tendency toward victim-blaming. He also eschews the radical-political model, with its emphasis on manipulating the social and political environment to address health issues at their roots. Airhihenbuwa notes that this model can be biased toward the interests of the medical interventionist while ignoring or seeing as secondary the interests and needs of the community.

Airhihenbuwa next turns to the self-empowerment model, with its emphasis on facilitating choices for individuals and communities within the context of their sociocultural and political environments. He notes that this model uses nontraditional teaching methods to supplement the community's health knowledge through values clarification and practicing skills in decision making. It draws on the positive elements found in the preventive-medical and radical-political models. However, Airhihenbuwa warns that the major limitation of the self-empowerment model is its emphasis on the self. In the end, this model places the burden of responsibility for health on the individual.

Thus, he and we turn to the cultural-empowerment model as a means to explore the possibilities of health and healing in the African American community. This model takes into consideration how health knowledge, beliefs, and actions are produced and interpreted on the micro (individual, family, and community/grassroots) and macro (national and international) levels. What this requires is an examination and understanding of the history and the present context in which African Americans hold their health beliefs and actions as a people.

## The PEN-3 Model

Airhihenbuwa employs the PEN-3 model as a method for moving through this process. This model consists of three interrelated and interdependent dimensions of health beliefs and behaviors: health education, the educational diagnosis of health behavior, and the cultural appropriateness of health behavior.[22]

### *Health Education*

This dimension yokes the person, the extended family, and the neighborhood in a dynamic interrelationship. Here, individuals should be empowered to make informed health decisions in consonance with their familial and community roles. Although the individual remains the focus, her or his extended family is also taken into account because recognizing the immediate context of a person's environment is important. Finally, the neighborhood is included because the involvement of community members and their leaders is crucial. This is the case because community leadership often defines communal boundaries, and it is critical for these leaders to define what constitutes their community or neighborhood at the beginning of any specific health-education and delivery project.

### *Educational Diagnosis of Behavior*

This is a dynamic mix of perceptions, enablers, and nurturers. The crux of understanding perceptions is realizing that attitudes, values, ways of knowing, and beliefs within a cultural context may be avenues for obstructing or motivating personal, familial, and communal change regarding health. Enablers are those cultural, social, systemic, or structural forces that can either enhance or impede change for a healthier lifestyle. Examples of this include the availability of resources, accessibility to health care and education, and employers. Finally, nurturers are the extended family, kin, friends, peers, and the community. These groups function to mediate health beliefs, attitudes, and actions.

### *Cultural Appropriateness of Health Behavior*

Again, a triad makes up this part of the PEN-3 model. Positive behaviors, existential behaviors, and negative behaviors form this framework. Existential behaviors are those cultural beliefs, practices, and/or behaviors that are group-specific and have no harmful health consequences. These are behaviors that do not need to be changed and should not be blamed for health-care strategies that fail simply because these behaviors are misunderstood. A challenge for all of us is to address the actual situation of a group and not impose what we believe ought to be happening in any cultural community outside our own. This does not preclude a call for accountability about harmful behaviors. It does mean that we must resist moralizing behaviors that are unfamiliar to us and that we do not understand. Because affirmation is critical to success and long-term healthy behaviors, positive behaviors that promote good heath are encouraged. Negative behaviors that are harmful to health must be examined and understood within their cultural, historical, and political context before attempting to change them.

## Health as Cultural Production

When communities of faith seek to respond to the health-care crisis in the nation, it is important that they recognize the ways in which health behaviors are culturally produced. This is doubly so for African American churches and churches in predominantly African American communities that seek to be in ministry with those folks indigenous to the community. Unfortunately, the majority of culturally sensitive health and health-care programs in African American communities tend to be based on White experience. More specifically, they rely on the individual and family psychology of Blacks.[23]

The principal weakness of these models is their failure to ground the person in her or his sociopolitical context. This devalues and dismisses the dynamic nature of who we are as individuals and the vital role communal cultural values play within any health condition. Airhihenbuwa uses teenage pregnancy to highlight the failures inherent in ignoring the impact of cultural norms.[24] He notes that most anti–teenage-pregnancy programs assume that these pregnancies are unwanted. The results are programs that concentrate on birth-control methods and abstinence. What this means is that for those teenagers who *plan* their pregnancies such health interventions are irrelevant. Airhihenbuwa notes that as the number of teenagers who plan pregnancies continues to climb for African Americans, programs need to be developed that address why children *want* to have children. This is a very different conversation and strategy from the assumption of unwanted pregnancy.

Culturally sensitive and relevant health care must recognize the daunting realities of Black health in the United States. In 1994, the top ten causes of death for African Americans were heart disease (27.2 percent), cancer (21.2 percent), stroke (6.4 percent), HIV infection (5.7 percent), unintentional injuries (4.5 percent), homicide (4.3 percent), diabetes (3.5 percent), pneumonia/influenza (2.5 percent), chronic obstructive pulmonary diseases (2.3 percent), and perinatal conditions (2.0 percent).[25]

In addition, Black mental health is very problematic. Most African Americans are referred to mental-health caregivers from the educational and legal systems. This tends to give mental health and mental-health care a negative gloss within the Black community. There is also a higher probability that Blacks will be misdiagnosed, will be underserved, and will receive poor mental-health care.[26] Because, in large measure, a lack of cultural awareness plagues the mental-health-care field, many mental-health-care professionals do not assess and treat African Americans effectively.

Alvin Poussaint, the director of the Judge Baker Children's Center in Boston and professor of psychiatry at Harvard Medical School, notes that

> if a clinician thinks Blacks are not supposed to get depressed . . . [he] will underdiagnose depression and overdiagnose schizophrenia. We know that Blacks have one-half the suicide rate of Whites, 2 per 10,000 as opposed to Whites' 5 per 10,000. Some people say this proves Blacks are "happy-go-lucky." This illuminates a cultural difference in Black people. Suicide rates may indicate the prevalence of depression in Whites, but not necessarily in Blacks, because it is more taboo in the Black community to commit suicide.[27]

Thomas Parham, the immediate past-president of the National Association of Black Psychologists, adds that

> Black people struggle with depression, which is the No. 1 issue in America, but our depression manifests itself differently. Instead of the classic "vegetative signs" one expects to see — lack of interest in activities, trouble sleeping, failure to eat — depressed African American patients often show increased activity — the proverbial "laughing to keep from crying."[28]

This example concerning depression points to the dangers of assuming a hegemonic stance relative to health and health care. A standard that assumes White American culture as the norm and as generalizable to other cultures means mis- and underdiagnosis.[29] Even more deadly is when certain cultures are labeled as pathological rather than as simply different. Such mental-health issues as high rates of undiagnosed stress, depression, and substance abuse — issues that may be, and often are, directly related to interstructured oppression — are left fallow in many African American communities.

As I have attempted to show in this book, Black health is under a plague. It should not be surprising that African Americans have a low number of annual medical visits and express a higher degree of dissatisfaction with the medical attention they receive. A fear of unethical studies such as the Tuskegee Syphilis Study, patronizing health care, and poor physician-patient communication mean that many African Americans tend to leave their doctor's office unsure of their medical problem or the different avenues for its treatment. When the shortage of Black doctors (3.6 percent of U.S. doctors) is added to lack of transportation, limited or no childcare, and no time off from work, African Americans face a daunting, but not an impossible, task in achieving accessible, affordable, and excellent health care.

A 1992 study showed that improving self-esteem, building skills, and providing support are three ways to promote positive behavior-change regarding health.[30] When employing a cultural-empowerment model for health and health care, a wide range of strategies can be helpful; among these are consciousness-raising, training health-care professionals in cultural awareness, identifying and building on existing strengths in the social and personal network of individuals and communities, analyzing the ways in which feelings of powerlessness are affecting the situation, identifying and using the sources of power present, mobilizing resources, and holding the person's or the community's welfare as primary.

These strategies depend on the community and the caregiver working together as partners in providing health care. The role the individual must take in adopting healthy life patterns — just as it is the individual voices who join the communal lament — calls the individual to accountability that is personal *and* communal. This enables individuals and groups to work together using positive strategies that enhance living rather than accepting an inadequate health-care system that does not deliver good health to many African American communities.

The yoking of responsibility and rights comes to the fore here once again. Ultimately Black health rests on our ability to take responsibility for our health and fight the individual and social forces that block liberating health and health care. This means, as I have argued previously, that we must demystify the medical-care system and realize that if our health is being treated as a commodity, it is a precious commodity that must be respected and cared for.

As individuals take responsibility for their health and health care, it is important to also realize the powerful roles that socioeconomics and environment play in the dynamic. For example, when it comes to food choices, we can celebrate the positive beliefs and actions found in the African American community concerning the custom of eating green vegetables. The positive beliefs and actions include drinking the juice from the cooked vegetables. The negative ones include eating greasy foods. However, we must recognize the greater availability of fast-food restaurants in Black neighborhoods. When joined with a preponderance of cigarette billboard advertising and the greater number of liquor stores, individual behaviors face a terrible onslaught that can only be countered by communal response. The social environment is a powerful factor in health and health care.

## Examples of Community-Based Health-care Programs

In the face of the immensity of the task of understanding and advocating for good health and good health care in Black America, it is important to hold the dynamic of the individual and the community in a liberating tension. There are community-based and religious-based programs within Black communities that are functioning and effective advocates and providers of health care.

John McKnight notes six common reforms to health care: ensuring equal access to medical care (which can lead to the assumption that the right to consume medical services is the central health-care issue); improving the quality of health care (which can intensify the popular myth that health-care professionals know what health is); attempting to deal with costs (which can lead to rationing); involving health consumers in the health-care system (which can co-opt advocates for health reforms); increasing concern about the ethical issues posed by modern medicine (which can lead to the usurpation of theologians and clergy by medical professionals); and, finally, emphasizing the preventive health-care movement (which can make every person a client or patient every day of her or his life). All these reforms have medical as well as sociopolitical and theo-ethical dynamics.[31]

Faced with the commodification of health care, some community groups have formed to combat any movement that devalues the individual in community. The People's Medical Society is one such organization. It has two basic goals: to exert popular control over the medical system and to develop information among its members so that they can respond to a medical system that can and does function as a monolith.[32] McKnight points to a low-income community where the people are experimenting with decommodifying their health care by transferring funds budgeted for health care into activities that involve community action to change the elements in the local environment that are causing some of the poor health in the community.

These kinds of local, often grassroots, movements for community-based health-care point to the kind of healing and salvation that comes from communal lament that is genuine and thoroughgoing. In various manners and to differing degrees, these groups and the ones that I will highlight next focus on social change, often work across racial-ethnic and class lines, include indigenous leadership and organizers, encourage diversity training as part of their ongoing outreach and training, emphasize the connections between local and national issues, value and support personal empowerment while working for communal empowerment, and seek to be flexible and adaptable to meet the changing needs of the community and the leadership styles of the participants.[33]

What is clear is that significant community-based health-care advocacy and health-care promotion and delivery must incorporate substantial investment in the community itself and in the resources found in that community. A community's assets, capacities, and abilities are its greatest resources — resources that are often neglected or overlooked both in the community and by those forces outside of the community. Jon P. Kretzmann and John L. McKnight note that "even the poorest neighborhood is a place where individuals and organizations represent resources on which to rebuild."[34] For them, central to community-based social-change programs is locating all the available local assets, connecting them together to enhance their viability and power, and harnessing local institutions that are not yet available or involved in local development.

In focusing on the assets of its residents, a community makes an inventory of their gifts, skills, and capacities. Kretzmann and McKnight see this as crucial in marginalized communities that often do not see the giftedness and potential of every one of their members. In the Kretzmann-McKnight approach, all members of a community must be seen and act as full contributors to the community-building process. When people turn to concentrate on the assets of their community, local institutions such as businesses, schools, hospitals, and parks are yoked with churches, block clubs, and cultural groups.

Highlighting assets does not mean that *all* the resources a community-based group needs are internal to the community. When addressing a complex issue such as health care, additional resources from outside the community *will* be needed. What Kretzmann and McKnight stress is that these outside resources be used more effectively *by* a local community that is mobilized and invested in itself and in the individuals that comprise it.

This asset-based approach begins with what is present in the community, not with what is absent or with what the community needs. It allows for the human dimensions and realities of the individual and the community to come to the fore and guide the ways in which the community responds to the various issues and problems within it — including health and health care. Kretzmann and McKnight note that this is an internally focused approach that concentrates on the agenda-building and problem-solving abilities of local residents, associations, and institutions.[35] Their aim is not to minimize the role external forces play in helping to create desperate conditions in lower-income neighborhoods or the need to attract additional resources to them. What Kretzmann and McKnight stress are the internal resources within a community that can point to communal investment, creativity, hope, and control.

Kretzmann and McKnight advocate a strong relational model that echoes much of what is required in the communal lament I argue for concerning health care in the African American community. Their model combines the features of the PEN-3 model with the community-assets-based model. All African American communities are not low-income and disempowered due to a devaluation of their resources, and when faced with issues of health and health care, many, if not most, African American communities function like the rest of society. They place far too little value in advocacy and education about the health-care needs of the individuals who comprise them. There is limited recognition of the ways in which health overall, and Black health in particular, is a cultural production and must be addressed beyond a medical model or an ill- or underinformed reliance on caregivers and health professionals. The Kretzmann-McKnight model speaks to the ways in which African American communities across the country can and must address the health and health-care needs of their members.

## High School–Based Clinics

In Kansas City, there are five school-based clinics in the eighty schools that make up the Kansas City School District.[36] The clinics are full-service health providers that have nurse practitioners who can prescribe medications, nutritionists, social workers who provide mental-health counseling, and doctors on call. The staff of these clinics fill a variety of roles outside of their official ones. An unofficial liaison works with the school-based clinics and the five hospitals and health centers linked with the schools.

Some students who have health insurance but cannot get their parents to take them to the doctor are able to receive care in the clinic. In some cases, clinic personnel have intervened with suicidal patients to have them admitted to inpatient psychiatric treatment directly from the clinic. In other cases, clinic personnel have helped generate positive attitudes toward education and learning in some of their patients through repeated conversations and encouragement.

These clinics survive in a school district in which most of the other seventy-five schools lack basic nursing care. Although the clinics are free to patients, they do bill insurance companies for those who have insurance coverage. Funding is an ongoing worry because most of the money that funds the clinics comes from Medicaid. With the changes in Medicaid still unfolding, but with a definite drive to require clients to enroll with managed-care plans, it is not clear what the future will be for these clinics. One school-based clinic that opened in 1995 has been successful in community outreach. In November 1996 it handled 327 patient visits — 125 were from the community. The reasons were simple. The nearest hospital was seventeen miles away; two-thirds of the residents in the community either were on Medicaid or have no insurance; and the staff of the clinic saw it as their mission to provide services for the community.

These kinds of school-based clinics can be one answer to providing affordable, accessible, and quality health care in poor communities and in African American communities. They help bring health care into communities that may be underserved and provide the opportunity for school personnel, students, and parents to have more direct control in helping shape the kind of health-care service available to the community.

## Responding to Tobacco and Alcohol Advertising

Tobacco and liquor companies have been committing substantial advertising dollars to periodicals geared for an African American audience. These ads try to make smoking and drinking look sensual and glamorous. A pointed economic reality of many African American consumer publications such as *Essence, Ebony,* and *Jet* is that they must rely on tobacco and liquor advertising more than other mainstream publications that have a wider readership.[37] This situation is set up by a historic, but quickly changing, reluctance on the part of some manufacturers of cosmetics, athletic shoes, and other products to buy ad space in Black magazines out of the fear of being mistaken as a producer of "Black products"; some of these companies also incorrectly believe that African Americans do not have enough income to buy their products.

The obscenity of the failed 1990 Uptown cigarette campaign points to how closely cigarette companies study Black folks. The cigarette was designed to appeal to Blacks. It was a mentholated brand (higher levels of tar and nicotine) because 69 percent of Black smokers preferred this flavor. The cigarettes were to be packed face down because African Americans open the packs from the bottom, and the name of the cigarette was chosen after it scored high in consumer surveys of African Americans.[38]

This cigarette and its ad campaign were derailed after a strong public outcry from prominent Blacks and African American community groups. This was a concerted effort to name the specific health risks associated with this cigarette, make this information available to the Black community, and use the media to both educate the general population and condemn this kind of deadly commodification of blackness.

In inner-city communities like Harlem, community groups whitewash billboards that advertise alcohol. They make a very public and visual statement about the incredible number of billboards advertising alcohol in urban Black communities. These groups also stake a claim for sending messages that do not encourage unhealthy and potentially addictive behaviors in their respective communities. These very doable and concerted efforts to combat cigarette and/or alcohol addictions are powerful ways to highlight issues of African American health and health care.

## HIV/AIDS

Across the country, poorer Black, Hispanic, and Asian peoples with AIDS are questioning how their communities are being served. African American leaders from government, academia, religion, and medicine met in October 1996 at Harvard University to urge Blacks to take action against the spread of HIV. Given that HIV/AIDS is neutral when it comes to income, the socioeconomic diversity in this call to action should not be surprising, even though it has been a long time coming.

In Wyandotte County, Kansas, the American Red Cross sponsors an HIV/AIDS program that has three foci. Girl Talk is a series of evening events for women who want a safe and private place to learn about HIV prevention. Each party is hosted by a woman who invites five to seven friends, co-workers, and/or neighbors to her home. The American Red Cross HIV/AIDS program staff is there to provide practical information and advice such as the best ways to negotiate condom use with a man. This program uses role play to help women get a sense of their options.

Teen Girl Talk is for senior high school students who must have parental permission to attend or host a party. The HIV/AIDS staff explains the ways in which HIV is transmitted in terms that those who are sexually experienced or inexperienced can understand. This program promotes abstinence and role plays a variety of ways to say "No." However, the staff will discuss in detail the precautions and preventions one must take if engaged in any form of sexual activity.

The Working Girl Luncheon was a biennial event originally designed to help prostitutes avoid contracting the HIV virus from their clients. The Wyandotte Red Cross recently expanded the lunches, and now they are called Just for Ladies. These luncheons now serve women from a variety of occupations and lifestyles. They maintain the focus of giving women information on how to avoid contracting the HIV virus.

## Grandparents Who Care

The Grandparents Who Care Support Network of San Francisco is a partnership among health-care providers at community-based health centers, patients, and grandparents. In San Francisco, poor, working-class, middle-aged, and elderly Black women comprise the bulk of grandparents who now have responsibility for raising their grandchildren. Most of these women are not and were not welfare mothers although many are single because of divorce or the death of a spouse. Many held full- or part-time jobs in either the service industry or professional fields until they had to resign because they could not resolve such issues as affordable childcare.[39]

The Grandparents Who Care philosophy is simple:

- The health problems of individuals relate closely to their family, home, and community situations.
- Cultural and institutional barriers often impede access to needed health care and other services.
- Professional health-care services alone are inadequate or inappropriate in meeting all the needs.
- Individual and collective empowerment of African Americans, grandparents, and community members is essential to maintaining health.[40]

The support groups that form the network meet weekly for one and a half hours. From two to twenty-five grandparents attend — mostly women. One group is for adolescents who are in the care of their grandparents. The groups use a social-support intervention model that incorporates emotional, informational, and practical aid for the members. This model is the basis, but each group takes on its own identity and strategies as it allows for the particular abilities of the facilitators (two health-care professionals) and the needs of the participants. A volunteer board composed of grandparents, community members, and professional health-care providers helps advise on policy issues.

Using the empowerment model, Grandparents Who Care has now begun training grandparents to be group facilitators in a four-week program. The grandparents also have been active in political advocacy and lobbying. For instance, the grandparents, in collaboration with a state legislator, helped draft legislation that would make it easier for grandparents who are raising their grandchildren to receive payments under the foster-care system.[41] Another part of empowerment for the group is that the women are learning to connect their health status to their lifestyles and environment through the education and sustenance they find in the group. The hope is that as the network grows and matures, it will expand opportunities for empowerment to other health and social issues affecting their neighborhoods.

This cursory look at forms of community-based programs that make use of the resources found within the community will, I hope, serve as an inspiration and guide for other communities as they analyze and address the many health-care needs that arise within them. It is important to keep in mind — both with regard to community-based programs and with regard to the religiously based programs I will discuss next — that there is an important difference between social service and social change. Genuine lament is a call for change, for salvation, for transformation.

## Examples of Religiously Based Community Health-Care Projects

There are two forms of caring, personal and social. The personal concerns our attitudes and personal traits — how sensitive we are, our sense of dedication to others, our willingness to learn and practice patience. However, it is the social dimension that I want to focus on in the remaining pages of this chapter. Social caring means organizing institutional support for those who are in need. This support provides comfort and security — it can help people either adapt to or resist their health situations in structured ways. There are many models of religiously based social care. The following are but two.

### *The Atlanta Interfaith Health Program*

The Interfaith Health Program (IHP) of the Carter Center in Atlanta began in 1992 and ended in 1996.[42] With faith communities as the base, IHP developed a national strategy for improving health. Thomas A. Droege, the director of the Atlanta Interfaith Health Program (AIHP–an offshoot of IHP), cites what he calls five major gaps that keep faith groups from fulfilling their potential for improving health.[43] First, there is the gap between having knowledge and not applying it. Second, a gap exists between what faith communities say about social justice and what they actually do. Third, there is the failure to make successful practices widely available for replication. Droege notes that there are churches, synagogues, and mosques involved in health ministries, but it is rare that successful models are recognized widely. Fourth, faith communities operate in isolation rather than as interconnected communities. For Droege, this is "perpetuated by narrow vision, empire building, a mentality of us versus them, suspicion born of mistrust, and a failure to see that there exists, beyond differences, a common concern for social justice and the improvement of health."[44] Fifth, there is a gap between future need and present greed — it is difficult to identify with those we are separated from by time and distance.

The AIHP was a three-year project that ended in December 1996. It sought to address the health needs in underserved sections of Atlanta. By building coalitions of congregations to improve health and training congregational health promoters (CHPs), the program attempted to close the five gaps Droege identified.

CHPs help people apply the information they receive from community-health agencies and remind the congregants in their respective congregations of their health mission and their commitment to social justice. CHPs also adapt successful health-ministry models used elsewhere and join with other CHPs and community-health agencies to overcome the isolationism that can be a part of congregational ministry. These coalitions of congregations are the voice of the dispossessed in this and future generations.

The lay health ministry of AIHP was compelling. Although parish nursing is now a rising feature of the health ministry of many local churches, many congregations cannot afford to pay for the nurses' expertise. The concept of the congregational health promoter, a lay minister in the congregation, fills this gap and allows the church, no matter its size, to begin with the resources from within it to reach out to advocate and practice health care in the community.

Many of the features found in the Kretzmann-McKnight and PEN-3 models are at work with CHPs. The ideal is that these are folks from the community who understand the local cultural and ethnic values and beliefs of the community. They receive twenty hours of training based on the participatory learning approach of Paulo Freire. AIHP saw that trainees were in a better position than the trainer to identify health-related problems and assets in the community.

Rather than stay within a specific congregation or community, the ideal of the IHP was that congregations form coalitions to work together on health promotion and advocacy. In the AIHP, three coalitions formed. The Brown coalition was thirteen African American churches in the center of Atlanta. The McNair coalition was nine churches and one mosque — mostly small, struggling racial-ethnic congregations. The Buford coalition was nineteen multiethnic congregations.

Representatives from the participating congregations made up a Health Ministry Council (HMC). In one coalition, this was composed entirely of clergy; in the others it was a combination of clergy and laity. In each case, the leadership came from within the churches that composed the coalition. The network coordinator (a half-time paid position) was selected by each HMC to stimulate interest in the project and strengthen the ties between congregations.

This program is currently under evaluation, so it not possible to point to its specific strengths and drawbacks. However, it is clear that such a community-based project may be a key way in which religious communities in distressed African American communities can acknowledge and address intracommunal health-care needs.

## *HIV/AIDS Ministries and the Black Church*

The Good Samaritan Project is an HIV/AIDS advocacy and care organization in Kansas City, Missouri. It has developed a Care Team Plan in which interested churches or other religious groups can establish a care team of ten to fifteen members.[45] For churches that do not have enough volunteers to sustain a single team, Good Samaritan arranges interfaith care teams. Each team is assigned one to four HIV-positive clients who are matched to the abilities and availability of the team members.

The goal of the care team is to help HIV-positive people to remain at home if their needs are such that extracommunity assistance can help them stay there. Shopping, meal preparation, assistance in bathing, and helping people get out of bed are ways that care team members help. The care team members are there to provide supplemental care — not primary care — but they can give primary caregivers a much-needed respite.

The Good Samaritan Project recognizes that many potential care team members may be unable or unwilling to provide personal care, so these members focus on meal preparation, shopping, yard work, and other nonpersonal chores that enhance the quality of life of the HIV-positive person. The point is that within the team, members are diverse enough in their interests and skills that the *team* can provide solid supplemental care.

Dr. M. Joycelyn Elders, the former U.S. surgeon general, has an eight-point call to the Black Church concerning HIV/AIDS. She believes that the church must

- be more than concerned about this problem; the church must be *committed.*
- use tools of commitment; give time, talent, and treasure.
- be the voice and vision for the poor and the powerless.
- begin to network and use its prestige, power, and passion to influence decisions.
- form partnerships and help to develop sound public health policy.

- reach out, be responsible, and be willing to take some risks to save our young people.
- educate our young people and ourselves, as well as people in our communities, our businesses, and our schools.
- claim victory in conquering this disease.[46]

Such a call must not go unanswered, and more and more Black churches are responding to this call. Although the numbers are growing, the Black Church is still woefully behind the need and the reality of Black suffering to which the statistics found in chapter 6 point.

Before a church begins an HIV/AIDS ministry, it is important to become knowledgeable about HIV/AIDS in general, to be clear about goals and objectives, and to make an honest assessment of the church's abilities in such a ministry. In Kansas City, Missouri, Calvary Temple Baptist Church has developed such a ministry to meet the needs found in its community. In its August 1996 newsletter, *Temple Times,* the church laid out its ten-point strategy for fighting HIV/AIDS:

1. Ask God for direction in making a start.
2. Speak to your pastor about starting an AIDS ministry at your church.
3. Learn the facts about AIDS by:
    - Participating in training offered by Calvary Temple (two hours)
    - Participating in Red Cross training (sixteen hours; Calvary staff will help to arrange it).
4. Participate in AIDS-related events and functions:
    - AIDS quilt
    - World AIDS Day
    - Black Week of Prayer for the Healing of AIDS
    - Walk for Life.
5. Volunteer to provide advocacy or education:
    - Make regular visits to nursing homes and skilled-care facilities
    - Become an HIV/AIDS educator
    - Make your food pantry available to people living with AIDS
    - Become a Care Team Volunteer
    - Assist a patient living at home by:

- Picking up prescriptions
- Grocery shopping
- Cleaning
- Making home visits to minister
- Being a friend by listening.

6. Teach, model, and encourage abstinence!
7. Collect special offerings designated toward the local or national AIDS service organization of your choice.
8. Make brochures available for your church tract rack that are sensitive to the needs of your church.
9. Be sensitive to the fact that there may be someone in your congregation that is living with the disease and afraid to tell. Be supportive.
10. Pray for a cure! Pray for healing! Pray for our compassionate response.[47]

The point of these forms of social care is to focus on care and healing rather than judgment, powerlessness, and illness. These are forms of communal lament that lead to the pathway of salvation.

> Then God became jealous for the land,
> and had pity on the people.
> In response to the people God said:
> I am sending you
> grain, wine, and oil,
> and you will be satisfied;
> and I will no more make you
> a mockery among the nations.
>
> Joel 2:18–19

## *Chapter 8*

# Searching for Paradise in a World of Theme Parks

## *A Womanist Ethic of Care and Healing*

*Hebrews 10:19–11:3*

when i was a little girl
  i spent a good deal of time trying to conjure up heaven
i thought that if i could just imagine those angels, those harps, those
    clouds
  then i wouldn't be so scared of this big angry white-haired, white-
  bearded, white furrow-browed God the minister preachified
  about on those Sunday mornings in Southern Pines, North Carolina
i thought if i could see those fluffy clouds
sit on those soft-with-goose-down couches
move around with grace and style as my walk was a *glide* all over heaven
  always being good, never having to worry about being bad
smell the tasty ('cause i just knew anything that had to do with heaven
had to be tasty) food
      the fried chicken
      the hot-with-butter rolls
      the spoon bread
      the gravy made from chicken grease
      the fresh greens
      the fresh string beans
      the big-grained rice
      the macaroni and cheese
      the mashed potatoes
      the candied yams, coming right from the ground
      the rib roast
      the salmon croquettes
      the salads — lettuce and tomato (with french dressing)
      the cakes — pound, coconut, chocolate

the pies — apple, sweet potato, chess, pecan
the kool-aid
the lemonade
the sweetened tea ('cause there was no such thing as
*un*sweetened tea when i was growing up)
and butter, butter, butter, butter
(i realize now that i was associating heaven with the way my
grandmama's house smelled on Saturday night and Sunday)
i thought if i could hear the good music — 'cause even my playmates
and i knew that all angels knew the beat, could carry a tune and played
a mean harp
then i wouldn't worry so much
when the men in white sheets marched through the black
section of town where my grandmother and all the other
loving people i knew lived
i thought if i could just conjure up heaven
in my mind
and in my heart
and in my prayers
then maybe
just maybe...
it seems interesting to me now, years later, that i never once consciously associated paradise with what i saw and felt on earth when i was a little girl
and now in our worlds of knowledge
and our ability to create and shape our environment
to fit our own levels of comfort
it is hard to imagine paradise
sometimes
that isn't beyond our technical expertise
we seem to be mired in a world of
facts
statistics
data
numbers
flow charts
pie charts
forecasts and projections
we seem to delight in our abilities to prove or disprove
anything
everything
and the reality of nothing

we use our technical brilliance to
explain
codify
compartmentalize
delineate
elaborate
we have created our own worlds and oceans of fun
flags over Texas
Georgia
St. Louis
river boats of delight
funhouses of sex
peep shows on paper and video and flesh
shooting galleries of death
and
enclaves of holiness
we seem to have so much knowledge
we are busy, oh so busy
searching for paradise in a world of theme parks
we have rushed in one too many times
to cover ourselves up with human-made delights so that life will not crush us
we have sought one too many easy answers
to the dilemma of shaping a faith that moves beyond shouting
that looks, feels, and sounds like a postmodern minstrel show
to one that endures and deals with the realities of what it takes to confess our sins in a world *we* have helped create
and it is often a mean, cruel, self-interested, selfish world
we have tried that one additional quick-fix
that has pushed us into empty living
empty worship
empty mission
empty witness
empty spirituality
empty faith
the writer of Hebrews reminds us
it is a fearful thing to fall into the hands of the living god
and so the writer reminds the people
"recall those earlier days when, after you had been enlightened, you endured a hard struggle with sufferings. . . . "
look back to your period of training before your baptism
look back on your baptism

look back on what God has done not only for you, but for your forebears
the believer, in Hebrews, is called to remember her or his faith
but not to linger in it
for the future is God's as well
the writer is also dealing with folks who had grown complacent,
who had lost (or were losing) their confidence in God's promises
brothers and sisters, you and i know — when we are honest with ourselves —
that the only thing more tenuously Christian than a Christian
who *only* knows success and gain and prosperity
is one whose faith is crafted out of shifting sands and therefore
cannot endure the tests and disappointments of living
so Hebrews tells the reader, you have to have endurance in your faith
your confidence in God is not out of place — get some staying power
and then the promise will be made real in your lives
if you don't
what you'll get is a God who is not happy with you
and this sounds all too familiar for us today
we are living in a world of deadly theme parks of our own making
*it is fatal to love a god (or gods) who does not love us*
who only takes from us
offers us false hope or temporary comfort
makes promises it cannot keep — and never intended to keep in the first place
who tells us to keep going when we should stop
and stop when we should be pressing on
oh yes, oh yes, oh yes: it is fatal to love a god who does not love us
instead of a God who comforts
leads
advises
strengthens
chastises
encourages
and enlarges our vision of ourselves
far too many of us have become beggars at the table of religions that sanction our own destruction
and some of us think that this is holy

## Eschatological Notes on Caring

i, quite frankly, have renewed my search for paradise

This paradise is not collapsed solely into a terrifying apocalypse howling in the end of human history. It is connected to an understanding of humanity, our value systems, and our world. Therefore, this paradise I seek is largely focused on this life, for it is intimately linked to a Hebraic focus on a good and long life as the goal of each person. This paradise causes us to hope to live on into the next generation and to expect God's judgment, God's salvation in this world — it is the Day of the Lord. This prophetic eschatology envisions God accomplishing divine plans within our context through human agents. And like the prophets, it calls the pyramidic towers of evil to beware. Yet it yokes with an apocalyptic eschatology that finds hope and judgment in the future. It may be that we are facing the terrible Day of the Lord and are failing to repent.

This Day of the Lord is eschatological and salvific. Eschatologically, the tension is between our present social order and the coming Day. It is historical and temporal in this regard and provides a theo-ethical foundation for the transformation of society. This search for paradise is not a desperate search for just any kind of revelation. It is a soul-deep and wish-filled conviction that our current circumstances are not ultimately definitive or inevitable. This eschatological hope seeks consolation and fortitude in a difficult reality — one in which far too many of us *cannot* receive adequate health care because it may be inaccessible, unaffordable, or unavailable.

Therefore, the salvific dimension of this paradise is not otherworldly. Salvation, here, embraces all of humanity, for it is our kinship and relationship with God and with one another. Through this embrace, we are transformed body and spirit, individuals and society, persons and cosmos, time and eternity.[1] It is transformatory. The salvation *we* seek must not be formed out of a rampant individualism. It is one that joins in community as God touches all of humanity in a caress that is neither sentimental nor spiritualized. It is one forged out of God's relentless love for us regardless of our willingness to recognize or accept such love. Yet when we enter into genuine lament out of the recognition that we need, if not yearn for, a balm and not human-made panaceas, then we open up the opportunity for God's salvation and healing to shower us with transforming power such that we can and do seek to form a world that holds the opportunity for each of us to live into health and wholeness — it is social and political.

It is important to note that everything we do is mediated by our bodies. Part of the dilemma the Christian community faces when addressing health and health care is rooted in a negative dualism that separates the body and the spirit. This Cartesian separation does more than split us apart — it fractures us in such a way that we often believe and live as if our bodies and spirits have no influence on each other. We live together in a somewhat uneasy coexistence with the splinters of this fracturing.

This is ironic given the way in which the material world is such a vital part of our lives. We eschew healthy living and health itself in relentless drives for status, money, power, and privilege. The plague of locusts that often descends on our values overshadows the need to nurture and cherish the human spirit. E. Anthony Allen notes that this deadly body-spirit dualism that is such an integral part of our churches is alien to the biblical view of the person.[2] He notes that the church is to span the physical, psychological, social, and spiritual in its concern for humanity and the whole of creation.

The theological root of the body-spirit fracture is the traditional Christian theological formulation of the meaning of incarnation in which being (our reality, our essence, our is-ness) is that which is in the body yet not of it. This Cartesian formulation belies the ways in which the body is basic to much of the imagery we have concerning Jesus from nativity to crucifixion, and it belies our own embodiedness as well. The nativity is a very embodied experience. Those who are reading these words and have spent any time in a stable are aware of the strong odors present. The nose, the eyes, and the ears are assaulted by the very fleshiness and fecundity of life that are part of a stable. The sights, smells, and sounds of birth, life, and death are very much a part of the living that happens in that environment. Yet our representations of the nativity, our conscious and unconscious imaginings of the scene, often take all the is-ness of the birth of Jesus away from us. We imagine and often worship an antiseptic scene that is pleasing to a deodorized faith.

Yet as we move from the birth to Jesus' life, we see the richness of the body returning again and again to the story of Jesus. He was a carpenter — a man who worked with his body to create that which was needed in his society. Carpentry is a very physical trade. It requires a keen eye and muscles toned to handle the sometimes intricate work needed as well as the force that must be employed. It requires maneuvering one's body and using one's body to maneuver objects. It can be hot and tiring work that causes sweat and smell and exhaustion. Yet we separate the reality of carpentry from Jesus far too often as we reflect back on these early days of his life — if we pause to consider the trade he practiced at all.

The stories of Jesus sharing meals with others are frequent in the Gospels. Yet we tend to "spiritualize" these stories and name them miracles — which they were. But we do so before we recognize the ways in which they provided concrete bodily sustenance to people. The story about turning water into wine and the story of the loaves and fishes are narratives that spark the mystery of miracles for us. Yet they are also stories that point to the physical needs we have for food and drink. When we separate the mystery from the way in which it touches our humanity to offer a window *into* the mystery, we invite a fracturing of body and soul.

Many of our Christian rituals take place on the believer's body. Most of them are a reenactment of the story of Jesus' body. In baptism, it is water that is washed on our bodies; in confirmation and ordination, we have the laying on of hands; in communion, we take in drink and bread. There is a very concrete and physical aspect to Christian faith that we often ignore because of the body-spirit fracture we have in our faith and in our understanding of faithfulness. When we live out of an incarnational understanding that takes us out of the *dynamic* dualism we have of body *and* spirit, then we lapse into the *deadly* dualism that tells us that the body is inferior, if not evil, and must be transcended by the spirit of Jesus.

This poses an interesting dilemma when we state that Jesus is fully human and fully divine. His humanity — his appetites, temptations, sufferings — tends to be devalued or moved into a spiritualized realm that takes him out of the world. We do not deal seriously with the fullness of Jesus' humanity. Instead, we hold him in a transcendent realm that really does not touch us in concrete ways. He becomes the Divine Wholly Holy Other and moves out of our sight and out of the possibility of our being able to really model our lives on his humanity. We are desperately "less than," rather than believers in the fullness of his humanity and the hope that brings for all of us.

This devaluing of the body takes many forms in our society. In some cases it manifests itself as ageism; in others it is racism, sexism, heterosexism, homophobia, classism. All of these fracturings of the body and the spirit destroy our health. We need to develop a sense of caring for each other and for ourselves; in order to bring us back together again and to heal, we need a communal lament that names, with precision and clarity, the ways in which we destroy our health.

Developing caring relationships, an ethic of care, is a key social ingredient in addressing health and health care in the United States broadly speaking and in African American communities in particular. Allen poses a tremendous challenge to the Black religious community at this juncture:

> One of the greatest causes of failure in the church's health and healing ministry is the positioning of congregations as theaters instead of healing communities. Chapels with platforms as stages for the clergy and robed choirs to perform are too often more the order of the day than are organic communities where each person is as important as the other and each has a friend. We cannot heal in isolation. We need others.[3]

We need each other. One way to begin to find ourselves is to develop a sense of empathy beyond the mere intellectual identification of ourselves with another. As a moral virtue, empathy means that we put ourselves in the place of another. This means sharing *and* understanding the emotional and social experiences of others and coming to see the world as they see it. We move away from "those people" and "they" language and behavior to "we" and "us" and "our" ways of living and believing.

Yet empathy is only one path to finding our way to health and establishing a health-care system that is equitable and just. We also need to reconfigure our understanding of love. In doing so, we begin to realize that we need to live our lives as if we are more united than separated. This does not mean a mindless and essentializing drive toward a unity fraught with hegemony. Rather it means moving in the direction of a commitment to deepen our understanding and respect for one another in our uniqueness and in our commonality without one overriding or subsuming the other.

This love, which is agapic *and* erotic, realizes the tensions and indecision with which we all live. The agapic dimension of this care is that which is unselfish and seeks the good for all of us — not just the common good. Therefore, it is concerned for self *and* for others. It is a very interested love that questions self-sacrifice, self-denial, genocide, and other forms of annihilation that are often held, by our cultures, as greater goods or necessary evils. The erotic dimension of this care is our individual and collective creative energy that makes us feel what we are doing passionately and fully.[4] The aim of our lives becomes making that which we do in our lives and in the lives of those generations yet to come richer and more viable. We live our lives from the inside outward in such a manner that we begin to take on a deep responsibility for ourselves and a sense of accountability to others. We move away from the ways in which we numb ourselves through food, drink, and acquisition. We choose a way of living that is an ever-evolving mutuality that seeks healthiness for all of humanity. This erotic dimension helps us care because we seek genuine change within the world rather than seek a shift of characters in the same weary drama.

## Hope

Richard Shaull has written:

> Our industrial society has placed a strong emphasis upon living for the future. But that was something quite different. It was a matter of *not* living in the present, of depriving ourselves of material things now in order to have more material things and enjoy a higher status later on.

> What I am getting at is an orientation toward the future that reveals *present* possibilities to us.... The future has already begun.[5]

And such is what the yoking of Joel and Hebrews brings us to: the call for genuine lament, the call to faithfulness as we live in the present to live into the future. If we want to understand what health and health care will look like for future generations — be they African Americans or others — we need only look at what we are doing now. Our future is conditioned on the present and the past. Our legacy, as a nation, is not always an admirable one when it comes to how we have treated one another's health. The task before us, as we lament and as we search for faithfulness, cannot be conditioned by disillusionment, fear, or cynicism.[6] Such reactions and the actions they spark are defeatist and nihilistic. The ethic of care that is rooted in a search for paradise must travel up the rough side of the mountain and retain its passion, its commitment, its vision, its hope — *regardless.*

We live in a time of gross imbalances: Medicare fraud in 1996 was roughly $17 billion; this is more than the federal government's bill for providing cash welfare assistance to poor families with children. We live in a time that demands a communal lament. The present realities and some of the history of what health care has been for Black folks in our country are our contemporary locusts. Our situation echoes that Joel describes:

> What the cutting locust left,
> the swarming locust has eaten.
> What the swarming locust left,
> the hopping locust has eaten,
> and what the hopping locust left,
> the destroying locust has eaten. (Joel 1:4)

It is time we blow the trumpet in our contemporary Zion and sanctify a fast. It will take all of us, peoples of color and White, male and female, young and old, to carry out a communal lament. But only a lament that comes from all of us can address the complexities of health and health care in our lives and the peculiar way in which these complexities affect the African American community.

The film *Daughters of the Dust,* by the African American filmmaker Julie Dash, is stunning in its power and scope. It tells the story of a Black sea island (or Gullah) family preparing to go to the mainland at the turn of the century. The story is told through the eyes of a character called the Unborn Child, who, though still in the womb, already loves her family, the Peazants, fiercely and who understands that she is traveling on a spiritual mission. But, in her own words, the Unborn Child also admits that "sometimes I get distracted."

The history and mythobiography of the film have captured me. There is a powerful speech near the end that simply takes my breath away and challenges me as I seek to respond to questions and answers I find piling up as I try to make sense of the system of health and health care we face in this nation and how health and health care find a peculiar home in communities of the dispossessed. The words are from the character Eula, who had been raped by a White man. The narrator, the Unborn Child, is her child. Only the audience knows that the child Eula carries is truly the one she conceived, in love, with her husband, Eli. As Eula speaks, she calls the women to task for ostracizing Yellow Mary, a prostitute who turned to prostitution after her own experience of rape. Yellow Mary has come home to the island to be with her family again and to heal. Eula reminds them all that the fate and hope of Yellow Mary are their own — no one escapes the ravages of evil; no one stands outside of the promise. Then she turns to the younger women and her words are for us as well:

> There's going to be all kinds of roads to take in life.... Let's not be afraid to take them. We deserve them, because we're all good women. Do you... do you understand who we are, and what we have become? We're the daughters of those old dusty things Nana carries in her tin can.... We carry too many scars from the past. Our past owns us. We wear our scars like armor,... for protection. Our mother's scars, our sister's scars, our daughter's scars... Thick, hard, ugly scars that no one can pass through to ever hurt us again. Let's live our lives without living in the fold of old wounds.

•

a lament *and* a cry for deliverance
  to break the fine rain of death that is falling in the lives of far too many black folk in the united states
    when it comes to our health and health care
to say, on one hand
  this is a demanding or difficult task
  that in some way we live in a health-care delivery system that in effect
  calls some of us to prove or justify our very lives in a court of science
  that may be structured so that some of us
    need not apply for justice or mercy or equality or harmony or peace
  that we see (when we do not sense) that there are false accusations lining the fabric of our lives
  that we are involved in an ill-designed and misbegotten contest
    that is deadly, oh so deadly
to say, on the other hand

that we have expectations of and for ourselves when it comes to providing
adequate and affordable health care
that we have dreams that can be more powerful than the nightmares
possibilities more radical than the realities
and a hope that does more than cling to a wish
or wish on a star
or sit by the side of the road, picking and sucking its teeth
after dining on a meal of disaster and violence
we live in a challenge that should compel us to cry out in a communal lament
that is brimming with hope
hope, that anticipation of a future that fulfills God's plans
and is based on God's covenant of faithfulness
and the very resurrection of Jesus, the living Christ
yet we are caught in a tension that rends the body and soul
one is Greek and classical
the other is biblical
the hope that is the standing ground for a womanist ethic of care is not the
Greek
it is not the hope of Pandora's box
for Pandora, hope is an evil that comes to confuse the human spirit
Pandora's hope is one that causes us to miss the opportunities of the
present because we are expecting something else
our spirits are in the future, not the present
and so we wallow in confusion in a melancholy and morbid
hopefulness for what will not come
it is not the hope of Aristotle
for he compares those who hope to naive youth
the hopeful are unrealistic
they believe too much in the good found in life
it is not the hope of Goethe
for Goethe believed "why roam in the distance? see, the good lies so
near. learn only to achieve happiness, then happiness is always there"
it is not the hope of Camus
for Camus's myth of Sisyphus was to teach us that we should "think clearly
and do not hope"
for Camus, hope is a tool of political and economic charlatans who sell
life-destroying illusions in the cold porridge of hopefulness
no, the cry of lament that leads to hope we must have must be unequivocal
and unambiguous
it is a hope that is found within the pages of scripture
it is enduring and pervasive
it is positive, it is the divine power of life

it is the expectation of a justice-filled future established on God's promise
and supported by our ever-evolving and deepening trust in God
it cannot detach the human spirit from the present through mad delusions
and flights of fancy
hope does not empty out our lives
it is the new heaven and the new earth
it is the eternal life of all God's creatures
who are brought to this place through God's justice
no this hope
is one that pulls the promise of the future into the present
and places the present into the dawn of a future that is on the rimbones
of glory

For hope lies in the midst of a lament that cries out for salvation that leads to healing. However, it is all-too-often true that we tinge our hope with skepticism. We seriously doubt the possibility of the very things we most want. We find ways to sell ourselves short, to deem others less than they are or can be, to give up on living a life of justice and mercy — because, after all, *we are only human*. For all that we dream about, we find ourselves content to live out the weary drama of the nightmare — to accept the is-ness of our lives as the ought and to find ways to short-circuit the hope found in possibilities and daring to reach beyond what we ever thought ourselves capable of. We forget or neglect the miracle of God working in us: that God takes our brokenness, the threads of our lives, and weaves masterpieces.

We say, both overtly and covertly, that true justice and equality will never be a part of the fabric of living in our lifetimes — that we will always have the poor with us; that some of us can access adequate, if not superordinate, health care while other will rely on a health-delivery system overburdened with the sheer force of numbers and acuteness of illnesses it must treat; that some of us are just destined to be wealthy and successful and others of us will naturally fall by the wayside into despair and hopelessness.

We are afraid to live our hopes. We look at struggle as a sign of discord and turmoil rather than realizing that our faith demands from us *seasons* of struggle and *moments* of glory. When we finally reach those places where we are close to attaining some measure of our best dreams, our moment of glory for ourselves and the world around us, we begin to get nervous; we begin to look around; we start looking over our shoulder; and we cannot *believe* that this moment is close at hand.

Hope that is birthed from lament is a strange thing, and each of us has suffered from a loss of hope. We feel that what we wanted to happen was simply beyond the believable. We are not unlike the disciples after the resurrection. They were people whose hopes had been crucified by the very nails that pinned Jesus to the cross. There was no confidence left in them; the future they longed for seemed to die with Christ. They had depended on him to bring about the fulfillment of the promise of God. With Christ dead, they had nothing to look forward to. Their hopes had been misplaced, and emptiness was all that remained; but the rumors began to come — he lives, some had seen him, and the hopes that were dying began to live again.

We must take our sometimes fractured hopes and breathe new life into them as we look at the worlds so many of the dispossessed endure. What a paradox we place ourselves in when we hope and yet are afraid to hope. Hope is powerful. It enables us to press onward when we feel like giving up. It enables us to draw strength from the future to live in a discouraging present. It makes it possible for us to see the world, not only as it is, but as it can be. Hope can move us to new places and turn us into new people.

Yet for all the possibilities in hope that bode well for us, we all know that hope is dangerous. It not only gives us strength, but makes us vulnerable. Sometimes the causes we support and the vision we have prove to be unworthy of our support, and the vision of the future we long for fades from our eyes — a cold and desolate wind blows in our hearts. Yes, the chill of despair is doubly cold for those who had their hearts warmed by hope. Hope can create new opportunities for pain and disappointment. It is undeniable that countless hopes have been short-lived and undependable. All of us are mindful of the tight circle in which our lives are lived. We know all the ways by which life closes in, stultifies, frightens, and disturbs us. We know those private regions of the heart where desires have their beginnings and the quiet anxieties of the spirit express themselves in many ways that defeat us.

To hope does not mean that we are now free to suppress the meannesses of life. But we are often tempted to do so in an ill-designed search for an otherworldly, heavenly utopia. This is a dangerous place for us to stand as well. Rather than hold the prophetic and apocalyptic together in our eschatological hope, we fracture them into so many pieces. And then when we piece together what is left, we do it in such a way that only a few can possibly benefit from this new design.

But there is something about hope, when it is grounded in the divine, that is solid enough to sustain our lives and overcome skepticism and doubt. It *is* frightening, this hope, because we know that God interrupts the mundane and comfortable in us and calls to us to move beyond ourselves and accept a new agenda for living. We are led into a life of risk. The hope that is to be found in God cannot simply be given a nod or quick recognition. It demands not only a contract from us, but covenant and commitment. It is to be engaged in — hope leads us into an exodus that crosses and transcends human-made boundaries.[7] When we truly believe in this hope, it will order and shape our lives in ways that are not always predictable, not always safe, rarely conventional. This hope will drive us to protest with prophetic fury the sins of an inequitable health-care system.

Hope and faith are inseparable dance partners in a womanist ethic of care. Hope nurtures and succors faith. Hope gives us the gumption to lay claim to the strength of our faith and the power of God's love for us! We are drawn again and again to a God who gives us the comfort of the familiar landscape that enables us to find our way even in the darkness of sin and sorrows. Hope gives us the ability to recognize that we must refuse to scale down our aspirations to the level of the facts in our present situation because God is always calling us to move beyond the present to shape and mold a better tomorrow. We wrestle with the problems of health and health care until they open, until they yield, until they break down and disintegrate under the relentless pressure of our ability to hope *and live in that hope.*

There is misery abounding in our world. We cannot hide from these miseries *or* from responsibility. We can choose to say that someone else is more qualified and more knowledgeable about equitable health care. We can be content to allow experts to debate the quality of *our* lives. We can wring our hands or, worse, turn our backs in indifference and callous disregard to the erosion of human rights. But this never relieves us of the responsibility we have to our generation and future generations to keep our hopes alive and vibrant.

Hope gives us the wisdom to know that God is not through. Our task is to take the challenge a lament that dares to hope gives us — the joy along with the disappointment — and work *with* God until our lives begin to pulse with something vaster and greater than anything we have known before. We are destined to reach for the skies and embrace life with songs of joy and justice. Hope gives us the will power it takes to look at all those people and situations that wish us harm and do us harm and decide that we are called to new life and not early death. Hope gives Black folks the stubbornness to survey our situations and work out a way of life that gives us health and growth despite the wearying paradox of our living.

With hope, we do not give up, for we answer life *with* life. The responsibility for living with meaning and health and dignity ultimately rests within us — not with managed care, health maintenance organizations, or preferred provider organizations.[8] Only a hope that is grounded in a faith that rests within God can see us through this miasma of life.

## Despair and Victimization

This hope is part of who we are, how we are, and is made manifest in our interactions with others. It reflects a trust in the goodness of a God who listens and responds to our communal lament that is a true act of repentance and trust. We are living in the midst of a plague of locusts. The health of Black America is under siege to a relentless army. It is the task of each of us, as we join with others, to cry out and then live out of a new vision for our lives. For we know that what we have now is not fated by necessity. We can and must act to change it.

We turn away from despair. For Jürgen Moltmann, despair is the "tacit absence of meaning, prospects, future purpose."[9] To despair is signaling that we have no confidence, no expectation, no yearning for a tangible justice or an immeasurable love. We have abdicated; we have given up. We have no confidence that our lament for salvation — our cry to our communities that we must, absolutely must, begin to choose health in whatever small or large ways we can — will do any good. So we sit and we walk and we crawl and we stumble and we run toward our own annihilation.

African Americans must also move out of a rhetoric of victimization. Health is indeed a cultural production, but we must also acknowledge our individual and collective choices of how we live our lives — even in the midst of death-dealing socioeconomic and cultural realities. If Black folks refuse even a limited agency when it comes to health and health care, then we abdicate our agency and place our fate in the hands of a powerful and absolute dominating Other that is not divine but all-too-human, if not inhumane. To assent to victimization — be that assent conscious or unconscious — is to live lives of hopelessness and despair. It is to believe the inaccurate but very effective media portrayals that African Americans are hopelessly trapped in pathologies of our own making without any recognition or analysis of larger social structures that defeat caring, compassion, and respect for all humanity and the earth itself.

The sometimes mindless, other times calculated, rhetoric of victimization is sinful. It does not place any of us on a higher moral ground but allows us to make claims that are often unjust and to abdicate from our responsibility to work with God as partners seeking health and wholeness. To give victimization such a large hand in Black lives means that we are no longer seeking mutual or harmonious relationships. Rampant individualism, which often fuels this rhetoric of victimization, has turned back on African American life in such a way that the moral arc of the universe bends toward the self (and its gain) rather than toward the community (and what it means to work and live in mutuality). Rather, we are falling into a weird solipsism in which we are bound within the walls of our ideologies rather than expanding our vision into a radical future based on justice.

James Gustafson provides a helpful warning at this juncture. He cautions us against

> excessively moralizing against those who are in despair and against a Pollyanna "pull yourself up by your own bootstraps" optimism. The presence of despair will not be overcome by bland assurances that the abyss of hope is deeper than the abyss of despair given to those for whom there is little or no confirmation of the reliability of persons and communities, of the openness of the future.[10]

Despair and the rhetoric of victimization are the natural enemies of hope. However, if we cannot provide a hefty hope that moves in transformatory ways that are concrete and specific as they also call for vision and trust, then we cannot expect any ethic of care — no matter how necessary it is to address the very real inequities of life — to have meaning for those who have either fallen into despair or been placed there by hegemonic forces.

This hope is far more than optimism. It moves beyond images and constructions of fatedness. This hope must be crafted out of the fight against despair and victimization. We begin this work by accepting individual and communal accountability and complicity in how we have and have not responded to the declining health of Black America and an inequitable health-care system that collides with all of U.S. culture.

Hope is based on possibilities and promises. Ultimately it rests on God's promise to us: "And my people shall never again be put to shame" (Joel 2:27). Yet this is joined by the admonition that "it is a fearful thing to fall into the hands of the living God" (Hebrews 10:31). Genuine lament guides us into a life-giving openness to the possibilities rather than miring our present or our tomorrows in narcotic selfishness and disinterest.

## Away (A Way) from the Theme Parks

hope is a spirit that is within and without us
it calls us to itself, to ourselves, to one another
it is a spirit that moves and shapes
  figures and reconfigures
  it is swift, it is slow
  it is time-less, it is time-filled
it is a spirit that leads us beyond what we can touch
  or see
  or feel
this hope is not discursive and discrete
  it is not rimmed with ontological categories that serve
  to keep us from our health

this hope
is lament
is community
is love
is justice
is healing
it is the very heart and soul of who we are and how we are and how we can be and how far we have yet to go
it is the spirit of promise
it is the spirit of refusing to accept the realities in which we all dwell
in which we try to survive — and do survive
in which we try to live and sometimes, through amazing feats of moving through
we not only live, but thrive
actually shimmer with life and hope and justice and righteous,
o so holy and righteous anger
this hope reminds us that we cannot accept the death-dealing and life-denying ways in which we have often structured our existences
or had our worlds ordered for us through the Tuskegees,
the HIV/AIDS, through the inadequate clinical trials, through
unaffordable health care, through unattainable insurance
we must act through a faith that is grounded in what the wise old folks tell
us about living and hoping and refusing and cussing and praying and doing
the work of love and justice to bring ourselves home again
to realize that our lives, our bodies, are precious
our minds are priceless
our souls are to be cherished
and we must resist the western model of ripping ourselves apart
the Christian dogmas that encourage us to neglect parts of blessed createdness
the made in America brand of violence against everybody and everything
and re-cast our ways of being
for many of our ways of being are killing us
none too softly and with a song that assaults our very souls and spirits
hope sustains us as we refuse to accept the smallnesses of life
the amazing acts of violence and hatred
the awful indignities we inflict on others and others inflict on us
and dis-eased and mal-nourished bodies we carry around like postmodern cadavers
performing morbid minstrel shows
that no longer entertain
and our black-face does not come off

hope reminds us to celebrate the spirit that lives and breathes life into us
beyond the seeing and knowing and believing we can do
it is a spirit that refuses destruction and is impolite when it says a
bodacious "no" to praxeological frameworks that serve the masters' and
mistresses' houses of hegemony

A womanist ethic of care prompts us to seek a communal lament that challenges us to stand in the midst of the flux of knowing that among the industrialized nations the United States has the highest percentage of children living in poverty; that the Black infant mortality rate is obscene; that heart disease, diabetes, sickle-cell disease, and stroke visit the lives of African Americans like plagues of locust. We know all this and more — and yet we must still theorize, strategize, and work to create a healthy life for us all.

all who take hold of their disbelief
and fashion a faith that does not let us go and holds us accountable to
ourselves and to God
all who recognize the cost of hope
and choose to live *in* it rather than circle it, dodge it, or turn from it
all who hope in Christ
have accepted a gift that will always challenge and always change us
it is a solid hope, a hope that will never fail us and never leave us alone and
without support
when it's the spirit showering us with grace and hope and love
then we are set free to serve
and free others
with full hearts — we can do this
with a full ministry — God's church is never put to shame
your sons and your daughters
your young and your old
your free and your slave
them is us
and *we* are the church
we are called to love ourselves
to love one another
*to love God hard* if we are to *live* out
the pouring of God's spirit into our lives
we must reach out to our brothers and sisters
and touch creation with our hearts and souls
the spirit will let us do much more
but it will not tolerate much less
and still allow us to name ourselves faithful

God's spirit is showering us
a womanist ethic of care asks us *these* questions
  will we stand in the midst of the flux
  seek forgiveness
    move on in faith
    and work to create a healthy life for us all
or will we wait
  for the trumpet blast
  and the swarm of locusts
  and the relentless, unswerving, devastating army

# Notes

## *Chapter 1: The Formfulness of Communal Lament*

1. Hebrew Bible scholar Harold Washington, who is my colleague at St. Paul School of Theology, argues that Joel is postexilic, proto-apocalyptic literature. In a conversation with me, Washington pointed out that "the disaster language is lifted free of any immediate, concrete historical situation, so it informs all the more readily the communities' response to crisis in later years. Also, the (judgment) Day of the Lord and outpouring of the spirit comport with proto-apocalyptic literature."

2. John D. W. Watts, *Joel, Obadiah, Jonah, Nahum, Habakkuk and Zephaniah,* Cambridge Bible Commentary, New English Bible (London: Cambridge University Press, 1975), 13.

3. James Limburg, *Hosea-Micah, Interpretation: A Bible Commentary for Teaching and Preaching* (Atlanta: John Knox Press, 1988), 59. See also Deuteronomy 6:7, following the Shema.

4. All scriptural references will be from the NRSV unless noted otherwise. I use inclusive language where appropriate for the text. The text of Psalm 78:2–8 is:

> I will open my mouth in a parable;
>   I will utter dark sayings from of old,
> things that we have heard and known,
>   that our ancestors have told us.
> We will not hide them from their children;
>   we will tell to the coming generation
> the glorious deeds of God, and God's might,
>   and the wonders that God has done.
> God established a decree in Jacob,
>   and appointed a law in Israel,
> which God commanded our ancestors
>   to teach to their children;
> that the next generation might know them,
>   the children yet unborn,
> and rise up and tell them to their children,
>   so that they should set their hope in God,
> and not forget the works of God,
>   but keep God's commandments;
> and that they should not be like their ancestors,
>   a stubborn and rebellious generation,
> a generation whose heart was not steadfast,
>   whose spirit was not faithful to God.

5. Claus Westermann, *The Psalms: Structure, Content, and Message*, trans. Ralph D. Gehrke (Minneapolis: Augsburg, 1980), 32.

6. Claus Westermann, "The Role of Lament in the Theology of the Old Testament," *Interpretation* 28 (1974): 20.

7. Ibid., 21.

8. Ibid.

9. Ibid., 22.

10. Ibid.

11. Ibid., 24.

12. Joel 1:15; 2:1, 11, 31; and 3:14.

13. Hans Walter Wolff, *Joel and Amos*, Hermeneia (Philadelphia: Fortress, 1977), 12.

14. Graham S. Ogden and Richard Deutsch, *A Promise of Hope — a Call to Obedience: A Commentary on the Books of Joel and Malachi* (Grand Rapids, Mich.: Eerdmans, 1987), 24.

15. Raymond Bryan Dillard, "Joel," in *The Minor Prophets: Hosea, Joel, Amos*, ed. Thomas Edward McComiskey (Grand Rapids, Mich.: Baker Book House, 1992), 266; and Richard L. Mayhue, "The Prophet's Watchword: Day of the Lord," *Grace Theological Journal* 6, no. 2 (1985): 244.

16. Mayhue, "Prophet's Watchword," 245.

17. Leslie C. Allen, *The Books of Joel, Obadiah, Jonah, and Micah* (Grand Rapids, Mich.: Eerdmans, 1976), 60.

18. Ibid., 67.

19. Wolff, *Joel and Amos*, 48.

20. Dillard, "Joel," 280.

21. Ibid., 295.

22. Wolff, *Joel and Amos*, 68.

23. Ogden and Deutsch, *A Promise of Hope*, 23. Washington notes that the "'private' (i.e., individual as opposed to communal) laments are raised in the setting of *community*, originally at Temple worship, before a priest and congregation, and later in the gathered scriptures of the community in the Psalms" (Washington, personal conversation).

24. Paul Wayne Ferris Jr., *The Genre of the Communal Lament in the Bible and the Ancient Near East* (Atlanta: Scholars Press, 1992), 10.

25. Walter Brueggemann, "The Formfulness of Grief," *Interpretation: A Journal of Bible and Theology* 31, no. 3 (July 1977): 265. Although Brueggemann uses the word "grief" in this essay, I believe that his remarks apply to the process of lament in Joel.

26. Walter Brueggemann, "The Costly Loss of Lament," *Journal for the Study of the Old Testament* 36 (1986): 59.

27. Ibid., 60.

28. Ibid.

29. Ibid., 63.

## *Chapter 2: Fragmented Efforts*

1. Barbara Ehrenreich and John Ehrenreich, "The System behind the Chaos," in *The American Health Empire: Power, Profits, and Politics* (reprint, 1970; New York: Meridian, 1990), 50.

2. Ibid., 51–61.

3. David Brizer, *Health Care for Beginners* (New York: Writers and Readers Publishers, 1994), 9.

4. The gross national product is the amount spent on goods and services each year in a country.

5. Brizer, *Health Care for Beginners,* 44.

6. Ibid., 45.

7. The following table is from Health and Human Services (HHS), *Poverty Guidelines for 1997:*

| *Year* | *First Person* | *Each Additional Person* | *(Four-Person Family)* |
|---|---|---|---|
| 1990 | $6,280 | $2,140 | ($12,700) |
| 1991 | 6,620 | 2,260 | ( 13,400) |
| 1992 | 6,810 | 2,380 | ( 13,950) |
| 1993 | 6,970 | 2,460 | ( 14,350) |
| 1994 | 7,360 | 2,480 | ( 14,800) |
| 1995 | 7,470 | 2,560 | ( 15,150) |
| 1996 | 7,740 | 2,620 | ( 15,600) |
| 1997 | 7,890 | 2,720 | ( 16,050) |

HHS cautions that this straightforward table does *not* reflect the procedure by which the poverty thresholds were originally developed or the procedure by which the poverty guidelines are calculated from the poverty thresholds each year. See http://aspe.os.dhhs.gov/poverty/97poverty.htm.

8. Robert Greenstein, Richard Kogan, and Marion Nichols, *Bearing Most of the Burden: How Deficit Reduction during the 104th Congress Concentrated on Programs for the Poor* (Washington, D.C.: Center for Budget and Policy Priorities [www.cbpp.org/104tTH.HTM], December 3, 1996).

9. Ibid., 12.

10. Brizer, *Health Care for Beginners,* 5–7.

11. "42 Million Lack Health Insurance," *Kansas City Star,* April 27, 1996, A11.

12. Ibid.

13. David U. Himmelstein and Steffie Woolhandler, *The National Health Program Book: A Source Guide for Advocates* (Monroe, Maine: Common Courage Press, 1994), 26.

14. Ibid., 27.

15. Ibid., 29.

16. Ibid., 30.

17. Brizer, *Health Care for Beginners,* 34. One of the major third-party payers is Blue Cross (Blue Cross/Blue Shield) Association. This is a group of over eighty independent insurance plans nationwide. Blue Cross pays for hospitalizations, and Blue Shield pays for hospital-related doctors' bills.

18. Ibid., 32.

19. Alan Bavley, "Parents Find Coverage for Children Elusive," *Kansas City Star,* May 19, 1997, A13.

20. Ibid.

21. Ibid.
22. Ibid.
23. Ibid.
24. Brizer, *Health Care for Beginners,* 35.
25. Jena Heath and Andrew Park, "Big Money Involved in Blue Cross' Future," *Sunday News and Observer* (Raleigh, N.C.), June 15, 1997, A1, A8.
26. Brizer, *Health Care for Beginners,* 42.
27. Health Care Financing Administration, *1996 Statistics at a Glance* (http://www.hcfa.gov).
28. Ibid.
29. John T. Dauner, "Man Sentenced to 10 Years for Medicare Fraud," *Kansas City Star,* March 11, 1997, B2.
30. "Twelve Charged with Defrauding Medicare of $15 Million," *Kansas City Star,* August 8, 1997, A16. Mederi had already ceased operation. The federal grand jury found that two administrators of the agency convinced doctors and nurses to aid in the fraud. Five of those charged are medical doctors.
31. Geraldine Dallek, *Learning the Lessons of Medicaid Managed Care* (Washington, D.C.: Families USA, December 1996 [http://www.epn.org/families/medicaid.html]).
32. See www.hcfa.gov/medicaid/mbfraud.html.
33. Judy Waxman and Joan Alker, *Highlights of the President's Medicaid Reform Plan* (Washington, D.C.: Families USA, December 1996 [www.epn.org/families/kids98a.html]).
34. Ibid.
35. Ibid.
36. Brizer, *Health Care for Beginners,* 16.
37. Ibid., 19.
38. Ibid., 22.
39. Ibid., 66.
40. John D. Lantos, "Life Support," *University of Chicago Magazine* (February 1997): 19.
41. Ibid., 20.
42. Steve Sakson, "Reaction to HMOs: Practice Managers," *Kansas City Star,* June 9, 1996, F12.
43. Ibid.
44. Ibid.
45. Ruth Baum Bigus, "More Doctors Choose Primary-Care Practice," *Kansas City Star,* June 9, 1996: F8.
46. Brizer, *Health Care for Beginners,* 55.
47. Ibid., 55–56.
48. Ibid., 73.
49. Ibid., 74.
50. Jane Bryant Quinn, with contributions by Julius A. Karash, "Patient's Fighting Medical Restrictions," *Kansas City Star,* February 16, 1997, F6.
51. Ibid.
52. Ellen Freudenheim, *HealthSpeak: A Complete Dictionary of America's Health Care System* (New York: Facts on File, 1996), 205.
53. Ibid., 204.

54. Eric Houston, "Cutting Back on Doctors — and the Community," *Emerge* (June 1997): 28.

55. Ibid.

56. An American Medical Association (AMA) study found that 46 percent of the patients of African American doctors are African Americans. This is twice the percentage of other doctors.

57. Houston, "Cutting Back on Doctors," 28.

58. Freudenheim, *HealthSpeak*, 238.

59. Brizer, *Health Care for Beginners*, 83.

60. Ibid., 94.

61. Jennifer Mann Fuller, "Doctors Take Health Insurance into Own Hands," *Kansas City Star*, June 9, 1996, B2.

## *Chapter 3: Shutting Down America*

1. Collins O. Airhihenbuwa, *Health and Culture: Beyond the Western Paradigm* (Thousand Oaks, Calif.: Sage Publications, 1995), x.

2. Barbara M. Dixon, *Good Health for African Americans* (New York: Crown, 1994), xvi.

3. "The Cervix Industry," review of *Public Privates: Performing Gynecology from Both Ends of the Speculum*, by Terri Kapsalis (Durham, N.C.: Duke University Press, 1997), *Village Voice*, July 22, 1997, 53.

4. Dixon, *Good Health*, 12.

5. Ibid.

6. Ibid., 13.

7. Ibid., 14.

8. Ibid., 16.

9. Ibid., 20.

10. Ibid., 24.

11. Paul Starr, *The Social Transformation of American Medicine* (New York: Basic Books, 1982), 180.

12. Ibid., 180–81.

13. Ibid., 184.

14. Ibid., 189.

15. Ibid.

16. Ibid.

17. Ibid., 191.

18. Ibid.

19. Ibid., 193.

20. Edward H. Beardsley, *A History of Neglect: Health Care for Blacks and Mill Workers in the Twentieth-Century South* (Knoxville: University of Tennessee Press, 1987), 128.

21. W. E. B. Du Bois, ed., *Efforts for Social Betterment among Negro Americans*, Atlanta University Publications, no. 14 (Atlanta: Atlanta University Press, 1909), 87.

22. Ibid.

23. Ibid.

24. Ibid., 88.

25. Ibid., 94–95.
26. Beardsley, *History of Neglect,* 129.
27. Ibid., 130.
28. Ibid.
29. Ibid., 131.
30. Ibid., 152.
31. Ibid.
32. Ibid.
33. Ibid., 154.
34. Ibid., 155.
35. Ibid.
36. Ibid., 158.
37. Dixon, *Good Health,* 27.
38. Ibid.
39. Ibid.
40. Cited in Beryl Byman, "Out from the Shadow of Tuskegee: Fighting Racism in Medicine," *Minnesota Medicine* 74 (August 1991): 18.
41. Sue Chastain, "A Magazine of Black Health: *HealthQuest* Is Finding a Niche Helping Blacks to Lead Healthier Lives," *Charlotte News and Observer,* May 16, 1995, 4E.
42. Dixon, *Good Health,* 31.
43. Ibid., 32.
44. Ibid., 27.
45. Ibid.
46. Ibid., 28.
47. Linda Villarosa, ed., *Body and Soul: The Black Woman's Guide to Physical Health and Emotional Well-being* (New York: HarperPerennial, 1994), 4.
48. Ibid.
49. Cited in ibid., 5.
50. Dixon, *Good Health,* 28.
51. Ibid.
52. Ibid., 29.
53. Villarosa, *Body and Soul,* 93.
54. Richard F. Gillum, "The Epidemiology of Cardiovascular Disease in Black Americans," *The New England Journal of Medicine* 334, no. 21 (November 21, 1996): Internet edition.
55. Villarosa, *Body and Soul,* 94.
56. Jing Fang, Shantha Madhavan, and Michael H. Alderman, "The Association between Birthplace and Mortality from Cardiovascular Causes among Black and White Residents of New York City," *New England Journal of Medicine* 335, no. 21 (November 21, 1996): Internet edition.
57. "Birthplace, Not Race, Sets Risk," *Kansas City Star,* November 21, 1996, A15.
58. Hypertension, or high blood pressure, is defined as a persistent elevation of blood pressure above the normal range while the heart is contracting or relaxing. For adults, the typical pressure reading is 120/80. The top number is the systolic pressure and measures the maximum pressure during contraction of the heart. The bottom number is the diastolic pressure and measures the blood pressure when the heart is at

rest between beats. As a rule, if one's blood pressure is consistently 140/90 or higher, the diagnosis is high blood pressure.

59. Olympia Duhart, "Killing Us Softly: The Hypertension Threat," *HealthQuest: The Publication of Black Wellness* (Black History Special) 12 (1996): 7.

60. Ibid.

61. Cited in ibid., 8.

62. Ibid.

63. Ibid.

64. Villarosa, *Body and Soul,* 97.

65. Ibid., 98.

66. Ibid., 107.

67. Ibid., 109.

68. Ibid., 111.

69. Ibid., 60.

70. Ibid., 62.

71. Robert Staples, "Substance Abuse and the Black Family Crisis: An Overview," in *The Black Family: Essays and Studies,* ed. Robert Staples, 5th ed. (Belmont, Calif.: Wadsworth Publishing, 1994), 261.

72. Ibid.

73. Villarosa, *Body and Soul,* 78.

74. Staples, "Substance Abuse," 263.

75. Ibid., 261.

76. "Black Patients Overmedicated," *Detroit Sunday Journal,* June 2, 1996, 14.

77. Villarosa, *Body and Soul,* 79.

78. Farai Chideya, *Don't Believe the Hype: Fighting the Cultural Misinformation about African-Americans* (New York: Plume, 1995), 211. National Institute on Drug Abuse, *National Household Survey on Drug Abuse: Population Estimates 1991* (Substance Abuse and Mental Health Services Administration Office of Applied Studies, U.S. Department of Health and Human Services, Public Health Service).

79. National Institute on Drug Abuse, *National Household Survey on Drug Abuse: Population Estimates 1991.*

80. Ibid., 213.

81. Ibid.

82. Ibid., 215–16.

83. Nanny L. Green, "Low Birth Weight and Infant Mortality in the African American Family: The Impact of Racism and Self-Esteem," in *The Black Family,* 187.

84. Ibid., 216.

85. Arline T. Geronimus et al., "Excess Mortality among Blacks and Whites in the United States," *New England Journal of Medicine* 335, no. 21 (November 21, 1996): Internet edition.

86. Ibid., 215.

87. H. Jack Geiger, editorial in *New England Journal of Medicine* 334, no. 11 (September 12, 1996): 815.

88. Ibid.

89. Ibid., 816.

90. Ibid.

91. Ibid.

92. See "What the Clinton Health Plan Means to Blacks," *Ebony* (March 1994): 25.

93. Ibid., 28.

94. When the NMA was founded in 1895, its founders recognized that Black health and Black health-care professionals were receiving short shrift in the medical community. The association now represents more than twenty thousand predominantly African American physicians in more than twenty-three medical specialties throughout the United States, Puerto Rico, and the Virgin Islands.

95. See "What the Clinton Health Plan Means," 28.

96. Anita Womack, "Years of Healing: The Legacy of the National Medical Association," *HealthQuest: The Publication of Black Wellness* (summer 1995): 30.

97. Ibid., 31–33.

98. "Whose Managing Your Care? A Conversation with Randall C. Morgan, Jr., MD, FACS," *Emerge* (July/August 1997): S4.

99. Ibid.

100. Ibid., S5

101. Laurie Kaye Abraham, *Mama Might Be Better Off Dead: The Failure of Health Care in Urban America* (Chicago: University of Chicago Press, 1993), 51.

102. Marian E. Gornick et al., "Effects of Race and Income on Mortality and Use of Services among Medicare Beneficiaries," *New England Journal of Medicine* 335, no. 11 (September 12, 1996): 791.

103. Ibid., 791–98.

104. Marian Gray Secundy, "Lack of a Moral Consensus on Health Care: Focus on Minority Elderly," in *"It Just Ain't Fair": The Ethics of Health Care for African Americans,* ed. Annette Dula and Sara Goering (Westport, Conn.: Praeger, 1994), 57.

105. Jerome P. Kassirer, "Our Ailing Public Hospitals — Cure Them or Close Them?" *New England Journal of Medicine* 333, no. 20 (November 16, 1995): Internet edition.

## Chapter 4: "The Doctor Ain't Taking No Sticks"

1. James H. Jones's *Bad Blood: The Tuskegee Syphilis Experiment,* new and expanded edition (New York: Free Press, 1993), remains the best extended treatment of this gruesome affair. Readers are encouraged to explore the new and expanded edition for a detailed account of the experiment and the principals therein.

2. David McBride, *From TB to AIDS: Epidemics among Urban Blacks since 1900* (New York: State University of New York Press, 1991), 10–11.

3. American Social History Project, *Who Built America? Working People and the Nation's Economy, Politics, Culture, and Society,* vol. 2, *From the Gilded Age to the Present* (New York: Pantheon Books, 1992), 300.

4. Ibid., 301.

5. Ibid., 405–6.

6. McBride, *From TB to AIDS,* 21.

7. Ibid., 21–22.

8. Ibid., 86.

9. Ibid., 27.

10. Ibid., 31.

11. Ibid., 32.
12. Ibid., 32–33.
13. Ibid., 70.
14. Ibid., 75.
15. Ibid., 76.
16. Ibid., 77.
17. Ibid., 78.
18. Ibid., 79.
19. Ibid., 86.
20. Ibid., 89.
21. Louis I. Dublin and Alfred J. Lotka, *Twenty-Five Years of Health Progress: A Study of the Mortality Experience among the Industrial Policyholders of the Metropolitan Life Insurance Company 1911–1935* (New York: Metropolitan Life Insurance Company, 1937), 372–72.
22. McBride, *From TB to AIDS*, 107–8.
23. Jones, *Bad Blood*, 62.
24. Ibid., 64.
25. Ibid.
26. Ibid., 76.
27. Ibid., 72.
28. Ibid., 73.
29. Ibid., 74.
30. Ibid., 80.
31. Ibid.
32. Susan Smith, *Sick and Tired of Being Sick and Tired: Black Women's Health Activism in America, 1890–1950* (Philadelphia: University of Pennsylvania Press, 1995), 110.
33. In lumbar punctures, a sample of fluid is obtained by inserting a needle directly into the spinal canal. The procedure was risky and could result in temporary or permanent paralysis. It was painful, and patients often endured severe headaches that could last for day or weeks as side effects.
34. Jones, *Bad Blood*, 106.
35. Ibid.
36. Smith, *Sick and Tired*, 109.
37. Ibid., 112.
38. Cited in ibid., 115.
39. Ibid.
40. Ibid.
41. Ibid.
42. Edward H. Beardsley, *A History of Neglect: Health Care for Blacks and Mill Workers in the Twentieth-Century South* (Knoxville: University of Tennessee Press, 1987), 171.
43. Ibid., 174.
44. Dublin and Lotka, *Twenty-Five Years of Health Progress*, 373–74.
45. Jones, *Bad Blood*, 123.

46. Vonderlehr to Clark, January 12, 1933, Records of the USPHS Venereal Disease Division, Record Group 90, National Archives, Washington National Record Center, Suitland, Maryland.

47. Clark to Moore, March 25, 1933, National Archives.

48. Undated letter attached from Vonderlehr to Clark, April 21, 1933, National Archives.

49. Jones, *Bad Blood,* 128.

50. Ibid., 128–29.

51. Ibid., 179–80.

52. Ibid., 190.

53. Ibid., 199.

54. Ibid., 202.

55. *Medical World News* (September 14, 1973): 58.

56. *HEW News,* Office of the Secretary, March 5, 1973.

57. See Beryl Byman, "Out from the Shadow of Tuskegee: Fighting Racism in Medicine," *Minnesota Medicine* 74 (August 1991): 17.

58. See Benjamin Roy, "The Tuskegee Syphilis Experiment: Biotechnology and the Administrative State," *Journal of the National Medical Association* 87, no. 1: 57.

59. Ibid., 61.

60. Martha Solomon, "The Rhetoric of Dehumanization: An Analysis of Medical Reports of the Tuskegee Syphilis Project," in *Critical Questions: Invention, Creativity, and the Criticism of Discourse and Media,* ed. William L. Nothstine, Carole Blair, and Gary A. Copeland (New York: St. Martin's Press, 1994), 311.

61. Ibid.

62. Ibid., 312.

63. Ibid., 313.

64. Ibid., 315.

65. Ibid.

66. Ibid.

67. *Atlanta Daily World,* August 3, 1972, 1.

68. Ibid.

69. Ibid., 8.

70. Roy, "Tuskegee Syphilis Experiment," 58.

71. Ibid., 64.

72. Ibid., 59.

## Chapter 5: It's Not Always Just in Her Head

1. Nancy Krieger and Elizabeth Fee, "The Biopolitics of Sex/Gender and Race/Ethnicity," in *Man-made Medicine: Women's Health, Public Policy, and Reform,* ed. Kary L. Moss (Durham, N.C.: Duke University Press, 1996), 17.

2. Ibid.

3. Ibid., 20.

4. Eileen Nechas and Denise Foley, *Unequal Treatment: What You Don't Know about How Women Are Mistreated by the Medical Community* (New York: Simon and Schuster, 1994), 24.

5. Ibid., 26.

6. Ibid., 21.

7. Ibid., 22. See also Lesley Doyal, *What Makes Women Sick: Gender and the Political Economy of Health* (New Brunswick, N.J.: Rutgers University Press, 1995), 17.

8. Nechas and Foley, *Unequal Treatment,* 22.

9. Doyal, *What Makes Women Sick,* 17.

10. Nechas and Foley, *Unequal Treatment,* 22.

11. Ibid.

12. Ibid.

13. Ibid.

14. Ibid., 23.

15. Ibid., 26.

16. Ibid.

17. Cited in ibid., 27.

18. Krieger and Fee, "Biopolitics," 21.

19. Nechas and Foley, *Unequal Treatment,* 35.

20. Ibid.

21. Sue V. Rosser, *Women's Health — Missing from U.S. Medicine* (Bloomington: Indiana University Press, 1994), 87.

22. Ibid.

23. Ibid., 88.

24. Ibid.

25. Tinker Ready, "Mammograms Advised Less for Blacks," *News and Observer* (Raleigh, N.C.), June 14, 1997, 3A.

26. African American women are almost ten times more likely to be tested and reported for drug use than White women. Eighty percent of cases prosecuted for drug use during pregnancy are against racial-ethnic women. See Rosser, *Women's Health,* 92.

27. Patricia Hill Collins, *Black Feminist Thought* (New York: Routledge, 1991), 64.

28. Rosser, *Women's Health,* 93.

29. Ibid.

30. Ibid.

31. Wilhelmina A. Leigh, "The Health of African American Women," in *Health Issues for Women of Color: A Cultural Diversity Perspective,* ed. Diane L. Adams (Thousand Oaks, Calif.: Sage Publications, 1995), 114.

32. Ibid., 121.

33. Ibid., 123.

34. Erma J. Lawson and Aaron Thompson, "The Health Status of Black Women: A Historical Perspective and Current Trends," in *The Black Family: Essays and Studies,* ed. Robert Staples, 5th ed. (Belmont, Calif.: Wadsworth Publishing, 1994), 286.

35. Leigh, "Health of African American Women," 125.

36. Lawson and Thompson, "Health Status of Black Women," 288.

37. Ibid.

38. Ibid., 126.

39. Institute for Women's Policy Research, *Women of Color and Access to Health Care,* briefing paper (1994), 1.

40. Willa Mae Hemmons, *Black Women in the New World Order: Social Justice and the African American Female* (Westport, Conn.: Praeger, 1996), 206.

41. Unless otherwise noted, the insurance statistics quoted in this section are from the Institute for Women's Policy Research's briefing paper, *Women of Color and Access to Health Care,* 1–7.

42. Hemmons, *Black Women,* 212.

## Chapter 6: And All the Colored Folks Is Cursed

1. Portions of this chapter appeared previously in "Writing the Right: Gender and Sexuality in African American Community" in my *In a Blaze of Glory: Womanist Spirituality as Social Witness* (Nashville: Abingdon Press, 1995).

2. Victoria Benning, "Police Investigating Whether Race Was a Factor in Black Man's Death," *Washington Post,* August 1, 1997, D5.

3. White House Domestic Policy Council, *Health Security: The President's Report to the American People* (New York: Touchstone, 1993), 2.

4. Laurie Kaye Abraham, *Mama Might Be Better Off Dead: The Failure of Health Care in Urban America* (Chicago: University of Chicago Press, 1993), 3.

5. See ibid., 206–8.

6. Stephen B. Thomas and Sandra Crouse Quinn, "The Tuskegee Syphilis Study, 1932 to 1972: Implications for HIV Education and AIDS Risk Education Programs in the Black Community," *American Journal of Public Health* 81, no. 11 (November 1991): 1498.

7. Barbara Justice, "AIDS: Is It Genocide?" *Essence* (September 1990): 78.

8. Cited in Thomas and Quinn, "Tuskegee Syphilis Study," 1499.

9. Ibid., 1500.

10. Ibid., 1502.

11. AIDS Council of Greater Kansas City, "HIV in the African-American Community," *Catalyst* (January–February 1997): 3.

12. See Thomas and Quinn, "Tuskegee Syphilis Study," 1499.

13. National Commission on AIDS, *The Challenge of HIV/AIDS in Communities of Color* (Washington, D.C., December 1992), 4.

14. Centers for Disease Control and Prevention, *HIV/AIDS Surveillance Report,* 1997, vol. 9, no. 1, tables 4, 5, 6.

15. Ibid., tables 17, 18, 19.

16. It is important to note that Native Americans and Asian Americans/Pacific Islanders are underrepresented among AIDS cases in proportion to their numbers in the total population. In 1996, Asian Americans/Pacific Islanders were 3 percent of the population and 1 percent of the AIDS cases. Native Americans were 0.8 percent of the population and 1 percent of the reported AIDS cases.

17. AIDS Council of Greater Kansas City, "HIV in the African-American Community," 4.

18. William Raspberry, "AIDS Is Becoming a Black Disease," *Washington Post,* October 11, 1996, A25.

19. Ibid.

20. AIDS Council of Greater Kansas City, "HIV and Teens: Some Experts Fear a Hidden Epidemic in the Making," *Catalyst* (July/August 1996): 1.

21. Ibid.

22. Ibid., 2.

23. Ibid.

24. Ibid., 3.

25. AIDS Council of Greater Kansas City, "HIV in the African-American Community," 1.

26. Ibid., 3.

27. Centers for Disease Control and Prevention, *HIV/AIDS Surveillance Report,* 1996, table 8.

28. Centers for Disease Control and Prevention, *HIV/AIDS Surveillance Report,* 1995, table 21.

29. "AIDS Increased Most Rapidly among Heterosexuals, CDC Says," *Philadelphia Inquirer* March 11, 1994, A18.

30. National Commission on AIDS, *Challenge of HIV/AIDS,* 32.

31. AIDS Council of Greater Kansas City, "HIV in the African-American Community," 4.

32. Lawrence K. Altman, "AIDS Deaths Drop 19 Percent in U.S., in Part from Newer Treatments," *New York Times,* July 15, 1997, A1.

33. Ibid. Protease inhibitors are used with other antiviral drugs in a combination that has the potential to suppress HIV for long periods. Included in this mix are Invirase, Crixivan, and Norvir. These drugs prevent or slow down the progression from HIV to AIDS. They can also reverse some of the effects of full-blown AIDS. For many people, but not all, protease inhibitors reduce the HIV to undetectable levels, but it is not clear that they will work indefinitely. Protease inhibitors function much like insulin does for diabetics — it is a way to control the disease, but it is not a cure.

34. Altman, "AIDS Deaths Drop," A14.

35. Harriet A. Washington, "AIDS and the High Cost of Living," *Emerge* (July/August 1997): 28.

36. Ibid.

37. Ibid.

38. Ibid.

39. Ibid.

40. Jennifer Oldham, "The Economic Cost of AIDS," *Los Angeles Times,* October 13, 1995.

41. Ibid.

42. Ibid.

43. Ibid.

44. Ibid.

45. Centers for Disease Control and Prevention, *HIV/AIDS Surveillance Report,* 1997, tables 5 and 18.

46. Catherine Teare and Abigail English, "Women, Girls, and the HIV Epidemic," in *Man-made Medicine: Women's Health, Public Policy, and Reform,* ed. Kary L. Moss (Durham, N.C.: Duke University Press, 1996), 125.

47. AIDS Council of Greater Kansas City, "HIV and Women," *Catalyst* (March–April 1996): 1.

48. Ibid., 2.

49. Cited in ibid.

50. Eileen Nechas and Denise Foley, *Unequal Treatment: What You Don't Know about How Women Are Mistreated by the Medical Community* (New York: Simon and Schuster, 1994), 91.

51. Ibid., 96.

52. Ibid., 102.

53. Cited in ibid.

54. "Panel to Review AZT Use during Pregnancy," *Washington Post,* January 9, 1997, A13.

55. Nechas and Foley, *Unequal Treatment,* 99.

56. Ibid.

57. U.S. Department of Health and Human Services, Public Health Service, *HIV/AIDS Surveillance Report,* vol. 6, no. 2:5. This report covers HIV and AIDS cases reported in the United States through December 1984.

58. *Health Advocate* 179 (spring/summer 1994): 10.

59. Ibid.

60. Ibid., 38.

61. Ibid., 45.

62. AIDS Council of Greater Kansas City, "HIV in the African-American Community," 5.

63. Thomas and Quinn, "Tuskegee Syphilis Study," 1503.

64. Ibid.

65. Revon Kyle Banneker, "Rev. Carl Bean," in *Sojourner: Black Gay Voices in the Age of AIDS,* vol. 2, *Other Countries,* ed. B. Michael Hunter (New York: Other Countries Press, 1993), 37–38.

66. D. Mark Wilson, "The Black Church and AIDS," *Voice of the Turtle* (summer/fall 1995): 6.

67. Alice Walker, *The Color Purple* (New York: Washington Square Press, 1982), 178.

## Chapter 7: Wounded in the House of a Friend

1. Farai Chideya, *Don't Believe the Hype: Fighting Cultural Misinformation about African-Americans* (New York: Plume/Penguin Books, 1995), 13.

2. Lewis W. Diuguid, "Marchers to Celebrate Surviving," *Kansas City Star,* October 14, 1995.

3. Ibid.

4. Ibid.

5. Ibid.

6. Ibid.

7. Mary P. Van Hook, "Rural Poverty: Christian Charity and Social Justice Responses," in *Welfare in America: Christian Perspectives on a Policy Crisis,* ed. Stanley W. Carlson-Thies and James W. Skillen (Grand Rapids, Mich.: Eerdmans, 1996), 357.

8. Glenn C. Loury, "Blind Ignorance," *Emerge* (December/January 1997): 65. Loury is quoting the March 1994 *Current Population Survey.*

9. Chideya, *Don't Believe the Hype,* 14.

10. Ibid., 16.

11. Ibid., 16–17.

12. Loury, "Blind Ignorance," 65. Black mean earned roughly 86 percent of the earnings of comparable White men. Black women earned 10 percent higher than comparable White women.

13. Loury, "Blind Ignorance," 65.

14. This study by Philip Cook of Duke University and Jean Ludwig of Georgetown University analyzed the *National Educational Longitudinal Survey for 1990.*

15. Julianne Malveaux, *Sex Lies and Stereotypes: Perspectives of a Mad Economist* (Los Angeles: Pines One Publishing, 1994), 11.

16. Ibid., 15.

17. Amitai Etzioni, *The Spirit of Community: The Reinvention of American Society* (New York: Simon and Schuster, 1993), 3.

18. Alan Keith-Lucas, *The Poor You Have with You Always: Concepts of Aid to the Poor in the Western World from Biblical Times to the Present* (St. Davids, Penn.: North American Association of Christians in Social Work, 1989), 52.

19. Etzioni, *Spirit of Community,* 27.

20. Collins Airhihenbuwa, *Health and Culture: Beyond the Western Paradigm* (Thousand Oaks, Calif.: Sage Publications, 1995), 7.

21. Ibid., 26–27.

22. Ibid., 29–34.

23. Ibid., 90–91.

24. Ibid., 94.

25. National Center for Health Statistics, "Advance Report of Final Mortality Statistics," *Monthly Vital Statistics Report* 45, no. 3(S) (September 30, 1996).

26. Harriet A. Washington, "Mental Health Care Can Help or Harm," *Emerge* (November 1997): 30.

27. Cited in ibid.

28. Ibid.

29. Such an assumption is suspect at its very roots. To assume that Whites in the United States form a monolithic community is ludicrous. This does not allow for the kinds of cultural diversity within White lives that are obvious. It also points to the class biases of many psychological theories that reify White middle-class values.

30. Airhihenbuwa, *Health and Culture,* 98.

31. John McKnight, *The Careless Society: Community and Its Counterfeits* (New York: Basic Books, 1995), 56–58.

32. Ibid., 66.

33. Linda Stout, *Bridging the Class Divide and Other Lessons for Grassroots Organizing* (Boston: Beacon Press, 1996), 105–16. Stout sees these seven principles as key for a successful and inclusive grassroots movement.

34. Jon P. Kretzmann and John L. McKnight, *Building Communities from the Inside Out: A Path toward Finding and Mobilizing a Community's Assets* (Chicago: ACTA Publications, 1993), 5.

35. Ibid., 9.

36. Lynn Horsley, "Road to Recovery — Special Section," *Kansas City Star,* February 6, 1997, 10–11.

37. Linda Villarosa, ed., *Body and Soul: The Black Woman's Guide to Physical Health and Emotional Well-being* (New York: HarperPerennial, 1994), 61.

38. Ibid., 61–62.

39. Margo Okazawa-Rey, "Grandparents Who Care: An Empowerment Model of Health Care," in *"It Just Ain't Fair": The Ethics of Health Care for African Americans,* ed. Annette Dula and Sara Goering (Westport, Conn.: Praeger, 1994), 222.

40. Ibid., 225.

41. Ibid., 230.

42. Unless indicated otherwise, the information in this section is from the Atlanta Interfaith Health Program website, http://www.interaccess.com/ihpnet/. This website contains a detailed manual (complete with training and development resources) that describes how to set up an interfaith health-care ministry. Interested parties may also contact the director of the Atlanta Interfaith Health Project, Thomas Droege, at tdroege@emory.edu.

43. Thomas A. Droege, "Congregations as Communities of Health and Healing," *Interpretation: A Journal of Bible and Theology* 49, no. 2 (April 1995) 123–24.

44. Ibid., 124.

45. AIDS Council of Greater Kansas City, "Keeping AIDS at Bay with Better Prevention Planning," *Catalyst* (November–December 1995): 3.

46. M. Joycelyn Elders, "AIDS: What the Black Church Must Do," *HealthQuest: The Publication of Black Wellness* (fall 1996): 10.

47. Calvary Temple Baptist Church, *Temple Times* 2, no. 4 (August 1996): 3.

## Chapter 8: Searching for Paradise in a World of Theme Parks

1. Gustavo Gutiérrez, *A Theology of Liberation: History, Politics, and Salvation,* rev. ed., trans. Sister Caridad Inda and John Eagleson (Maryknoll, N.Y.: Orbis Books, 1988), 85.

2. E. Anthony Allen, "The Church's Ministry of Healing: The Challenges to Commitment," in *Health, Healing, and Transformation: Biblical Reflections on the Church in Ministries of Healing and Wholeness,* ed. E. Anthony Allen et al. (Monrovia, Calif.: MARC/World Vision International, 1991), 12.

3. Ibid., 31.

4. Audre Lorde, "The Erotic as Power," in *Sister Outsider* (Trumansburg, N.Y.: The Crossing Press, 1984).

5. Richard Shaull, "The Death and Resurrection of the American Dream," in Gustavo Gutiérrez and Richard Shaull, *Liberation and Change,* ed. Ronald H. Stone (Atlanta: John Knox Press, 1997), 134, 146.

6. Ibid., 120. Shaull states: "The disillusioned, the frightened, the cynical — be they conservatives, liberals, or radicals — do not lead the way to the future, no matter how profound their insights may be regarding the nature of the present crisis. That journey is reserved for women and men of passion."

7. Jürgen Moltmann, *Theology of Hope* (New York: Harper and Row, 1975 [1967]), 19.

8. David Brizer, *Health Care for Beginners* (New York: Writers and Readers Publishing, 1994), 62–66. As of 1994, thirty-six million people in the United States belonged to HMOs (health maintenance organizations). People may join by paying a monthly, quarterly, or yearly prepayment fee that covers all health-care services. There is often a small fee (five to ten dollars) when an HMO member visits the doctor. Patients may or may not be able to choose their own doctor. PPOs (preferred

provider organizations) are like HMOs in payment method. In a PPO, certain hospitals and doctors agree to provide their services to employees at a company at a reduced, prearranged rate. The term "managed care" refers to a variety of programs in which companies will only pay for medical procedures and hospitalizations that they have preapproved.

9. Moltmann, *Theology of Hope*, 24.

10. James M. Gustafson, *Christ and the Moral Life* (Chicago: University of Chicago Press, 1968), 250–51.

# Appendix

The Atlanta Interfaith Health Project lists the following resources for building coalitions of congregations to improve health and help train health-care promoters.

*Training for Transformation: A Handbook for Community Workers*
Anne Hope and Sally Timmel
Mambo Press, Zimbabwe
Available through Grailville Bookstore
Loveland, Ohio 45140
513-683-0202

*Helping Health Workers Learn*
David Werner and Bill Bower
The Hesperian Foundation
2796 Middlefield Rd.
Palo Alto, CA 94306
415-325-9017

*From the Ground Up! A Workbook on Coalition Building and Community Development*
Tom Wolff and Gillian Kaye
AHEC/Community Partners
24 South Prospect Street
Amherst, MA 01002

*Community Health Education: The Lay Advisor Approach*
Connie Service and Eva Salber (eds.)
Order from:
Ethel Jackson
University of North Carolina, School of Public Health
Rosenau Hall
Chapel Hill, NC 27599
919-966-3910

*Community Health Advisors.* Vol. 1, *Models, Research, and Practice.* Vol. 2, *Programs in the United States*
Technical Information Services Branch
National Center for Chronic Disease Prevention and Health Promotion
Centers for Disease Control and Prevention
4770 Buford Hwy, NE, Mailstop K-13
Atlanta, GA 30341
770-488-5080

*Health Promoter's and Trainer's Manuals English/Spanish*
Providence Holy Cross Medical Center
Parish Nurse Partnership, Latino Health Promoters Program
15031 Rinaldi Street
Mission Hills, CA 91345
818-898-4683

*The Technology of Prevention Workbook: A Leadership Development Program*
William Lofquist
Associates for Youth Development, Inc.
PO Box 36748
Tucson, AZ 85740
602-297-1056

*Called to Care: A Notebook for Lay Caregivers*
United Church Press
700 Prospect Avenue
Cleveland, OH 44115
800-325-7061

*The Health Promotion Resource Catalog*
Stanford Center for Research in Disease Prevention
1000 Welch Road
Palo Alto, CA 94304-1885
415-723-0003

*The Lafiyia Guide: A Congregational Handbook for the Whole-Person Health Ministry*
Association of Brethren Caregivers
145 Dundee Avenue
Elgin, IL 60120
800-323-8039

*Beginning a Health Ministry: A "How-To" Manual*
Health Ministries Association
PO Box 7853
Huntington Beach, CA 92646
800-852-5613

*The Community Health Advisor Network*
Agnes Hinton, Director
206 West Pearl Street, Suite 1010
Standard Life Building #822
Jackson, MS 39201
601-354-4225

# Index